POLITICAL *and* MILITARY SOCIOLOGY

Editors
Neovi M. Karakatsanis
Indiana University South Bend
Jonathan Swarts
Purdue University North Central

Book Review Editor
Jonathan Swarts
Purdue University North Central

Board of Associate Editors

Sergei Baburkin, *Yaroslavl State Pedagogical University*; **Amir Bar-Or**, *Sapir College*; **Robert Benford**, *Southern Illinois University*; **Hans Born**, *Geneva Centre for the Democratic Control of Armed Forces (DCAF)*; **Clem Brooks**, *Indiana University*; **Michael Conniff**, *San José State University*; **Gebretsadkan Gebretensae**, *Center for Policy Research and Dialogue, Addis Ababa*; **Metin Heper**, *Bilkent University*; **Nila Kapor-Stanulović**, *University of Novi Sad*; **Savvas Katsikidis**, *University of Cyprus*; **Anicia Lala**, *Higher Institute of International Relations (ISRI), Maputo*; **Dominique Maillard**, *University of Paris XII*; **David Mares**, *University of California, San Diego*; **Leonardo Morlino**, *University of Florence*; **Riefqi Muna**, *Indonesian Institute of Sciences (P2P-LIPI)*; **David Pion-Berlin**, *University of California, Riverside*; **Karthika Sasikumar**, *San José State University*; **Robert K. Schaeffer**, *Kansas State University*; **Riaz Ahmed Shaikh**, *Shaheed Zulfikar Ali Bhutto Institute of Science and Technology, Karachi*; **Henning Sørensen**, *Institute for Sociological Research*; **Marybeth Peterson Ulrich**, *U.S. Army War College*; **Laurence Whitehead**, *Nuffield College, University of Oxford*; **Jerzy Wiatr**, *European School of Law and Administration, Warsaw*; **Daniel Zirker**, *University of Waikato*; **Marian Zulean**, *University of Bucharest*

POLITICAL and MILITARY SOCIOLOGY

POLITICAL AND MILITARY SOCIOLOGY

AN ANNUAL REVIEW

VOLUME 40

NEOVI M. KARAKATSANIS
JONATHAN SWARTS

Routledge
Taylor & Francis Group
New York London

First published 2013 by Transaction Publishers

Published 2017 by Routledge
711 Third Avenue, New York, NY 10017, USA
2 Park Square, Milton Park, Abingdon, Oxon OX14 4RN

First issued in hardback 2017

Routledge is an imprint of the Taylor & Francis Group, an informa business

Copyright © 2013 by Taylor & Francis.

All rights reserved. No part of this book may be reprinted or reproduced or utilised in any form or by any electronic, mechanical, or other means, now known or hereafter invented, including photocopying and recording, or in any information storage or retrieval system, without permission in writing from the publishers.

Notice:
Product or corporate names may be trademarks or registered trademarks, and are used only for identification and explanation without intent to infringe.

ISSN: 0047-2697
ISBN 13: 978-1-4128-5149-7 (pbk)
ISBN 13: 978-1-1385-3004-1 (hbk)

Contents

Volume 40, 2012

Potestas and *Violentia* Power in the Doctrine of "Military Operations in Urban Terrain" (MOUT): State Sovereignty and Biopolitics in 2000–2011 Urban Warfare
Maria Markantonatou 1

Postmodern or Conservative? Competing Security Communities over Military Doctrine: Israeli National-Religious Soldiers as Counter [Strategic] Culture Agents
Udi Lebel 23

Doing Army or Feeling Army? What Makes Women Feel Organizational Belonging in the Israeli Defence Forces?
Orlee Hauser 59

Reconsidering the Defense–Growth Relationship: Evidence from the Islamic Republic of Iran
Bruce D. McDonald, III 97

Rethinking the Legacies of the Iran–Iraq War: Veterans, the Basij, and Social Resistance in Iran
Neema Noori 119

Justifying War in Post–Cold War Conflicts
Molly Clever 141

Relational Dialectics in the Civil–Military Relationship: Lessons from Veterans' Transition Narratives
Christina M. Knopf 171

American White Nationalism: The Ongoing Significance
of Group Position and Race
David Bugg and Dianne Dentice 193

The Illinois State Chapter of the Moral Majority: A Study of a
Religious Right Organization at the State Level
and the Perception of Power, 1980–1988
Aaron K. Davis 217

Book Reviews 243

In This Issue 255

Potestas and *Violentia* Power in the Doctrine of "Military Operations in Urban Terrain" (MOUT): State Sovereignty and Biopolitics in 2000–2011 Urban Warfare

Maria Markantonatou
University of the Aegean

Political and Military Sociology: An Annual Review, 2012, Vol. 40: 1–21.

This article discusses "Military Operations in Urban Terrain" (MOUT), arguing that MOUT is a doctrine that systematically blurs distinctions observed in traditional warfare, such as those between public and private space as well as those between military forces and civilians. Moreover, through a series of administrative mechanisms, MOUT seeks to legitimate psychological warfare techniques and to broaden social control over various populations. The article also reviews some of the arguments that rationalize the new political and academic interest in urban warfare. It investigates topics such as global urbanization, the increase in low-intensity conflicts, and the paradigm shift in military sociology (from Clausewitz to "new warfare"). The article suggests that MOUT seeks to justify a conflation between two forms of violence, potestas and violentia, namely military repression and administrative/biopolitical social control over populations. I argue that the doctrine cannot be analyzed simply through appeals to state sovereignty or the implications of biopolitics, as has become customary. The article concludes with an examination of the conflation between potestas and violentia in "Operation Enduring Freedom" in Afghanistan after September 11 and in a series of Israeli operations in Palestine following the outbreak of the Second Intifada in the year 2000.

Cities *qua* Battlefields

Military operations in urban areas have become a prevalent feature of the "War on Terror" and its associated pre-emptive interventions. Urban warfare is indeed characterized as "having the potential to become a critical security issue in the 21st century" (Hills 2004:3). Urban warfare is clearly not a new phenomenon; on the contrary, cities have been significant battlefields since antiquity and, according to one school of thought, the birth of the city was itself a result of war and the preparation for war (see Virillio and Lotringer 2007:19). The belief that cities provided defenders, rather than invaders, with a strategic advantage was established after the Second World War, and this assumption persisted more or less until the 1990s. According to this view, operations in cities should have been avoided and open-field combat should have been preferred, even if this was not always possible. During the Cold War, there was not much discussion of urban warfare, as NATO conceived of a clash with the Soviets as something that was more likely to occur on the plains of northern Germany and central Europe (Spiller 2004:90).

Operations in cities became more frequent with the post–Cold War "humanitarian wars" of the 1990s. These wars were conducted against armed groups whose activities were deemed incompatible with U.S. conceptions of human rights or appeared to constitute an impediment to U.S. political goals. It soon became evident that aerial bombing and the deployment of high technology weapons were insufficient in themselves as a means of securing and retaining military supremacy (Spiller 2004:90). Thus, the military analysis of urban operations gradually became more systematized. As a result, the idea of annihilating the enemy is being conflated with that of providing humanitarian help. The U.S. Navy's late-1990s "Three Block War" doctrine is an illustration of this concept. In this approach, conventional war is first conducted in the traditional bellicose manner, followed by "peace operations" inside the cities, with "humanitarian relief" measures bringing the operation to an end (see Evans 2004:28).

By the end of the Cold War and, more intensively, after the attacks on the "axis of evil" after September 11, 2001, the renewed interest in systematizing a broader strategy for urban operations was further refined by circumstances such as the continuing war in the Afghanistan–Pakistan zone (Afpak War), the intensification of Israeli attacks in the populated areas of Palestine and Lebanon after the 2000 Intifada, and the escalation of attacks in Iraq after 2003. The renewed interest in tactics and technologies of urban warfare was evidently a by-product of the strategic choice of humanitarian wars in the 1990s. This interest intensified in the decade between 2001 and 2011. The primary characteristic of the intensification was the U.S. War on Terror after September 11 and Israel's operations in response to the outbreak of the Second Intifada in October 2000. In both cases, a "state of emergency" was declared against asymmetric threats. More recently, the unrest in Tunisia, Egypt, Syria, Yemen, and Algeria in early 2011, not to mention NATO's operations in Libya, have once again transformed cities into theaters of war that are characterized by civilian deaths, police repression, violence, asymmetrical conflicts, and the destruction of urban and social infrastructures. Nevertheless, due to the rapidity of developments, it is not yet clear how urban warfare in these countries is likely to evolve.

Cities have undoubtedly become "areas of careful study" (Boniface 2004:193). Modern strategic studies have clearly placed urban areas at the center of their analyses, drawing on sociological theories of globalization and cosmopolitanism, as, for instance, in Kaldor's (2003) approach to "new wars," in the thesis that the state's monopoly of violence has been weakened (Wulf 2005), and in the idea regarding the "transformation of war" (Creveld 1991). Moreover, theories of social architecture in urban planning, urban design, urban management, urban geography, and land use are being elaborated in a large number of generously funded educational and strategic research institutes that have been established over the course of the last few decades to analyze urban warfare (Weizman 2006:2).

Theoretical Justifications for the New Urban Wars

A number of sociological arguments have been put forth to legitimate the renewal of interest in urban warfare, though some of these arguments have characteristically been detached from the specific circumstances of the "state of emergency" and/or the "war on terror" and the assertion of their necessity. The chief claims and arguments that have been put forward in support of urban operations can be summarized as follows:

(a) *Demography and the intensification of global urbanization.* According to statistics provided by Spiller (2004:86), the world population has doubled in the last 40 years, with half of the people now living in cities and towns. The total global population is expected to reach 7.2 billion in 2015, an increase of 1.1 billion from 2000, with 95% of the increase occurring in developing countries and almost entirely in cities (Hills 2004:16). The phenomena of overpopulation, spatial and social mobility, the accumulation of wealth, and increased life expectancy are observed in cities, which, according to Boniface, give rise to "misery and vengefulness" and "create reactions of violence and despair," because they are "unable to satisfy needs ... due to the coexistence of slums and wealthy neighborhoods, of misery and luxury" (2004:192). As the near totality of human activity is transferred to cities, the demographic and global urbanization argument maintains that conflicts become more intense and war spreads.

(b) *Globalization and low-intensity conflicts.* Globalization is seen as leading to a loss of control by national governments and their military forces due to developments in technology, the growth of immigration, the spread of illegal weapons and uncensored information, as well as illegal transborder trade flows. Moreover, the global cities of the West are now regarded as hothouses of terrorism. To this end, it is often repeated that the executors of the September 11 attacks did not live in "rogue" states, such as Afghanistan, but in urban centers in the United States and Europe, which "provide more cover and better command-and-control opportunities than do caves in central Asia" (Hills 2004:21). At the same time, NGOs, private military companies (PMCs), clan militias, mercenaries, and gangs in "shadow states" and in "war economies" seek to fill security gaps (Hills 2004:17), creating new sources of insecurity and aspects of imbalance at the international level (Wulf 2005:197). The disorderly character and the precariousness of globalization require that more effective control should be exerted over such groups. As a result, it is argued that flexible special units trained in guerrilla warfare and prepared to carry out attacks on houses, other buildings, and, indeed, on entire neighborhoods are required, as conventional armies would be ineffective in such settings.

(c) *Paradigm Shift in Military Sociology: From Clausewitz to "New Warfare."* This type of analysis takes as its point of departure the idea that Clausewitz's approach to war applies to wars between well-defined states of the Weberian type (Bassford and Villacres 1995:16). In his description of the new forms of non-conventional warfare, Creveld's analysis of the "decline of the state" employs the concept of "non-trinitarian war," rather than Clausewitz's "trinity" (Creveld 1991:45–51). Creveld interprets the Clausewitzian concept of "trinity" as "trinitarian war"—that is, as a war predicated on an indissoluble link between the state, the people, and the army.[1] Given the alleged contemporary retreat of the Western state model, Creveld regards Clausewitz's conception as historically outdated, centered on an excessively rational understanding of war that is plausible only in the case of conventional warfare between nation-states of the Westphalian type. Further, in keeping with what Virillio and Lotringer have described as the "end of the political war à la Clausewitz" (2007:8), contemporary urban warfare is integrated into a broader paradigm of "new wars" that are subdivided into "pre-modern," "modern," and "postmodern," corresponding to the related ideal types identified in state theory.[2] As Evans (2004:24) argues, "under new global security conditions the postmodern has collided with the pre-modern and the cosmopolitan has confronted the parochial"; thus, all forms of war merge when contemporary urban wars are conducted. In an era in which wars between nation-states are for the time being not the dominant paradigm, the study of urban wars and operations corresponds with the need to better understand the transitions in contemporary warfare.

For all their factual correctness, the reasons set forth in the three preceding arguments drape urban operations in a cloak of necessity; in a world characterized by "global anarchy" and insecurity, peace needs to be "maintained" even if the enemy is not always visible. Moreover, even though the discussion is enriched by these arguments, the problems of economic and military asymmetry that give rise to urban warfare and "small wars" are neglected. For example, the view that "information technology is being exploited by both conventional militaries and networked terrorist groups" (Hills 2004:4) is conspicuously present. What this approach neglects, however, is the fact that asymmetrical wars are not the cause, but the effect, of the correlations and balance of power between those engaged in armed conflict. Even if the existence of super-weapons that are supposedly possessed only by the United States is assumed to be a marketing myth that is propagated by the superpower (Grivas 2008:163), it is precisely the incontestable military and technological superiority in a states' conventional forces and information technology that creates what Boniface (2004:21) describes as the problem of "dissymmetry"—namely, the type of military supremacy which paves the way for terrorist or asymmetric threats. Enemies seek to deceive the conventional forces and drive them out of the open field—where their advantages are indisputable—and into more precarious places, such as hideouts, mountains, and the inhabited labyrinths of the city.

The new significance of cities as battlefields, as illustrated by conflicts in the Gaza Strip, the American intervention in Mogadishu, and the Russian intervention in Grozny, is the reason why urban wars in Leningrad, Stalingrad, Singapore, Hue, and elsewhere are being studied anew. The revision of the American doctrine of "Military Operations on Urban Terrain" in 2002 testifies to this renewed focus on cities.

The Doctrine of "Military Operations on Urban Terrain"

The more severely a regular army is disciplined, the more correctly it distinguishes between military and civil, and only the enemy in uniform is considered an enemy. A regular army becomes more sensitive and more nervous when it encounters a non-uniformed, civilian population on the other side of the struggle. Then, the military responds with harsh reprisals, on-site inspections, hostage taking, destruction of villages, and considers this to be the correct self-defense against treachery and perfidy. (Schmitt 2007:34)

The subject of military operations in cities was introduced for the first time in 1979 in the U.S. Military Field Manual, *Military Operations on Urban Terrain (MOUT)*. "Operations in built-up Areas" (OBUA), "Fighting in built-up Areas" (FIBUA), and "Urban Operations" (see Spiller 2004) are British variants on MOUT. In 2002, the American "Doctrine for Joint Urban Operations (JUO)" was issued. It was broader in scope, including joint operations of American land, sea, and air forces and introducing new areas of complex urban field interventions.

The JUO doctrine is tautological in the way it links the idiosyncratic nature of urban operations to the city environment. It conceives of urban operations simplistically as "military operations on, or against, objectives within a topographical complex and its adjacent natural terrain, where manmade construction or the density of noncombatants are the dominant features" (JUO 2002:9). Likewise, it defines the "urban triad" in a descriptive manner as consisting of three distinctive features. The first has to do with "the physical terrain of an urban area that consists of three-dimensional surface areas; internal and external space of buildings and structures; subsurface areas; and the airspace above the topographical complex." The second is "the noncombatant population that is characterized by the interaction of numerous political, economic, and social activities," whereas the third is the "physical and service infrastructure" (JUO 2002:9).

The strategic analyst Daryl Press noted the growing importance of urban warfare in a lecture delivered two years before September 11. According to Press, given that "Americans will frequently be drawn into cities because no enemy's military can compete with U.S. forces in open terrain" (Press 1999:5), American troops should take into account such parameters as risk, casualties, and expected benefits when conducting urban operations. Press discerns three types of military intervention: policing operations, raids, and sustained urban combat. He notes that police missions are undertaken when the risk is low and the benefit is limited. Raids (e.g., on embassies, nuclear construction facilities, and the hiding places of enemy leaders, among others) involve both greater risk and benefits. Press urges the American political leadership to be cautious when proceeding with urban operations (Press 1999). Interestingly, he predicts a casualty ratio of 20:1 for milder interventions in cities, such as police missions and raids:

> Even a 20:1 exchange rate might not be a big enough advantage for US forces because the political goals which motivate most policing missions and many raids are not sufficiently critical to U.S. national interests to justify the loss of many troops. (Press 1999:2)

Combat within cities is high risk and quite problematic. Long-range weapons and missiles prove much less useful in the urban environment. Indirect fire support becomes rigid. Close-contact clashes are dangerous, as civilians may be involved or attackers may find themselves under friendly fire (Press 1999:10). Since problems of this kind are hard to solve, a thorough cost-benefit analysis is imperative. The leadership should weigh its priorities, taking public opinion into account well before making any decisions on which operations might be necessary. According to Press,

> [I]n a conventional war between NATO and the Warsaw Pact, a 10:1 exchange ratio in NATO's favor would have been a tremendous victory for the West. But in a conflict in 1993 between U.S. soldiers and Somali gunmen, a 25:1 exchange rate in America's favor was considered to be a terrible defeat. The difference between these two scenarios is obvious: Americans believed that defending NATO from a Soviet attack was worth the lives of thousands of Americans; arresting the Somali Warlord Mohammed Farah Aidid, on the other hand, did not merit the loss of even eighteen soldiers. (Press 1999:10)

In short, the doctrine of urban operations establishes a number of priorities: "Situational awareness" of a unique nature and the distinctiveness of each particular circumstance; an in-depth understanding of people's habits and of "the local psychology"; air, naval, and land "joint operations"; coordination with international NGOs and with private security and policing companies; readiness for various forms of "unconventional warfare" employing tried and tested techniques (e.g., that of "military deception" in support of friendly missions); and "defensive and offensive operations for information" designed to protect networks, digital media, and information systems while destroying or weakening the enemy's systems in the context of cyber defense and "consequence management" (e.g., medical assistance to civilians injured in explosions triggered by the attackers or by their deployment of biological or chemical weapons) (JUO 2002:143).

The distinguishing trait of these new types of operations is their situationally determined, flexible, and individualized nature. The conflation of enforcement practices, humanitarian actions, and claims of being engaged in "state restructuring" is also characteristic of new urban warfare. It is typically assumed that lethally aggressive actions in the field are a *sine qua non* of anti-terror police operations, such as the arresting of warlords or designated terrorists. On a different, but related, question, counterinsurgency operations are thought to require the type of advantage that is gained by securing control over the population (e.g., by means of infrastructural funding, administrative mechanisms, etc.). Counterterrorism and counterinsurgency are perceived as being "two different trends" with separate implications for "the future philosophical orientation of the Army" (Anderson 2010:2). However, they are subsumed in a one-piece control strategy of humanitarian violence and endorsed as variants of urban warfare.

Micro-tactics comprise the central core of urban missions. They include attacks on small or larger conurbations, city blocks, camps, neighborhoods, houses, infrastructure, or, alternatively, on villages and districts purported to be "terrorist" hideouts. The logistics of attack change when the enemy is engaged at such close quarters. This affects not only matters such as ammunition, but also water, food, and medical provisions (Hills 2004:7). As Grivas (2008:176) points out, in urban warfare, there are not "just friendly and hostile battalions, one next to the other, but friendly and enemy forces side by side." The complexity of this context necessitates the adoption of correspondingly sophisticated operational maneuvers: lightning-fast encirclement of buildings, terraces, and courtyards without any warning; "mopping-up" operations that involve entire streets; and precision sharpshooting. Moreover, spying technology, including scanning devices such as sniper radars, satellites, and remote-controlled miniature robots, which make objects visible by means of micro cameras that are digitally connected to a distant operator, is necessary for this type of operation.

The JUO doctrine also foresees the employment of a number of specific practices in urban operations, openly proposing, for example, such methods as arson. In dealing with the technical difficulties of arson, it counsels:

> Fires may be used to isolate the urban area and, particularly with precision munitions, to engage adversary targets within the urban area. Noncombatant casualties and collateral damage have the potential for adversely affecting operational objectives and thus fires require careful planning and coordination. (JUO 2002:10)

The psychological factor in warfare is also emphasized, including how to control the flow of true and false information, influence public opinion, and manipulate both opponents and civilians:

> The key to success in urban operations may lie in the ability to control the information environment and influence the thoughts and opinions of adversaries and noncombatants through information operations, in particular, psychological operations. (JUO 2002:10)

It is also characteristic of JUO doctrine that it is not only flexible in its approach to actions prohibited under international law, but, despite these prohibitions, also positively disposed to these actions, given the necessities of new urban warfare. It is interesting to note that many of the micro-tactics and indeed the more general orientations of those who plan and conduct urban operations are not in conformity with the Geneva Conventions. This is true in relation to a number of issues, from the treatment of civilians to genocide, including such cruelties as infanticide, mistreatment of prisoners of war, damage to property and infrastructure, and others. The JUO doctrines, therefore, recommend the prioritization of securing legal cover:

> Because urban areas contain the potential for significant noncombatant suffering and physical destruction, urban operations can involve complex and potentially critical legal questions and issues, requiring strong support from military legal advisors. (JUO 2002:11)

Although MOUT and JUO are American doctrines, this does not mean that the practices mentioned earlier are not followed by other countries. Nor does it mean that American doctrines are not influenced by other countries' urban warfare strategies. Operations such as those of the Israeli Defense Forces (IDF) in Palestine, not to mention a number of American operations in Afghanistan and Iraq, have been to some extent collective undertakings. As Graham points out:

> [I]t is increasingly apparent that the battle of Jenin was actually planned, prosecuted, and evaluated in very close partnership with specialists in US Military Operations on Urban Terrain (MOUT). Keen to address the closely built-up, labyrinthine Islamic cities that would inevitably be the focus of their ongoing global war on terrorism (Kabul, Kandahar, Basra, Fallujah . . .), the US military, given their intimate connections with all parts of the IDF, have sought to make the most of the Jenin battle as a learning experiment. (2004:211)

Graham also suggests that the 2002 Israeli "Operation Defensive Shield," a reprisal for the Hamas suicide bombing in Netanya that had killed 30 Israelis, brought about a "Palestinianization" of Iraq for the United States (2004:212). By the end of 2003, similar tactics were being followed by the United States: search-and-seize operations, round-the-clock surveillance of suspected centers of guerilla activity by unmanned aerial vehicles, and, last but not least, what Graham calls, "urbicide by bulldozer"—the destruction by D-9 bulldozers of homes and built-up areas in Iraqi cities (2004:195).

Despite the variation in national military doctrines and significant differences in the goals being pursued, the causes of conflict, and the outcome of these confrontations, the affinities between United States and Israeli practices testify to a shared orientation. Given their economic and military supremacy, the attacks to which they seek to respond are asymmetrical ones, which are typically assigned to the category of "terrorist threats." The methods employed encompass both military enforcement and the assertion of state sovereignty through administrative, psychological, and biopolitical mechanisms of social control. These wars, as Bitsakis and Belantis have noted, are "waged by armies that are neocolonial: armies of global conquest, occupation and policing at the same time" (2005:346).

Urban Warfare through *Potestas* and *Violentia*

MOUT combines two forms of violence that resemble the two forms of Roman Law—*potestas* (force) and *violentia* (violence)—discussed by Walter Benjamin in his "Critique of Violence" (1986), which includes an analysis of their complicated conflation in the modern state in the form of *Gewalt*.[3] In the context of urban warfare, *violentia* is the violence of military enforcement, violent suppression, and direct power over human life and space. *Potestas* can be understood as the legal and administrative power that classifies individuals in accordance with norms, legitimizes and delegitimizes behaviors, regulates and deregulates, and imposes the discipline of power relations on subjects. In terms of current sociological analysis, and particularly vis-à-vis urban warfare, the theoretical perspectives of the *violentia* discourse apply notably in cases such as those of the United States and Israel, critiquing their behavior as belligerent from the viewpoint of international law and putting forth arguments in favor of social justice (e.g., on issues such as the safety of civilians).[4] By contrast, Foucault-type biopolitical analysis focuses more on *potestas*. It is not the "state-subject" that is central to this analysis but the disciplining strategies and the modes of governance that construct subjects as such through a series of micromechanisms of power and war, transforming them into "bare life" (Agamben 1998).[5]

Both approaches offer important insights into the nature of modern urban warfare. They are also limited, however, due to their points of departure and assumptions. Typical of the analysis of *violentia* is its fixed definition of state sovereignty, as if sovereignty remained historically unalterable or settled in permanent actions and measurable results. It seeks to systematize how this fixed sovereignty interacts or conflicts with international law and, thus, how sovereignty is either reasserted or eroded. This line of analysis precludes an understanding of sovereignty as a "contingent political effect" (Doty 1996:143), which is continually reconstructed through dynamic political processes. By conceptualizing sovereignty as something static, the reality that "the social construction of sovereignty is a never-completed project whose successful production never can be counted on totally" is neglected (Doty 1996:143). Focusing the critique almost exclusively on how states violate international humanitarian law causes us to fail to perceive, as Gregory (following Foucault) suggests, the law itself "as a tactic" (2006:207). It is precisely the changing tactics and micro-tactics of power and the construction of power relations that are important for biopolitical analysis, much more so than the orientations of a fixed sovereignty and its possible erosion through asymmetric threats.

However, critiques of the state sovereignty paradigm have also emerged. Thanks to the influence within the social sciences of deconstructing paradigms, such as cosmopolitanism and globalism, and the prevalent assumption that the historical model of the "nation-state" is giving way to other forms of networked, diffused, and biopolitical power, the focus has begun to shift to *potestas*. This has had a number of effects on the conceptualization of urban warfare, extending so far as to totally delink it from the paradigm of the nation-state. In terms of this logic, then, "genocide"[6] is replaced by more elusive concepts, such as "spaciocide"[7] or, even, "ethnocide," "politicide," "classicide," and various other "-cides."[8] The danger with such biopolitical analyses is, of course, that state strategies of social control—e.g., territorialization though colonizing, nuclear armament, urban militarism, dissymmetry, and the international enforcement of the divisive ideology of the "war on terror"—will be subsumed within a mechanical functionalism where the emphasis will be on micromechanics and the matrix of automatic actions. In this spirit, a number of issues—issues that within the classic state sovereignty paradigm were subjected to a liberal critique—can be stripped of their political importance. As Žižek points out in his critique of Agamben's concept of "Homo Sacer," this is the means by which the image of an "administered world"—a world in which "the topics of human rights, democracy, the rule of law and so on, are ultimately reduced to a deceptive mask for the disciplinary mechanisms of 'biopower'"—is constructed (2002:95). Stateless biopolitical interpretations ensure that criticism is limited to the exiled "bare life" of "Homo Sacer," to his marginal existence in the interstices of the "state of exception" and to his severe detachment from political life and the realm of law. One, and only one, phenomenon is subjected to critical scrutiny: the passivity of life in the "administered world" (Žižek 2002:100).

As demonstrated by the rhetoric of MOUT, contemporary urban warfare is not to be understood simply as the expression of a "timeless principle of sovereignty" (Biersteker and Weber 1996:2) and/or of a hegemony that is attributable simply to economic and technical-military supremacy. Moreover, it cannot be understood through biopolitical models of a stateless globalization or an uncoordinated diffusion of the microphysics of power. The tactics that followed September 11 in cities and inhabited areas in Afghanistan, Iraq, and Palestine reveal that the contemporary form of urban warfare does not derive from one or the other specific forms of violence—that is, neither exclusively military enforcement and state sovereignty nor wholly biopolitics—but from a more or less successful effort of conflating them. State sovereignty and military suppression mingle with policing and biopolitical surveillance via a range of administrative organizations and bureaucratic mechanisms as well as through humanitarian actions. As Gregory suggests, the war on terror and the resulting strategies of urban warfare "can be understood as a dispersed series of sites where sovereign power and bio-power coincide" (2006:206). Two brief overviews of U.S. operations in Afghanistan and of Israeli operations in Israel/Palestine after the Second Intifada may suffice to demonstrate this conflation of control through both *potestas* and *violentia*.

Afghanistan

The war in Afghanistan, which Herold described as the "ultimate asymmetric war" (2006:315), is illustrative of the conflation of military violence and administrative social control of the population. In Afghanistan, the Bush administration initially followed a relatively inexpensive strategy of "light footprint,"[9] with only limited numbers of land forces (Peceny and Bosin 2009:27–31). However, aerial bombings with Precision Guided Munitions (PGMs) and civilian deaths reached unprecedented heights. In the first eight weeks of the bombardment, the United States used many of its most effective weapons—smart bombs, depleted uranium bombs, BLU-82 bombs, and tons of long-range munitions—killing indiscriminately and poisoning through radiation those who did not die immediately (Misdag 2006:247). The ratio between the numbers of civilian deaths and the tons of munitions used indicates that attacks on civilians were not accidental "collateral damage," as suggested by the military authorities, but were targeted attacks on high-population-density urban areas (for statistics on the ratio between civilian deaths and the use of munitions, see Herold 2006).

American forces rapidly destroyed what had been left from the 10-year-long Soviet–Afghan war and the ensuing civil war in the 1990s.[10] Hospitals, houses, schools, mosques, and natural resources were obliterated. This destruction was executed not only through close air support, but also through strategic bombing, which avoids frontal attacks in order to target such military infrastructure as radars, airports, and military vehicles (Herold 2006:319). As was the case with the Bush administration, so also under Obama, the "war on terror" remained a fundamental priority, with an increase in troop numbers and an intensification of military efforts. Furthermore, apart from Bagram, one tactic of the U.S. Army has been illustrated by incidents such as the one in the Hajibirgit village: The village was evacuated, inhabitants were ordered out of their homes, the village elder was shot dead, men believed to be "suspicious" were taken to camps in Kandahar for interrogation, and women, children, and other residents were kept in cells pending their release (see Gregory 2004:72).

However, within the framework of Afghanistan's restructuring through Operation Enduring Freedom,[11] this military violence (*violentia*) was conflated with *potestas*. When the Karzai administration had been established and the National Afghan Army (today numbering about 90,000 men) created, Afghanistan was divided administratively into three zones: the North, the West, and the Kabul zone, with resulting heterogeneity in administrative tasks and military operations (Misdaq 2006:252). The idea was to cooperate with local warlords with a view to getting them to fight the Taliban and the groups and factions who were friendly to them (Peceny and Bosin 2009). These developments were accompanied by a biopolitical treatment of the population. A plethora of agents, officials, and bureaucrats—military and other—set about promoting a range of unclear objectives for "restructuring and development" by, on the one hand, inflicting military violence and, on the other hand, providing humanitarian assistance. In this way, as is also suggested by MOUT, the agents just mentioned mapped out a "gray area" that was situated somewhere between the operations of the military and those of the humanitarian aid organizations (Gregory 2006:73). In one of the world's poorest countries, lacking a central decision-making apparatus, social control is now being exercised by an array of international organizations—NATO commissions and subcommissions,[12] EU agents,[13] private security companies, and international NGOs—for the declared purpose of preventing terror and making use of the "restructuring" instrument, as defined under the terms of the 2006 Afghanistan Compact.[14]

Thus, it is in this spirit that a specific conjunctural situation has become permanent: precision bombing and the destruction of an urban area that is believed to be the home of terrorists along with humanitarian aid to civilians and other survivors. In this way, as MOUT suggests, humanitarian war can be justified. It is by these means that the image of "humanitarian biopolitics" where "the American war plane is flying above Afghanistan—and one is never sure what it will drop, bombs or food parcels"—has acquired a paradoxical iconic status: "the ultimate image of the treatment of the local population as Homo Sacer" (Žižek 2002:94).

Israel

Another conflation of *potestas* and *violentia* can be observed in the very different political and military context of the Israeli–Palestinian conflict. Azoulay and Ophir characterize it not as *potestas* and *violentia* but as "eruptive" and "withheld" violence (2009:101). Up to and including the first Intifada, "withheld" violence predominated, with "eruptive" violence being merely sporadic and exercised primarily in the form of clashes with armed Palestinians, followed by subsequent torture, home demolitions, and arrests (Azoulay and Ophir 2009:108). Immediately after the outbreak of the Second Intifada in October 2000, Israel placed a prohibition on Palestinians entering Israel and closed the "safe passage" between the West Bank and Gaza. After Sharon's election in February 2001, the Israel administration aligned itself demonstratively with the United States. The new administration experimented with ways of presenting the Palestinian Authority as the "Al-Qaeda of Israel" (Žižek 2002:155–156) and the suppression of Intifada as a "War on Terror." It seized the opportunity to associate the September 11 attacks with Palestinian attacks on Israel and to "place both of them under the heading of 'international terrorism' wherein bin Laden and Arafat became one and the same thing" (Said 2002:21).

This was followed by the division of the Gaza Strip in three, the first attack on the West Bank (on a Nablus prison), and the establishment of a checkpoint separating Jerusalem from Ramallah and the rest of the West Bank. Several other tactical innovations were implemented, such as the creation of the "agriculture security fence" along the Green Line and a series of IDF house demolitions in the Rafah refugee camp. In 2002, suicide attacks came as a prelude to the terrorist attack on the Park Hotel in Netanya, where 30 Israelis were killed, triggering Israel's Operation Defensive Shield. The IDF invaded Jenin and Jericho and bombed inhabited urban areas, including homes in Gaza, Ramallah, Beit Sahour, and Beit Jala, causing hundreds of casualties (children and adults) and destroying infrastructure (for the course of events, see Handel 2009:603–634).

The tactics followed by the IDF in this phase are instructive. In the retaliatory operation mounted in Nablus in 2002, several MOUT-like techniques were employed for the purpose of avoiding clashes on the streets between Palestinian guerrillas and soldiers. "Infestation," as Weizman describes it, was one such technique (2006:4). The IDF blew up walls and floors inside buildings, irrespective of whether people were inside or not. (If people were present, the IDF locked residents in one room). In this way, the IDF created an "overground tunnel," moving horizontally and vertically by breaking through adjacent buildings (Weizman 2006). The Israeli troops thus attempted to "redefine inside as outside, and domestic interiors as thoroughfares" (Weizman 2006:6). As described by General Kokhavi in an interview, these were practices of "inverse geometry" adapted to "the reorganization of the urban syntax by means of a series of micro-tactical actions." Just as MOUT proposes, public and private space was strategically merged; "the IDF's strategy of 'walking through walls' involves a conception of the city as not just the site but also the very medium of warfare—a flexible, almost liquid medium that is forever contingent and in flux" (Weizman 2006:6).

In the fierce Jenin battle that occurred in March 2002, the IDF employed armored bulldozers and demolished hundreds of houses with their Palestinian residents inside, often burying them under the ruins of their houses. Through the use of D-9 bulldozers, the refugee camp was left virtually leveled, and the IDF used noncombatant Palestinians as "human shields" to protect Israelis as they moved from door to door (Hajjar 2006:29). The Jenin attacks, which sparked widespread criticism from a number of governments and international organizations,[15] were succeeded by an extreme form of spatial exclusion, by the establishment of a permanent barrier in the West Bank to separate Israel from the West Bank, and by "Operation Determined Path," which imposed a more than 2-month curfew on Palestinians (Handel 2009:626). Still later, after the outbreak of the Second Lebanon War and 6 months after the election of Hamas in Gaza in January 2006, there was an increase in the number of deadly attacks against Hezbollah targets in Lebanon, which, in a vicious circle of asymmetric violence, continue to the present day. This *violentia* of the bloody military operations, the bombardments, the deaths of so many people, and the destruction of so much geographical space goes hand in hand with *potestas*. A variety of social controls over Palestinians is exercised through administration: control of the passage of people and goods through checkpoints at the borders, control of the water system, control of air space and the sea, as well as control of the personal data of inhabitants. The collection of data on the Palestinian population and a series of other bureaucratic practices are, as Parsons and Salter maintain, part of a wider administrative strategy of discipline and biopolitical governmentality that is aimed at managing Palestinian geographic and social mobility: "Control over Palestinian mobility takes place at discontinuous and non-obvious sites: the issuances of passports, identity cards and transit permits, as well as the discretionary moments of checkpoints, the poignant but 'anonymous, one-time encounters' between occupier and occupied" (2008:704). Microtactics are implemented both by the army in the cities as well as by the legal agents of social control (e.g., administrative personnel, policemen, and guards at checkpoints), ones who weigh significantly on the everyday lives of Palestinians.

The indirect aim of such tactics is to erect insurmountable ethnic, geographic, and economic obstacles to groups fighting for recognition, power, and resources. For instance, Israelis divided Palestinian territory into zones, designated as A, B, C, H1, and H2. The Israeli policy toward each of these zones fluctuates in accordance with shifting goals and anticipations of threat, making it impossible for Palestinians to solve various administrative problems, ranging from water supply to political representation (see Hanafi 2009:108). What one is dealing with as one confronts the controlling and disciplining agents is, as described by Parsons and Salter, "a heterogeneous set of neocolonial agents" that elaborates a "postmodern map," a "matrix of control," wherein the activities of the military, government agencies, architects, real estate companies, and others are not easily distinguishable (2007:706).

Final Remarks

If, according to Clausewitz, "war is the continuation of politics by other means" (1982:119), and if Foucault's well-known inverse also applies—that "politics is a continuation of war by other means" (2003:15)—then MOUT neither contradicts Clausewitz's instrumentalization of war by state sovereignty nor conflicts with Foucault's radical account of politics as a means of war. As demonstrated by the operations in Afghanistan and Palestine, biopolitical and bureaucratic mechanisms, micropractices, and urbicide/spaciocide are not, as is often suggested, replacing state sovereignty. They are simply some of the changing ways in which sovereignty is being constructed. It is a sovereignty that is biopolitical in its conception and perpetuated through micro-tactics.

According to Clausewitz, war is a "chameleon". Modern urban warfare is a particular form of war in which specific powers have both the intrinsic capacity and the practical means (institutional, legal, political, and technological) to adjust their strategies in one direction or another, toward *potestas* or toward *violentia*, depending on their own inclinations and their own goals. Not all states have the expertise, resources, and international support required for the successful conduct of urban operations, and success is not guaranteed even for the powerful players. The Palestinian resistance to Israel and the resistance in Afghanistan to U.S./NATO forces show that the dynamics, the outcome, and the length of a conflict may be unpredictable. A hegemonic state may enjoy military and economic supremacy, but this may not be enough to safeguard it from a desperate plebeian resistance, by any and all means, from suicide bombings to urban guerrilla warfare.

Notes

1. For a different interpretation of the Clausewitzian concept of "trinity," see Bassford and Villacres (1995). These authors interpret "trinity" as a set of forces and potentials and not as a concrete grouping of actors. Creveld's notion of the trinity as "army, people, government" (or, in a similar version, as "army, society, state") may be extrapolated from Clausewitz's position but does not exhaust the content of the trinity. It is a reading that "derives from an *illustration* of Clausewitz's key concept, not the concept itself" (Bassford and Villacres 1995:15; emphasis in original). Bassford and Villacres (1995:18), thus, suggest a broader interpretation of Clausewitz's trinity, expanding it to include "emotion, chance, [and] rationality." Violent emotion or irrational forces point to a broader debate on Clausewitz's work, encompassing ethical issues that are raised by war, including Clausewitz's position that the feature which distinguishes war from other forms of human interaction is organized political violence. The elements of "chance and probability" reflect Clausewitz's ideas on military intelligence and the creative spirit, both of which are indispensable owing to the operational nature of warfare (Bassford and Villacres:14).

18   Political and Military Sociology

2. According to Evans' (2004) presentation of this tripartite distinction, "modern war" corresponds to conventional warfare between states (e.g., World War II); "postmodern war" is centered on the idea of reducing casualties by means of high-tech air operations and high-precision bombing, in accordance with "the West's cosmopolitan political values of a limited war, peace enforcement, and humanitarian military intervention"; and "pre-modern war" makes use of asymmetric methods. It informs the conventional military actions of "failed states" with ethno-cultural claims against the Western liberal value system, "reflecting a mix of sub-state and trans-state warfare based on age-old policies of identity, extremism and particularism" (Evans 2004:28–29).
3. Benjamin (1986) designates *Gewalt* as the complex amalgamation between law, police, and the state's claim on the monopoly of violence.
4. For instance, Hajjar emphasizes how after September 11, 2001, the United States and Israel adopted similar strategies, in violation of the Geneva Conventions. Hajjar suggests that, given their economic and military power, states such as the United States and Israel resort to policies of "alternative legality" for the purpose of achieving legitimacy for their urban operations (2006:37).
5. Reid offers a uniquely biopolitical conceptualization of war. He regards war as constitutive of human life itself: "Examining this war [War on Terror] biopolitically means attempting to think more rigorously about the actuality of relations between the problems of life and politics which are constitutive of it. . . . [I]t is a war over the political constitution of life in which the limitations of liberal accounts of humanity are being put to the test, if not rejected outright" (Reid 2006:1).
6. For instance, in his analysis of the Israeli–Palestinian conflict, Hanafi (2009:110) argues that Israeli strategies are not implemented in the traditional context of state sovereignty but in that of biopolitics. Their effect is to transform the political life of Palestinians into "bare life," where people are neither entitled to defend their rights nor concede "the right to have rights" (Hanafi:111). The fundamental priority is to establish "a delicate balance," and the attempt to achieve this objective is understood to be a "political and scientific problem" (Hanafi:113). In this connection, Hanafi suggests that the dynamics of the Israeli–Palestinian conflict cannot be understood if one insists on employing the concept of "genocide" as an analytical tool. In terms of casualties, he maintains that the 60-year period of the Israeli–Palestinian conflict cannot be compared with the 6-week massacre in Rwanda or the 4-year Bosnian–Serbian war (Hanafi:111): "Any reading of the Israeli-Palestinian conflict using genocide as a measure of the extent of the colonial violence will be incapable of understanding the dynamic of this conflict" (Hanafi:111). In order to understand genocide quantitatively in terms of the number of casualties, one should overlook the structural character of genocide in war (see Shaw 2004:149–153). The distinguishing of genocide from war does not result in the inclusion of any new factor. This is why Shaw (153) emphasizes that, "while historically cities have been implicated in wars and specific anti-urban violence has been a feature of recent warfare, it does not make sense to separate urbicide (or other "'-cides'") from genocide or genocide from war."
7. "Spaciocide," in contrast to genocide, foreshadows pre-emptive actions of classification, clearing, disciplining, and social exclusion in the context of a decentralized biopolitical strategy that is targeted at "bodies" which are in the process of being transformed into Homo Sacer (Hanafi 2009:110).
8. These concepts place the emphasis on different consequences of military destruction. See Shaw (2004:151) for a critique.
9. The "light footprint" strategy in Afghanistan has been described in a report by the Secretary General of the UN as an intervention strategy "relying on as limited

10. an international presence and on as many Afghan staff as possible, and using common support services where possible, thereby leaving a light expatriate 'footprint'" (2002: 16).
10. For an overview of a series of U.S. operations in Afghanistan, see also Gregory (2004); Ali (2008); and Lister (2007).
11. Indicative of the ideology of the "War on Terror" is the history of the names given to the operation. The initial name employed by the Bush administration was the "Crusade Against Terrorists." Due to its associations with Christian crusades and suggestions of intolerance, this was, however, soon replaced by the name "Operation Infinite Justice." This second title was also criticized, as, in the eyes of critics, the United States appeared to be implying that it was a power which was capable of establishing infinite justice. Finally, on July 10, 2001, the campaign was named "Operation Enduring Freedom."(For more information on the process of naming these operations, see Misdaq 2006:253–255).
12. In the framework of the International Security Assistance Force (ISAF), a number of teams have been created, such as the Provincial Reconstruction Teams (PRTs), the Operational Mentoring and Liaison Teams, for police and humanitarian missions, as well as a variety of local councils and commissions that support military and political targets: the "Action Plan on Peace, Justice, and Reconciliation"; the Afghanistan Independent Electoral Commission; and others.
13. Apart from the UN's Assistance Mission in Afghanistan and the different UN programs, the European Union has also participated in the operations by deploying more than 22,000 troops under NATO supervision. In the context of the EU's Common Foreign and Security Policy (CFSP), the EU-Police Mission in Afghanistan (EUPOL Afghanistan) was approved in 2007. Between 2007 and 2010, 610 million euros were earmarked for the Islamic Republic of Afghanistan and the National Afghan Army.
14. Not only at the London International Conference on Afghanistan in 2010, but also at a conference in Kabul in 2010, which, for symbolic reasons, was the first to take place in Afghanistan, with 76 countries participating and draconian security measures in force, the basic line was similar: Afghanistan must be "reconstructed;" the Taliban poses an extreme threat to international security; and the Afghan Government, with its new Constitution and in co-operation with NGOs and other international organizations, is required, under the terms of the Afghanistan Compact, to establish functional social institutions (including schools, public administration, police, courts, and prisons), promote economic development and the creation of jobs, fight drug trafficking, establish border police, and further women's rights (http://afghanistan.hmg.gov.uk/en/conference/).
15. In response to the international criticism, "humanitarian" excuses were offered to justify the Jenin raid. Henkin (2003:15) illustrates this point: He says that given the IDF's training in urban warfare, neither did the IDF commit war crimes in the course of its "wide-ranging anti-terrorist campaign" at the Jenin refugee camp, nor was Jenin a "massacre of innocents," as presented by foreign media. These actions were rather "the result of decisions made by both the military command and the civilian leadership as part of a deliberate policy aimed at keeping civilian casualties to a minimum." In what way does the IDF differ from other armies engaged in urban wars? According to Henkin (15), the IDF did not show the same brutality in Jenin as the Russians did against the Chechens in Grozny in 1999. The IDF neither attacked the city with all its force nor destroyed it completely as the Russian army had done in the case of Grozny. Events in Jenin, therefore, "testify [to] the high moral standard employed by the IDF—a rare demonstration of humanity in the midst of battle" (15).

References

Agamben, Giorgio. 1998. *Homo Sacer: Sovereign Power and Bare Life*. Stanford, CA: Stanford University Press.
Ali, Tariq. 2008. "Afghanistan: Mirage of the Good War." *New Left Review* 50 (March–April):5–22.
Anderson, Gary. 2010. "Counterinsurgency vs. Counterterrorism." *Small Wars Journal* 2. Retrieved March 3, 2010 (http://smallwarsjournal.com/jrnl/art/counterinsurgency-vs-counterterrorism).
Azoulay, Ariella and Adi Ophir. 2009. "The Order of Violence." Pp. 99–140 in Adi Ophir, Michal Ginovi, and Sari Hanafi, eds. *The Power of Inclusive Exclusion: Anatomy of Israeli Rule in the Occupied Palestinian Territories*. New York: Zone Books.
Bassford, Christopher and J. Edward Villacres. 1995. "Reclaiming the Clausewitzian Trinity." *Parameters* XXV (Autumn):9–19.
Benjamin, Walter. 1986. "The Critique of Violence." Pp. 277–300 in Peter Demertz, ed. *Reflections*. New York: Schocken Books.
Biersteker, Thomas J. and Cynthia Weber. 1996. "The Social Construction of Sovereignty." Pp. 1–21 in Thomas J. Biersteker and Cynthia Weber, eds. *State Sovereignty as Social Construct*. Cambridge: Cambridge University Press.
Bitsakis, Eftychis. and Demetris Belantiss. 2005. *Οι Πόλεμοι της Νέας Τάξης* (The Wars of the New Order). Athens: Proskinio.
Boniface, Pascal. 2004. *Οι Πόλεμοι του Αύριο* (The Wars of Tomorrow). Athens: Papazisis.
Clausewitz, Carl von. 1982. *On War*. London: Penguin Books.
Creveld, Martin van. 1991. *The Transformation of War*. New York: The Free Press.
Doctrine for Joint Urban Operations (JUO), Joint Publication 3-06, Joint Chiefs of Staff, 2002.
Doty, Roxanne Lynn. 1996. "Sovereignty and the Nation: Constructing the Boundaries of National Identity." Pp. 121–147 in Thomas J. Biersteker and Cynthia Weber, eds. *State Sovereignty as Social Construct*. Cambridge: Cambridge University Press.
Evans, Michael. 2004. "Clausewitz's Chameleon: Military Theory and Practice in the early 21st Century." Pp. 26–45 in Michael Evans, Alan Ryan, and Russell Parkin, eds. *Future Armies, Future Challenges: Land Warfare in the Information Age*. Crows Nest, NSW: Allen & Unwin.
Foucault, Michel. 2003. *Society Must be Defended*. New York: Picador.
Graham, Stephen. 2004. "Constructing Urbicide by Bulldozer." Pp. 192–213 in Stephen Graham, ed. *Cities, War and Terrorism: Towards an Urban Geopolitics*. Oxford: Blackwell Publishing.
Gregory, Derek.2006. "Vanishing Points Law, Violence, and Exception in the Global War Prison." Pp. 205–236 in Derek Gregory and Allan Pred, eds. *Violent Geographies: Fear, Terror, and Political Violence*. New York: Routledge.
Gregory, Derek. 2004. *The Colonial Present: Afghanistan, Palestine, Iraq*. Oxford: Blackwell Publishing.
Grivas, Konstantinos. 2008. *Το Τέλος του Πετρελαίου και η Αρχή της Νέας Αμερικάνικης Γεωστρατηγικής* (The End of Oil and the Emergence of the New American Geostrategy). Athens: Livanis.
Hajjar, Lisa. 2006. "International Humanitarian Law in 'Wars on Terror:' A Comparative Analysis of Israeli and American Doctrines and Policies." *Journal of Palestine Studies* 36(1):21–42.
Hanafi, Sari. 2009. "Spacio-cide: Colonial politics, Invisibility and Rezoning in Palestinian Territory." *Contemporary Arab Affairs* 2(1):106–121.

Handel, Ariel. 2009. "Chronology of the Occupation Regime, 1967-2007." Pp. 603–634 in Adi Ophir, Michael Ginovi and Sari Hanafi, eds. *The Power of Inclusive Exclusion: Anatomy of Israeli Rule in the Occupied Palestinian Territories*. New York: Zone Books.
Henkin, Yagil. 2003. "Urban Warfare and the Lessons of Jenin." *Azure* 15 (Summer). Retrieved December 12, 2008 (http://www.azure.org.il/article.php?id=240).
Herold, Marc W. 2006. "Urban Dimensions of the Punishment of Afghanistan by US Bombs." Pp. 312–329 in Stephen Graham, ed. *Cities, War and Terrorism: Towards an Urban Geopolitics*. Oxford: Blackwell Publishing.
Hills, Alice. 2004. *Future War in Cities: Rethinking a Liberal Dilemma*. London: Frank Cass Publishers.
Kaldor, Mary. 2003. *Global Civil Society: An Answer to War*. Cambridge: Polity Press.
Lister, Sarah. 2007. "Understanding State-Building and Local Governance in Afghanistan." Working Paper no. 14. London School of Economics, Crisis State Research Centre.
Misdaq, Nabi. 2006. *Afghanistan: Political Frailty and External Interference*. London: Routledge.
Parsons, Nigel and Mark B. Salter. 2008. "Israeli Biopolitics: Closure, Territorialisation and Governmentality in the Occupied Palestinian Territories." *Geopolitics* 13(4):701–723.
Peace, Reconciliation and Justice in Afghanistan: Action Plan of the Government of the Islamic Republic of Afghanistan. Retrieved April, 22, 2011 (http://www.aihrc.org.af/).
Peceny, Mark and Yuri Bosin. 2009. "Counterinsurgency in Afghanistan: Lessons and Perspectives." Paper Presented at the Annual Convention of the International Studies Association, New York.
Press, Daryl. 1999. "Urban Warfare: Options, Problems and the Future." Paper presented at MIT Security Studies, Conference of the MIT Security Studies Program, Hanscom Air Force Base, Bedford, MA. Retrieved February, 2, 2010 (http://web.mit.edu/ssp/Publications/confseries/urbanwarfare/urbanwarfare.html).
Reid, Julian. 2006. *The Biopolitics of the War on Terror: Life Struggles, Liberal Modernity, and the Defence of Logistical Societies*. Manchester: Manchester University Press.
Report of UN Secretary-General, UN Doc A/56/875-S/2002/278, March 18, 2002.
Said, Edward. 2002. *Η Τρομοκρατία και η Κοινωνία των Πολιτών* (Terrorism and Civil Society). Athens: Metehmio.
Schmitt, Carl. 2007. *Theory of the Partisan: Intermediate Commentary on the Concept of the Political*. New York: Telos Press Publishing.
Shaw, Martin. 2004. "*New Wars of the City: Relationships of 'Urbicide' and 'Genocide.'*" Pp. 141–153 in Stephen Graham, ed. *Cities, War and Terrorism: Towards an Urban Geopolitics*. Oxford: Blackwell Publishing.
Spiller, Roger. 2004. "Sharp Corners: Combat Operations in Urban Areas." Pp. 82–95 in Michael Evans, Russell Parkin, and Alan Ryan, eds. *Future Armies, Future Challenges: Land Warfare in the Information Age*. St Leonards, NSW: Allen & Unwin, Crows Nest.
Virillio, Paul and Sylvere Lotringer. 2007. *Pure War*. Los Angeles:Semiotext(e).
Weizman, Eyal. 2006. "The Art of War: Deleuze, Guattari, Debord and the Israeli Defence Force." *Frieze Magazine: Art and Architecture* 99. Retrieved January 17, 2010 (http://www.frieze.com/issue/article/the_art_of_war/).
Wulf, Herbert. 2005. *Internationalizing and Privatizing War and Peace*. Hampshire: Palgrave Macmillan.
Žižek, Slavoj. 2002. *Welcome to the Desert of the Real: Five Essays on September 11 and Related Dates*. New York: Verso.

Postmodern or Conservative? Competing Security Communities over Military Doctrine: Israeli National-Religious Soldiers as Counter [Strategic] Culture Agents

Udi Lebel
Ariel University Center
Samaria and Jordan Rift R&D Center

In this article, I refer to "strategic culture" as a conceptual locus and describe the implications of the increasing number of religious-Zionist youth recruited into the Israeli military. Against the background of a postmodern versus traditional army, I argue that the motivating force for the nostalgic return to the martial values of Israel's early wars is rooted in a conservative backlash against liberal and "humane" considerations, rather than in religious ideology. The war against terror requires the same attitudes that more traditional battlefield confrontations do.

In recent years, public attention has been growing with regard to two demographic trends in the Israeli Defense Force (IDF):

a. Members of the middle class—western, secular, and left wing—have ceased to regard the military as an arena for integration, investment, and service (Peri 2007:128). The social elites, to which the majority of the military commanders belong, experienced a "crisis of motivation" in the final years of the millennium, and their sons "ceased to regard the military path as the dominant way to advance their personal careers" (Peri 2007:125).

b. At the same time, we are witnessing a growing trend for integration of the sons of religious Zionists in the IDF as officers, commanders, and fighters in elite and combat units, where their numbers as a percentage of the total are much higher relative to those of the general population (Cohen 2005). This was achieved through educational institutions that imparted religious, normative, and civic values which were pertinent to their integration in commanding positions in the military.

These two processes transformed the Israeli military command, which originally tended to be secular and identified with the socialist parties of the past and, still later, with the upper-middle classes, allowing it to be increasingly dominated by more peripheral elements—new immigrants, minorities, and, above all, by religious soldiers whom Peri (2007) identified as the "new military elite."

This change in the military's demographic characteristics has already been addressed in several contexts:

a. First to be addressed is the effect of the army's social composition on civilian criticism and protests related to security issues. The argument here has been that the more that fighters and casualties belong to ethno-republican groups, the less critical and more friendly the atmosphere in which the military operates will be (Levy 2010). This is especially the case with regard to public reactions to casualties (Lebel 2010, 2011).
b. The process by which religious groups are joining the military reflects a change in religious social thinking. Here, we are dealing with a society that, for years, has educated and encouraged its youth to acquire intellectual religious skills and has regarded the military profession as extraneous. However, since the 1990s, such groups were subjected to processes of militarization and began to regard war as a part of the normative Jewish experience (Cohen 2005).
c. As more and more religious groups were recruited to join the army, increased research on the issue of diversity management in the IDF emerged (Lumsky-Feder and Ben-Ari 2003), identifying an inherent conflict, especially between religion and gender.
d. Research also focused on the dilemmas faced by the religious soldier, involving a conflict of loyalties—one between obedience to military commanders and the instructions of his rabbinical educators (Cohen 1993; Rosman-Stollman 2008). This led to research on how such a religious soldier would react to orders contrary to his ideology, such as settlements evacuation, for example (Bick 2007; Lebel 2008; Levy 2007a).

It should be mentioned that both among the public and in the media discourse on this topic, the growing numbers of religious soldiers in the armed forces caused considerable moral panic, focusing on three issues:

1. The implication of this integration on the status of women in military service;
2. Possible future reactions of religious officers to orders related to the removal of settlements in the West Bank; and
3. The future work of military rabbis, who might strive to shape the entire military rather than just the religious soldiers according to Jewish norms and values.

The Research Approach, Its Aims, and Uniqueness

This article does not intend to analyze the integration of the new groups—particularly the religious groups—in the IDF from the point of view of secularism and religiosity but, rather, on a continuum of conservatism–postmodernism. Namely, it aims at examining the effect of demographic changes in the IDF on military doctrine and conduct. In doing so, the article will not focus on extreme cases that are not a part of everyday military life (such as the removal of settlements) or on the cultural implications (the status of women, for example), but rather on the implications of the demographic change on the military's daily conduct—its decisions, its theory of warfare, its fight against terrorism, and the way it frames threats and challenges. I argue that after years in which the IDF had become a postmodern army, the integration of religious Zionists into the army constitutes a counterculture and is an attempt to render the military as conservative as it was before having undergone the postmodern revolution. In other words, it has been an attempt to revive its activist ethos and initiative so as to prevail in war without being encumbered by ethical–legal–civilian considerations and ideologies, which have prevented it from crushing terrorism. Here, I refer to a nostalgic practice—an aim to "restore the army" to what it was at its founding—one required to lead conventional warfare, rather than fighting a guerilla and terrorist war.

The IDF in the Postmodern Condition

From the beginning of the 1990s, Israeli society has become increasingly exposed to what has been termed "the postmodern situation." This term refers to processes that affected the generation following the "founding elite" of the State. The latter were, for the most part, individuals with an upper-middle class, secular, western background with center-to-left political orientations. The second generation acquired values that were characterized by individuation, pragmatism, and privatization, accompanied by a discourse of rights containing sentiments of victimization. The second generation's ethos was only slightly imbued with the founding national ideology, and its adoption of a postnationalist outlook tended to regard the national-Zionist undertaking as aggressive, colonialist, and militaristic. These processes were a part of an attempt to formulate a liberal–secular–global civil society that would compete with the ethno-republican-local civil society which began to gather force among groups outside the ruling elite, with the religious Zionists being among them (Shafir and Peled 2002).

From the time these post-national processes began to influence the Israeli elite, the senior ranks of the IDF also began to exhibit characteristics associated with what has been termed a "postmodern army," a process in which armies reformulate their values, organization, and operations in a manner reflecting the culture of the social elite (Ingelhart 2000). This led to a civil-military gap, in turn, in which the cultural values of civil society do not match those required of an army geared to defend its civilian population. The gap is also reflected in the differing social profile of army personnel vis-à-vis the dominant class as well as the ethnic and religious composition of the civilian establishment. The postmodern army, thus, adapts itself to the outlook of the civilian elite it serves, while at the same time engaging in a process that diminishes its concern for issues of national security, in general, and the valorous military experience in particular. By undertaking missions in alternative arenas (economic, academic, media, and legal) and adopting organizational values associated with these missions, the army becomes thoroughly postmodern (Morgan 2001). These processes characterize the upper-middle class, the first to experience the processes of globalization, individuation, and post-nationalism, to be more sensitive to the costs of war in terms of money and casualties, and which attaches lesser honor to heroism (Higley and Pakulski 2007). This class also rejects the legitimacy of resorting to violence and prefers resolving conflicts through diplomacy and compromise. The military leadership, whose senior officers and high command come from the dominant social strata in society, reflects this postmodern *Weltanschauung* and manages to overcome the "cognitive dissonance" (Simionato 1991) by means of a strategic and tactical military policy, attempting to minimize losses through defensive and preventive approaches to war. Moreover, senior military echelons express support for the civilian-directed military policy and lobby only half-heartedly against budget cuts, conceding that there is no need to swell the ranks of the military and agreeing to a reduction of training maneuvers for ground troops.

Characteristics of the Postmodern Army

Legalization

The incorporation of human and civil rights discourse by the liberal elite led to the internalization of codes of behavior that were influenced by international laws of war and upheld by international courts of law (Singer 2004). The IDF also yielded to these legal orientations, a fact that affected tactical decisions in battlefield operations. This has resulted in increased legal supervision of military operations by civilians (Meydani 2007), especially by military attorneys who now play an important role in policy formulation regarding the deployment of forces (Chouchane 2009).

Operations Other than War

Since the main arena of combat has shifted to the West Bank, the IDF turned into an army that trains its forces to fight terror as well as to employ a variety of policing strategies pertaining to the maintenance of order—ones which characterize a humanitarian army (Weiss and Campbell 1991). These elements suit an army operating in civilian areas prepared to undertake additional roles, such as the promotion of democracy, the maintenance of peace, and the like (Burk 1997).

Civil Society, Civilian Discourse, and Communication

Similar to other postmodern armies, the IDF has become an army whose policies are influenced not only by civil society (Kaldir 2003), particularly human rights organizations and social movements (Helman 2001; Peri 2001), but also by an increased sensitivity to media coverage (Peri 2007).

Post-Heroism, Absence of Decisive Outcomes and Casualty Panic

As a part of its tendency to display casualty phobia and casualty panic, Israeli military policy now exhibits an anti-combatant orientation, preferring this to the allocation of time for military maneuvers (Avidor 2008). With regard to doctrine, the tendency involves relying on the air force, long-range artillery, and special forces because of the fear of political backlash over endangering soldiers' lives in land campaigns (Bracken and Alcala 1994; Gordon 1998). "Post-heroic" combat, as defined by

Luttwak (1995), has led the IDF to conduct or even to cancel missions on the basis of the degree to which solders will be endangered (Lebel 2010). As a part of this tendency, it distanced itself from the notion of "a decisive campaign outcome," conveyed through the term *Revolution in Military Affairs* (RMA)[1] (Everts and Isernia 2005), and replaced decisive conclusion by the "management of confrontation" concept (Merom 2003:15).

It should be noted, here, that the concept of a postmodern army refers not only to military operations but also to ideology (Moskos 2000a). In this regard, after the Oslo Accords, a part of the Israeli liberal elite wished that the IDF would become an army of peace, whose soldiers would engage in non-aggressive missions (Kasher 2001). It should be noted that this conception is foreign to Israeli military doctrine. From the very inception of the IDF, its values have been based on notions such as commitment to mission, transferring the war to enemy territory, a swift conclusion of military operations, achieving deterrence and recognition, attributing importance to control of territory, and a readiness for sacrifice (Kober 1996; Merom 1999; Lebel 2010).

Research Argument

Culture is, by definition, a process of negotiation between ethos, myths, and values. The postmodern situation is a state of conflict between the dominant and counter cultures (Bauman 1987). Familiar examples might include conflicts between the local and global, men and women, as well as between heroic and victim cultures. Our millennium is one in which, according to Inglehart (1990), culture shifts have occurred. These affect not only consumerism but also national and security issues.

According to the argument presented here, the Israeli military is an arena in which cultural negotiations are conducted, and the religious-Zionist group is a cultural agent, leading and promoting what I will call, "the conservative security culture," acting as a counterculture to the idea of a postmodern military. I argue that this is likely to affect military doctrine in the future.

According to Ben-Eliezer (2001:62), "if society enters the post-modernist mode and promulgates peace—its army will follow suit." The presence of religious Zionists in the IDF serves as an avant-guard for the advancement of a conservative counterculture opposed to the culture that has turned the IDF into a postmodern army. This vanguard has been termed "an oppositionary security community" (Adler and Barnett 1998), promoting an anti-hegemonic counter-discourse (Desmond, McDonagh, and O'Donohoe 2000; Teridman 1985). It reflects a venue shifting "from counter-culture to subculture to (strategic) culture" (Walter 1981). In our case, a quasi-romantic aura infuses this military counterculture. The religious Zionists envisage a nostalgic return to authentic martial values and are motivated by opposition to a hegemony that they believe has betrayed the basic founding ideals of the IDF. One of their central goals is to upgrade military performance to its optimal level to enable it to fulfill its primary public objective, namely guaranteeing security to all residents of the Jewish state and the state's survival through the elimination of terrorism.

On a continuum ranging from conservatism to postmodernism, this may be viewed as an effort to nudge the army toward the conservative end of the spectrum in all matters connected to its functioning—its combat doctrine, its missions, its organized values, and particularly its readiness to combat terror. With regard to the fight against terror, the conservative elements regard current efforts as limited confrontations rather than as a war that should be won. This orientation is not conducted in the language of religious discourse, but rather through the employment of a wistful narrative that appeals to republican standards of virtue, civic duty, courage, and resoluteness. There is a longing to return to a strategic realism of the kind posited by Huntington and Clausewitz in order to counter the adoption of postmodernism.

This is a tendency toward conservatism, rather than religiosity. Religiosity is the opposition to secularization (Hervieu-Leger 1990; Troper 2000; Tschannen 1991). However, the community of religious Zionists, as I analyze, is also and, perhaps, first and foremost, an opposition to postmodernism and neoliberalism.

The origin of this claim resides in the school of strategic culture, which maintains that security policy and military doctrine are dependent on the culture of the communities serving in the armed forces, in general, and in positions of senior command, in particular. Gray (1999) regards strategic culture as related to military thinking and action and follows Freedman (2006), who maintained that a security community will act in a certain way under the influence of its cultural narrative; namely, it will follow a course of interpretation or understanding of itself and the reality in which it operates. Security communities think, understand, and operate in conjunction with a plot or dominant cultural narrative in which they are embedded. Burk (1998), who titled his book, *The Adaptive Military*, did so to convey the idea that a political culture, which brings with it new narratives for understanding reality, will shape the army and its military doctrine accordingly (see also Kier 1995). Moreover, the structure of the army and its objectives are attuned to public opinion and to the social groups that man its ranks.

This article will focus on the influence of the accelerated entrance of religious Zionists into the army and on the army's strategic culture (i.e., on what Horowitz [1970] termed "flexible responsiveness"). The notion of flexible responsiveness illustrates that military conduct in the IDF depends no less on the attitudes of the military commanders than on the decrees of the political echelons. Moreover, the Israeli army is an institution that shapes policy, rather than merely carrying it out—a fact which turns its commanders into partners in shaping Israeli security policy, as Peri (2007) has shown us in his research. As a result, any change in the composition of the army is likely to have political significance in the future.

Methodology

The research analyzes texts written by opinion leaders (the religious Zionists). These are individuals who enjoy public esteem on account of being considered exemplary moral members of their communities. They are also perceived as being eminently suited to act as mediators and interpreters on intellectual matters, in general, and on issues of security, in particular. Cohen has explained that religious-Zionist soldiers have been operating under two different authorities—the military and the civilian (social–cultural–rabbinical) (Cohen 2000). In this research, I examine the security discourse of the civilian authority, deliberately avoiding senior military personnel from the ranks of the religious Zionists. These leaders of civilian public opinion act as mediators and intensifiers of public discussion (Habermas 1974:53). They are people representing the accepted values that guide behavior in all areas of life (in this case, that of security). They are also people who facilitate the framing of military and security issues for the entire community (Hedley and Clark 2007). Obsborne (2004) called such individuals "public intellectuals" and maintained that, from the public's point of view, such individuals have the moral authority to extend or withdraw the legitimacy of the state's discourse. Coining the term "the intellectual as mediator," Obsborne (2004:430) maintained that such people influence the acceptance of a policy, the demands of the state, and everyday events—those occurring below and among the followers of such intellectuals.

In the current research, the religious Zionists whose discourse is analyzed serve as public intellectuals—those people who founded settlements or who have headed public institutions, rabbis—especially those heading "Yeshivot Hesder" (Israeli yeshiva programs that combine military service with Torah studies)—or pre-military academies, editors of sectarian newspapers, and publicists. The texts analyzed are policy documents, interviews in the media, opinion columns, and *Responsa Literature* (a customary pedagogical tool dating to ancient times, where individuals submit questions regarding contemporary issues to the rabbi or a group of rabbis who then deliver the response via public pronouncements).

In this study, I have adopted the method of frame analysis—combining the theories of social constructivism, symbolic politics, and discourse applied mainly in research based on documentary analysis (Johnston 1995). This methodology is well suited to a community frame analysis (in this case, a security community), claiming that in all communities a discursive solidarity exists, consisting of individuals with relatively homogeneous attitudes who provide a narrative identity for each member of the community. This is an attempt to identify a "narrative identity card" (Spector-Marzel 2010) that is a series of arguments, emotions, and demands and particularly the interpretative package through which the community's members comprise its identity and understand reality.

Findings

"Shooting and Crying"—The Debate Over the Trauma, Ethics, and Human Rights Discourse of the IDF

Morals versus Victory

In the first and, especially, in the second Intifada, there was a rising incidence of "shoot and cry" discourse among the Israeli elite. This victimized discourse describes the Israeli soldier as pained by the demand to kill and conduct other warfare activities and has been labeled "the beginning of the decadence of the Israeli ethos" by the former Chairman of the Council of Judea and Samaria (Harel 2009).

The growing concern with ethical dilemmas intensified (Gal 1990) to the point where it became a discursive genre bearing testimony to the suffering fighter who regards himself as a victim because he is victimizing others. The fighter is traumatized because he is required to deviate from moral standards in his behavior toward Palestinians. This phenomenon culminated politically and manifested itself through a variety of institutionalized settings (for example, the protest group Breaking Silence) that encouraged soldiers to circulate a narrative based on therapeutic testimonies in order to encourage them to refrain from serving in the Israeli-administered West Bank and Gaza Strip.

Against the background of the phenomena just mentioned, the IDF was inclined to adopt a human rights discourse, drawing on international laws of warfare, which reflected efforts to minimize inflicting injury on a category of people in the war-zone defined as "uninvolved," with all the difficulties entailed therein under combat conditions.[2] The IDF established an Ethics Committee, which formulated "an ethical code for the war on terrorism" and convened assemblies of combat echelons serving in the administered territories to discuss the operational aspects of the "ethical combat against terrorism" (Kasher and Yadlin 2005) implemented during the second Intifada. For example, at a conference, titled "To Attain Victory and Remain a Human Being," which took place in the Judea and Samaria Division of the IDF, it was emphasized that achieving a definitive resolution of a conflict did not enjoy priority over values, such as "purity of arms," and that the challenge of the educational command in the IDF was "to impart qualities of restraint and control to the soldier" though he was trained to be pugnacious and aggressive in the face of the enemy. In this human rights discourse, terms such as "containment" as well as "the ability to listen, to understand, and to respond,"[3] were adopted (Raveh and Pakar-Rinat 2000:23). Senior army officers went as far as to say that this new military culture was expected to instill the notion that the ethical behavior of combatants was a more exalted value than commitment to the military mission (Gordon 2002: 87).

Amos Yadlin addressed the question of the IDF's handling of Palestinian terror during the second Intifada. Yadlin, a pilot who had also served as commander of the military war colleges and, later, as head of Military Intelligence, was not referring to a concept of operations that was related to the objective needs of security operations but rather to those based on "other" values. Thus, his pronouncements described the postmodern situation that downplayed control, in general, and military sovereignty, in particular:

> The magnitude of our operations was limited by the extent of legitimacy accorded to us. What is Europe prepared to tolerate? What are the Americans prepared to accept? What does the Security Council have to say? . . . All this was achieved through focused action against terror while trying not to inflict injury upon innocents. . . . We examine the possibility of striking against terror without harming innocents and whether we abide by ethical criteria. (Lord 2003)

Amnon Lord, as editor of the weekly *Makor Rishon*, a newspaper associated with religious Zionists, commented: "It should be clearly stated that although the IDF abides by ethical criteria, it does not abide by basic criteria adhering to its most important mission, that of defending the nation, defending the Israeli civilian" (Lord 2003).

Religious Zionists point to the Supreme Court as the agency responsible for the IDF's deviation from its operational obligations while enforcing limitations on its activities. In their view, the Court's rulings and values prove that its justices prefer to protect the lives of the enemy over the lives of Israeli soldiers and restrict the IDF's efforts to eliminate Palestinian terrorism. This preference is consistently expressed in legal decisions dealing with combat restrictions, such as its decision to render the neighbor procedure as illegal,[4] intervention in the designated positioning of the separation barrier,[5] and matters concerning the military's policy of targeted killing[6] (Sultany 2007). The Supreme Court was accused of representing the preferences of the cosmopolitan over the local, the post-national over the Zionist, and, especially, of turning its back on the soldiers of the nation by limiting their ability to fight. For example, after Operation Defensive Shield,[7] the Supreme Court was criticized for abandoning IDF soldiers through its rulings, as soldiers were not allowed to bomb terrorists' hiding places because of the potential harm to innocent civilians. Instead, soldiers had to fight face to face with terrorists, inducing more soldier casualties. Avoiding mass artillery and preferring to risk soldiers'—rather than Palestinian—lives was believed to reflect the high court's values and decisions.

According to Rabbi Eliezer Melamed, "judges of the Supreme Court are the main establishment institution [sic] preventing the IDF from attacking and neutralizing the enemy as would usually be expected." With regard to what he called the "harm" caused by the Court's decisions and its influence on Operation Defensive Shield, he wrote:

> [The judges of the Supreme Court] forbade the bombing of terrorist houses by the IDF ... [and] as a corollary they (the IDF) refrained from bombing the Palestine refugee camps (which led to the death of dozens of soldiers). (Melamed 2008)

The Supreme Court, however, is no more than a symbolic representation of the post-national culture. Thus, for example, after what was perceived as the failure of the second Lebanese War, contrary to all the calls for the resignation of the Defense Minister, the Prime Minister, and the Chief of Staff, the manifest position of many public opinion leaders from the religious-Zionist camp was that it was the strategic culture which caused the IDF to lose the war. According to a publicist writing in the weekly magazine, *B'sheva*, which has a wide readership among the religious public and the settlers in the administered territories:

> The central problem of this War was the conception of victory with hands tied. The total failure emanated from the assumption that it was possible to achieve victory by using tweezers, with a minimum of injury to civilians, unlimited openness to the media, a restricted time schedule, and an excessively powerful urge to appease the world. . . . And a Christian morality (such as not to bombard houses even after their occupants were told to leave). . . . As long as we are still prisoners of an overstated morality . . . the morality of restraint, we are likely to lose the next war, even if another thousand Prime Ministers and two thousand Defence Ministers were to resign. (Segal, September 7, 2006)

Operation Cast Lead, in which Israeli forces entered the Gaza Strip in order to put an end to the missiles fired by Hamas, was perceived as a moment of insight, in which the right conclusions were drawn from Operation Defensive Shield, and the army was freed from the fetters of postmodern combat. This military operation was perceived as dominated by the conservative security community in the IDF. As soon as the yeshiva soldiers from Shala'bim set out to battle, "the head of the yeshiva gave them clear instructions regarding the ethics of combat required in the light of Jewish law (*halakha*), relying upon the medieval Jewish thinker, Maimonides, and others," making it clear to his students that:

> in a situation of war in all situations in which their lives or the lives of their comrades were regarded as sufficiently endangered and the choice was to endanger the lives of innocents—there should not be a moment's hesitation. . . . There should be no doubts as to who should be preferred. (quoted in Rotenberg 2010)

As a former tank crew man, the rabbi made it even more clear to his pupils, who served in the armored corps, that "If a tank crew man, in a position where he is about to open fire, hesitates even for a moment for fear of harming innocent civilians—he is liable to endanger his tank, himself and his comrades" (quoted in Rotenberg 2010).

Reserve General Avihai Ronzki, another former chief rabbi in the army who had commanded troops in Operation Cast Lead, was convinced that

> if the issue is whether endangering your life to enter a house, to check a suspicious object, or to choose the alternative of endangering someone residing there, your life should definitely take precedence over that of the other, even if it is not the enemy but some person in this house. (quoted in Rotenberg 2010)

In this Operation, commanders instructed the soldiers "to choose the right victim," that is, to prefer endangering the enemy population rather than IDF soldiers.

> In contrast to past deviations, the Office of the Chief of Staff instructed combat soldiers ... that in any doubtful situation they should favour their own life over that of the enemy, and this declaration of values brought Ashkenazi—the Chief of Staff—unmitigated praise. (Shilo 2011)

From a Decisive Campaign Outcome to Conducting a Restricted Confrontation: The Foundation of OTRI (The Operational Theory and Research Institute)—The Agent of Postmodernism in the Military

"Limited confrontation" was a doctrinal order circulated by the IDF in 2001, entailing several assumptions, including that of not perceiving terror as a vital threat and abandoning the view that a decisive outcome vis-à-vis terror is possible or even required. This instruction was expressed in the language used in the framework of the campaign—in this case, "prolonged attrition,"[8] a term expressing readiness to conduct a drawn-out war, which was contrary to the customary Israeli military doctrine that Israeli society and its economy are unable to endure combat over an extended period of time (Wagman 2002). The doctrine of limited confrontation distinguished between the political and military echelons of terrorist organizations and refrained from striking the former and granting immunity to it (Laqueur 1996). According to this approach, an army that is anxious to cope with terror should not operate in a traditional way as a decisive combat force. This approach is known as "operations other than war" (OOTW) and is a part of the RMA concept. In order to create a firm base for this new doctrine and allow the army to adapt itself to appropriate values, consciousness, and behavior, the IDF introduced special activities at the OTRI.

Specifically, following the Oslo Accords, the IDF established an institute for the purpose of developing a doctrine of military campaign. Dov Tamari and Shimon Naveh, two retired senior officers and brigadier generals in the reserves who also held Ph.D.s in history, were entrusted with this undertaking. The institute was to be responsible for the formulation of a new military doctrine in the areas of combat principles, perception of reality, military concepts, and especially military language. Established in 1955, the institute was to serve as an agent of change to incorporate the values, language, and conceptions that would make the IDF into a postmodern army and enable it to internalize the conception of RMA (Kober 2011:720). According to Kober, the revolution in combat doctrine promoted by the institute envisaged an army operating with a minimum of casualties, depending mainly on technology and using a language with a postmodern intellectual aroma (Kober 2011:719–720).

It was this institute that was responsible for the directions which guided the actions of the IDF in the West Bank at the outbreak of the second Intifada. It was designed to turn the soldier from a combatant into an interpreter and from a soldier into a diplomat regarding his mission—not as something that should be completed at all costs but, rather, in a limited and restrained way (Raveh and Pakar-Rinat 2000). This required combatants to internalize their situation as part and parcel of the political system as well as that of the army—as part of the peace regime rather than the war regime (Moskos 2000a, 2000b). As testified by two of the proponents of this approach: "[O]ne of the principles of war cherished by the IDF since its inception, is initiative and aggressiveness—in the West Bank the IDF must occasionally close itself off and refrain from action"[9] (Idan and Pakar-Rinat 2000:5). In the words of one battalion commander in the West Bank: "In limited confrontation, a company commander today is required to be part of the political system. . . . The definition of his mission is vague and requires contextual interpretation" (Idan and Pakar-Rinat 2000:25).

Let the IDF Win

The responses of opinion leaders in the religious-Zionist camp can be attributed to the school of strategic realism, which opposes this postmodern option. In a variety of writings, publicists, and retired officers, settlers and rabbis have earnestly spoken out against restraining the army, which, in their view, has betrayed its core objectives. As such, they have called for a return to the era of modernity, where the enemy is clearly defined, missions are carried out in a traditional way, aggression is met with aggression, and soldiers are expected to foster an instinct for battle and a striving for a decisive victory. This means, of course, a return to the era when the soldier was a fighter, and the army provided security and did not become entangled in political and diplomatic considerations.

This was how the army's Chief Rabbi, Brigadier General Avihai Ronzki, expressed it in a conversation with students of the "Hesder" yeshiva in Karnei Shomron. Voicing his dissatisfaction with the concept of limited confrontation, he exclaimed, "[D]amned be he who spares the life of the enemy in war" (Pepper 2009:3). Others demanded a return to the concept of "total war," based on Clausewitz's war terminology, maintaining that victory is not only a fight to achieve an objective in the present but also to eliminate the enemy's ability to fight in the future. According, for example, to Rabbi Eliezer Melamed:

> We must strive to attain a total victory, namely the complete surrender of our enemy in order to deter and to punish. . . . It is important that the victory be forceful and painful so that our enemy is deterred and the punishment is equivalent to an eye for an eye. What they intend to do to us, we will do to them. . . . When one sets off on a battle with the enemy whose intent is to annihilate us, the goal is not only to save Israel and to deter those who hate Israel, but also tear the evil ones apart and banish them from the face of the earth. (Melamed n.d.)

In making such arguments, the writers went as far as to restore legitimacy in the option of a preventive and pre-emptive strike—a method that had become illegitimate within the liberal camp's definition of a war of choice. In their view, this attitude had turned the IDF into a reactive, rather than a proactive, army: "David did not engage in defence alone; he also took the offensive against the enemies of Israel. David's army does not deserve to be called the "Israel Defence Force," but rather the "Israel Attack Force" (Melamed n.d.).

The main idea expressed by all these individuals was the necessity of reaching a decisive outcome in the confrontation with the enemy. Limited confrontation was perceived not only as a military doctrine, but also as an ideology negating the possibility of victory. This alternative doctrine was developed in the first Intifada in the context of the confrontation with Palestinian terrorism in the West Bank. At that time, senior echelons in the army, the majority of whom belonged to the Israeli elite, originating in the secular, left-wing middle class, did not believe that the Intifada could be vanquished in a decisive fashion. For example, Dan Shomron, the chief of staff, declared at its outbreak that there was no military solution to terror (Huberman 2008); Amon Lipkin-Shahak, the chief of staff, teaching a course for company and battalion commanders, argued that "it is impossible to win a victory over guerrilla warfare" (quoted in Hankin 2006:40); and General Ya'akov Or, coordinator for Israeli actions in the administered territories, claimed that "there is no military answer to popular national confrontations" (Wagman 2004). At a discussion at the National Security College, Shaul Moufaz, the chief of staff, maintained that "in a situation of limited confrontation in a context of total war, I believe that the word 'decisiveness' has no relevance" (Wagman n.d.). At the same forum, Dan Halutz, then-commander of the IDF, said that "the IDF must abandon several anachronistic assumptions, the first of which is that victory equals territory. I maintain that it does not. The notion of 'physical decisiveness' must also be removed from the lexicon and replaced by 'conscious, decisive victory'" (Wagman n.d.). Above all, military doctrine came to be characterized by "consciousness of expressions," as suggested by Brigadier General Eival Giladi, head of the Section of Strategic Planning, General Staff Headquarters. Giladi strove to replace the effort to subdue the Palestinians completely by, what he termed, "an alternative to victory" or "an appearance of victory" (*Ma'ariv*, January 2, 2004). In military operations against terrorists, the use of air power was preferred to the use of ground forces (Yadlin 2004).

The slogan "Let the IDF Triumph," countering the perceived military policy of restraint, made its appearance.[10] This catchphrase challenged the conventional view, emphasizing that counter-terrorism could employ the traditional strategy and tactics of general warfare, even when the battlefield contained territories that were densely populated by civilians. The desirable state of affairs was that every soldier should consciously place the fight against terrorism within a context of war with the intention that the determination to vanquish terror was not subject to the individual soldier's interpretation. Rabbi Shlomo Aviner expressed this point of view:

> "Hear O Israel, ye draw nigh this day unto battle against your enemies . . . for the Lord your God is He that goeth with you, to fight for you against your enemies, to save you" (Deut. 20:3–4), and thus we shall be practicing the Biblical injunction: "I have pursued mine enemies, and overtaken them; neither did I turn back until they were consumed." (Psalm 18:38) (quoted in Pepper 2009:3)

In Operation Cast Lead, the leaders of religious Zionism saw a kind of minor transformation and were satisfied with the performance of the soldiers in this campaign. Their mindset was summed up by Rabbi Ronzki:

> One of the major innovations in this Operation was its combat management, unlike any past operation or arresting action. Everyone fought with all his heart and with all his soul; this, of course, entails courage, but also fighting with all the available means. To fight—in order to really bring about a decisive outcome. (quoted in Pepper 2009:3)

Discussion: From Political to Military Sociology—Cultural Confrontation over Military Doctrine

Religious Zionism and the Rise of Neo-Conservatism

In recent years, the rise of neo-conservatism in the Western world has been identified in groups aspiring to return to the guiding principles of nation-building societies before these societies were exposed to globalization and post-nationalism in terms of values (Apple 2004), religion (Stiltner 1999) and even military strategies (Vaisse 2010). In the Israeli context, various groups participated in this trend (Ben-Porat and Yuval 2007). Israeli conservatives, for their part, joined the neoliberal trend, supporting the 1993 Oslo Accords and the newly created ideology of globalization and privatization. However, after the alleged appeasement of the Palestinians—which was expected to promote what Shimon Peres termed, "the new Middle East" (Peres and Naor 1993)—turned out to be an illusion, peripheral groups that had never been a part of the ideology of globalization (minorities, Asians, and new immigrants), along with elements of the founding elite who regretted the decline of collectivist values and the rise of post-national individualism, created a novel community despite differences of opinion on political and legal issues. Their common denominator was a national-republican ideology and opposition to various elements of postmodernism and neoliberalism (Shafir and Peled 2002).

Two large groups in this new conservative camp in Israel are the religious Zionists and the new immigrants from the U.S.S.R. Although the first group has a religious orientation and the second is secular, both are political hawks that support military activism as a solution to the problems of terror and security (Epstein 2006; Filc and Lebel 2005; Mozes 2009). As for their presence in the army, the size of both these groups, as a percentage of the total, is several times larger in the army than in the general population (Peri 2007:127). If these groups are joined by others—Ethiopians, minorities (Druze and Arabs), residents of border settlements, and, especially, settlers in the territories—together they comprise the "Army of the Periphery," according to Levy (2007). In the 1990s, the Oslo Accords were promoted and enjoyed legitimacy within the Israeli army, which was led by senior commanders belonging to the neoliberal elite and under whose leadership the military had become a postmodern army; whereas in 2000, by the time of the al-Aqsa Intifada, many neoconservatives (especially religious Zionists) had penetrated the fighting unites as well as the junior and middle ranks.

Unlike the various groups belonging to the Army of the Periphery, none of the groups in Israeli-Zionist society equals the influential intellectual leadership and agenda of the religious-Zionist group. In spite of differences of opinion in this camp, religious Zionism should be regarded as a counterculture that is opposed to many postmodern ideas. One of the most popular thinkers among religious-Zionist youth explained that the issue is an issue of war: "a war is being waged in the nation: a war of culture, of beliefs and opinions" (Horwitz 2007:68–69). According to him, the weakening trends are the postmodern elements: "the dominant culture of our time is the post-modern culture eliminating all that is sacred and dear to us from our minds" (Horwitz 2007:84). He claims that "the post-modern generation to which we belong today" promotes "life without a purpose and with no commitment whatsoever" (Horwitz 2007:150) and that the sons of the religious Zionists are the avant-guard destined to restore the sense of commitment and mission which had inspired us in the past. "We are small but we carry immense responsibility. First and foremost we must recognize our responsibility for the Jewish people" (Horwitz 2007:120).

The attitude just described expresses the main trends in the religious-Zionist community, characterized by hostility toward those social institutions affected by the postmodern generation. According to this opinion, these institutions spread neoliberal values, favoring the global over the local. To this end, in 2009, more than 90% of the adherents of the religious-Zionist ideology regarded the Supreme Court, the cultural academic elite, and the media as hostile or very hostile to the values of religious Zionism (Mozes 2009). Interestingly, before public leaders commenced their culture war, they turned first to the military arena to cleanse it from what they believed to be harmful postmodern elements.

National Religious Military as a Counter-cultural Avant-garde

The amazing increase in the number of religious Zionists in combat units and as pilots in the junior and intermediate military command was not unplanned. As Peri wrote,

> [T]he growth should be attributed primarily to the conscious effort of the religious Zionist leadership . . . by encouraging youngsters belonging to this camp, to choose a military career and to prefer combat units, especially elite units . . . and fighter pilots, formerly the domain of secular youngsters. This was advanced by the establishment of pre-military academies. (2007:126)

These pre-military academies are educational institutions to which religious-Zionist youngsters are accepted at the age of eighteen, which allows them to postpone their recruitment with the endorsement of the state.

In their research, Soffer, Kassan, and Shohat (1993) use the phrase "launching pad" to describe the role of parents in the context of military service—that is, in preparing youth for significant army service; providing them with the best possible resources with regard to emotional, psychological, financial, and educational values; and sending them to do army service which will prove their parents' success. "Pre-military academies" can be defined as *institutional launching pads* that do not exist in any other sector. Here, students, unlike others, receive physical training and lessons in Jewish studies and the scriptures dealing with issues related to life in the army. The majority of the instructors in these institutions and their rabbis are combat officers in the reserves, and they compete over the numbers of students who join the elite units. The academies operate under the auspices of the Ministry of Defense and are financed by it. The Ministry of Defense has identified them as excellent resources that motivate graduates into "full and significant service in the IDF and voluntary combat units, elite units and careers of officers and military commanders" (Ministry of Education, quoted in Avspenger 2011:63). Interestingly, the percentage of combat soldiers from these academies is twice as large as that of the general population of recruits; the number of commanders from the academies is three-and-a-half times larger than that of other recruits; and the number of officers is three times larger.

Although the majority of the religious-Zionist society belongs to the upper-middle classes, resides in urban areas, and practices the free professions (Leon 2009:120), its sons regard military service as the primary means of self-realization, affecting not only the students of the pre-military academies but also those of the "Yeshivot Hesder" and the religious high schools. All these young men participate in a republican-militaristic contest regarding the percentage of volunteers required to serve in combat units.

One of the unique attributes of the IDF is that the main part of the professional capital of the military commander is his experience and excellence in comparison to that of his colleagues. The IDF, according to Gal (1986), is an army that is characterized by flexible promotion: All the recruits begin their service as regular recruits, and the outstanding ones from among the highly motivated recruits are promoted to the ranks of commanders and officers. This stands in sharp contrast to the tradition of the U.S. Army, for instance, in which recruitment to the rank of officer is primarily based on elite recruits, identified from the start and sent to military academies for officer training. In Israel, the pre-military academies provide their graduates with considerable advantages, as they begin their army service with a greater chance of becoming a commander and an officer on account of the cultural and professional capital given to them. From this point of view, the pre-military academies should be regarded as institutions that are similar in spirit to the American military academies. Their graduates are bound to become the reservoir of the future military command.

It should be stated that the pre-military academies, similar to the "Yeshivot Hesder" and the entire religious-Zionist camp, do not regard the military solely as an appropriate framework for investment and integration, as do other conservative elements in society. Instead, these academies provide graduates with a unique class consciousness. The graduates, thus, help shape the army and become a counter-elite to its present leadership. This is done not only during their study in the pre-military academies or in the Yeshiva, but also during their military service, in the course of which they return to their Yeshiva or pre-military academy. There, they find a place where they can discuss military operations, ethical dilemmas, and the military assignments that they are expected to fulfill. This is carried out in semi-organized meetings with their rabbis and teachers who are themselves senior officers in the reserves. Thus, the pre-military academies, armed with a coherent orientation regarding their cultural role in Israeli society, in general, and in the IDF, in particular, constitute socialization agents, stimulating their students to influence the military by moving it toward a more conservative model and distancing it from its postmodern orientation.

As Rabbi Horowitz wrote:

> As long as there is a desire to achieve "general cosmopolitan peace," such peace is bound to fail. Unless we are prepared to go to war—we will not achieve true peace ... failing to defend Israel's honor and the decline of Israeli heroism supposedly deriving from the desire for peace, are immoral, hindering humanity from achieving true peace.... The way to peace is not by avoiding war.... [W]hat is required are heroism, coping, victory, sometimes even waging war against those fighting against us and impeding our footsteps. (Horwitz 2007:218–249)

Interestingly, the findings just cited are not unique to Israel. According to Inbody (2009), the U.S. Army also has become increasingly an ideological arena, exhibiting homogeneous and Republican characteristics.

Accordingly, only a minority of American army officers identify with liberal ideology (Holsti 1999; Morgan 2001:117). Moreover, cadets and their families show signs of resentment and hostility toward the media and the political elite (Inbody 2009:10). They consider themselves not only as Republican, but also as ultimate loyalists to the values of the founding fathers—a patriotic and conservative avant-guard. Retired Colonel Michael Wyly wrote in the *Marine Corps Gazette* that those in military service "must lead it, not politically, but culturally, for it is the culture we are defending." (quoted in Ricks 1997)[11]

In December 1994, an article in the same publication, by William Lind, a military analyst, claimed that American culture is steadily collapsing:

> Starting in the mid 1960s, we have thrown away the values, morals, and standards that define traditional Western culture. In part, this has been driven by cultural radicals, people who hate our Judeo-Christian culture. Dominant in the elite, especially in the universities, the media and the entertainment industry . . . the cultural radicals have successfully pushed the agenda of moral relativism, militant secularism and sexual and social "liberations." The agenda has slowly codified into a new ideology, usually known as "multiculturalism" or "political correctness" that is in essence Marxism translated from economic into social and cultural terms. (Lind, quoted in Ricks, 1997:18)

In his conclusion, Ricks (1997:18) wrote: "The next real war we fight is likely to be on American soil." He added, "[The American army is] socially isolated . . . [and] politically conservative." Although the Israeli army is not a volunteer army, the groups comprising it share a considerable resemblance with their parallels in the United States.

Generational Struggle in the IDF: On the Constitution of a New Conservative Military Coalition

As shown, soldiers from the religious-Zionist community serving in the IDF are a reinforcing vanguard for the conservative security community, maintaining a different and even a competing worldview to that of the postmodern security community. They aspire to return to earlier notions of military consciousness and doctrine. This group may be labeled "a nostalgic community," and its leaders express a longing "to return to what we were" (Shamir-Doner 2009:51). "[T]he values that fused the IDF as an Israeli army that developed in a specific reality, in a known context, in the face of defined enemies, are currently suppressed. They did not atrophy, but were choked and repressed" (Lord 2000:36). They act as an opposition to "declamations of 'limited warfare' that those weaklings have brought about on Israel" (*B'Sheva*, May 13, 2007, letter to the editor). They seek to break away from "the conception that a country can be defended without paying a price by the Air Force and by surgical and thus sterile tricks" (Scheinwald 2010:14).

Similar to the American soldiers, the avant-guard conservative religious-Zionist soldiers regard themselves as following the path of the generation that founded the IDF. A social entrepreneur attempting to persuade the public to carry out a reframing of reality, the avant-guard conservative religious-Zionist soldier will make use of significant crises in an effort to convince the public to doubt the dominant frames and consider adopting counter-framing (Boin, Hart, and McConnell 2009). In this case, the helicopter catastrophe of 1997—a collision of two helicopters on their way to Lebanon, resulting in the death of 74 soldiers—paved the way for these social movements to strive to convince the Israeli public of the need to retreat from the security belt in South Lebanon. By doing so, they spread the idea of reframing the sojourn in Lebanon from a security requirement to a burden costing an unnecessary price of soldiers' lives.

The postmodern orientation of the Israeli army, its tendency to reject the concept of *activism and prevailing war*, as it became more and more restricted in its use of violence, has led to increased frustration among the conservative groups, especially among the religious, many of whose sons—the settlers—lived in the territories during the Intifadas when the IDF was obliged to fight a guerilla war that involved civilians. By definition, this kind of war had greater media exposure, faced greater ethical dilemmas and legal constraints, and saw the involvement of human rights organizations in the course of peace negotiations, which encouraged the idea that the army would become a combination of the RMA and an organization engaged in peacemaking assignments. The military command and the liberal groups perceived the confrontation as one that could be framed as a low-intensity conflict which could be contained and managed, whereas the conservative groups promoted a reframing, arguing that the army was confronted with a conflict in which it should prevail. Later, the Second Lebanon War served as a catalyst for spreading the conservative counter-framing. It was a war in which the general public was exposed to the postmodern character of the army and to the fact that framing the war as a small, low-intensity conflict deprived it of the ability to identify and win the real war which it was facing, all the more so, as the conflict involved guerilla organizations, rather than a conventional army. Since wars are perceived as a catalyst for social and political changes (Aronoff 1999), the Second Lebanon War promoted a sociopolitical process through which many members of the founding generation of the IDF joined the religious Zionists in their criticism of the doctrine, the army's readiness, and military culture. The general public, for its part, demanded that an investigation committee be formed and that the chief of staff, the prime minister, and the minister of defense be dismissed (Kober 2006). In this way, it also expressed its indignation at the army's grave error, as its supreme commander (the Chief of Staff Dan Halutz) declared at the beginning of the war that this was not a "war" but a "campaign" (Mor 2012).

After what was regarded as the failure of the IDF in the war, a "conservative military coalition" suddenly emerged in opposition to the postmodern army. The religious Zionists were joined by representatives of the generation of the senior military command, which was no longer a part of the office of the chief of staff and that now replaced the postmodern mindset. Their outlook coincided with that of the religious Zionists who had been critical of conventional military thinking.

In two meetings between Dan Halutz, the chief of staff, and a large number of IDF reserve generals, most of who were secular and on the left wing of the Israeli political spectrum, the reservists voiced criticism that was, in effect, an attack on the postmodern orientation of the army. These "men of yesterday"—people who had served in the armored corps and the infantry and who had been trained in ground warfare—emphatically expressed their resentment. They complained about the excessive number of air force officers in senior command positions at the expense of armored officers and experts in ground warfare. This practice led to an overreliance on the air force and to a reduction in the training and deployment of reservists. The reservists also complained that, rather than leading the front-line attack forces, army commanders were directing the war from their computer screens. However, another objection focused on the prevalence of equivocal and complicated army language and on the fact that the goals of the campaign were being disregarded due to a fear of loss. The main complaint, however, was that soldiers were performing police tasks rather than displaying fighting skills, making them unable to identify their task as a war mission.[12]

It should be noted that such criticisms were voiced not only by retired officers. Even the Winograd Commission,[13] which investigated shortcomings in the conduct of the Second Lebanese War, claimed that the intractability of the army, with its postmodern orientation, led it to regard every fighting situation as a "low intensity conflict." This not only confined it and left it without critical fighting skills, but also prevented it from seeing that the Lebanon challenge required a different framing—that is, an understanding that this was a case of war.

> The IDF was not prepared for this war, partly because some of the political and military echelons held the opinion that the era of war had passed. There were those who claimed that Israel had the necessary means to respond to those who threatened her. There was a widespread assumption that Israel would not initiate any war in the future, and that the challenge facing the ground forces would be conflicts in which a low-level of force would be required. On the basis of this analysis, there was no need to make preparations for war nor to update the security orientation of the IDF. (Winograd 2008:328)

In addition, the Commission criticized the postmodern language imparted by OTRI. In fact, although considered by its architects to be high academic language, in reality, it was obscure and compelled those using it to resort to contradictory interpretations, creating a "Tower of Babel" in the organizational communication structure of the army (Kober 2011:720).

Apparently, a mid-level echelon of command also existed within the IDF, representing the conservative viewpoint, although the viewpoint of the secular Ashkenazi majority adheres to a liberal and postmodern ideology (Lebovitz 2010). In the war against Palestinian terrorism, the senior command strove to achieve "quiet as the goal and restraint as the way," identifying success as "the absence of military action" (Idan and Pakar-Rinat 2000:11). To this end, the senior officer ranks disseminated the new military language, which, as stated earlier, required a decisive military outcome but used words, such as "attrition," "restraint," "forbearance," and "containment." As an operative corollary to these conceptual definitions of reality, they imposed constraints on the armed forces—constraints that were in addition to those imposed by the political echelon.

The mid- and lower levels of command objected to these restrictions and expressed frustration at what they saw as the emasculation of their traditional missions "since their objectives were deterrence and military action, and the way to fulfil them was through a demonstrative presence and the implementation of missions" (Idan and Pakar-Rinat 2000:5-6). Not surprisingly, many voices are calling for a return to conservatism and the expunging of the postmodern consciousness within the IDF:

> The IDF needs more than rehabilitation. It needs a thorough shake-up, the erasure of the diskette that was written for twenty years, and of the principles on which an entire generation of senior officers was reared. . . . For many years now, the high command of the IDF has been locked in a conception of limited confrontation and a political solution. (Shilo 2006:26)

The position of mid-level commanders from the religious-Zionist camp makes many in the conservative, extreme right optimistic and points to a different future, one in which the IDF strategic culture will return to its former roots. In the words of Israel Harel:

> Fortunately for the Israeli nation, it now has an echelon of the best and most professional, and also the most humane and intelligent brigade commanders that the Israeli nation possesses. Thanks to these people, I believe I can look forward with hope that there will not be a division. (Lax 2005)

In order "to return the army to its military essence," the religious-Zionist camp should be mobilized, and this mobilization signals no less than saving the IDF from its commanders who are influenced by a variety of harmful and emasculating agents. As Rabbi Yosef Weitzan remarked:

> Our mission is to serve at the front. What weakness and weak heartedness would befall the nation if we did not courageously carry out this mission? . . . We must be the medicine against the disease of "the Four Mothers."[14] . . . And act as a dam against the collapse of national stalwartness. (Weizan 2001:29)

Summary: A Negotiated Strategic Culture

This article has demonstrated that the IDF constitutes an arena in which negotiations related to Israeli strategic culture are conducted. Since the 1980s, especially as a result of the cultural changes that occurred in the groups from which the high and middle echelons of the military command were drawn, the IDF was shaped into a postmodern army (Moskos and Burk 1998). As a result, the IDF began to establish its military doctrine on the basis of several revolutionary principles reflecting its postmodern orientation:

1. Control over territory does not contribute to victory.
2. Terror cannot be decisively defeated.
3. A high sensitivity is demonstrated toward casualties.
4. Reserve forces are sparingly used.
5. The war is not transferred to enemy territory.
6. Control over territory is not considered an important goal, as territory is not viewed as important for the outcome of the war.
7. There should be an extensive reliance on air power.
8. A tendency not to pursue decisive outcomes, but rather a victory of consciousness, is emphasized.

Contrary to the doctrine just cited, this article shows that conservative groups—those who in their daily lives are not subject to the postmodern situation and who possess an ethno-republican identity—are anxious to "return the army to what it had once been," to the thinking of Clausewitz—an army that prevails in battle, every battle, even when fighting against terror and guerillas means inflicting harm on civilians and sacrificing the lives of soldiers in order to complete the mission successfully.

Although Zeev Drory (2008) referred to Israeli society as a group with a monolithic identity and regarded the IDF as an organization with a monolithic military culture, today, Israeli society is no longer monolithic. Israel, similar to many other societies, has become fragmented and divided into many groups, each of which promotes different and competing values. As long as this situation prevails, the Israeli army, consisting of compulsory recruits, will also reflect the different societal fragments.

To this end, any option of strategic culture involves a different framing of the political and security situation. The Second Lebanon War (2006), perceived by the Israeli public as a distressing failure, provided the opportunity for the supporters of the conservative voice to spread their worldview among the wider public outside the religious-Zionist camp. Being a war in which a terror organization prevailed over a regular army, soldiers were killed in face-to-face combat (rather than by conducting bombings), and critical actions for achieving victory were cancelled for fear of a loss of soldiers' lives, a situation that might have led to public protest. Being a war in which the main effort was assigned to the air force and the artillery, while avoiding the sending of ground forces, and, especially, that it was not identified by the chief command of the postmodern army as a war, but rather as a continuation of the customary low-intensity campaign, was certainly a severe blow both to the postmodern doctrine and to the social elites that promoted it.

By contrast, the Cast Lead Operation (2009) was perceived as a kind of rehabilitation, a success and a beginning of something new. This operation was perceived as a correction, enabling the army to return to itself and fight, even though it meant inflicting harm on the civilian population while endangering military forces on the ground fighting in the heart of Gaza (Cohen 2009).

Competing Security Communities

Every security community has institutions of its own that shape its discourse. For example, the neoliberal community has shaped the postmodern army to a considerable extent with the help of the legal elite (Zamir 2007). In addition to the Supreme Court, many of whose court rulings shaped the postmodern doctrine of the IDF, other actors also have participated in the promotion of liberal values within the military arena. For example, the Israeli Institute for Democracy, originally a research institute dealing with parliamentary and governmental issues that provides a neoliberal perspective to public discourse, became an institute preparing a variety of position papers, research, and policy documents for the army to promote the postmodern and neoliberal revolution within it. In 2001, the institute began to organize meetings with senior military commanders—the chief of staff, the deputy chief of staff, five major generals, and brigade and battalion commanders. In 2005, the project "Army-Society," a cooperative project between the Institute for Democracy and the army, was launched. The institute—which supported the Supreme Court's restriction of the army in its fight against terror, subjecting it to international law (Kremnizer 2006)—took part in shaping military policy by, for instance, carrying out the disengagement plan (The Institute for Democracy 2005).

On the other side of the spectrum, the religious Zionists had a number of pre-military academies, Yeshivot Hesder, and institutes devoted to military ethics, military thinking, security doctrine, and related issues. The use of religious language often conceals the fact that they are intellectually engaged in military studies and whose main goal, as shown in this article, is to move the armed forces closer to the conservative pole.

From the point of view of these religious Zionists, in addition to their commitment to influence military doctrine, this group also has a sense of a cultural mission, enabling its members to make their sons feel similar to a Jewish avant-guard vis-à-vis the liberal elite. Rabbi Elyakim Levanon, head of the "Alon Moreh" Yeshivat Hesder, expressed this in the following statement: "Today the public consists of two parts: one, idealistic, with firm convictions that believes, plants and acts, and another—good in itself, but lacking firm convictions, and suddenly lightening comes down from the sky and carries it along" (Lax 2005).

The Cast Lead Operation, referred to earlier, made it easy for religious-Zionists to convince the public that their worldview leads to major military gains; whereas the neoliberal, postmodern worldview caused the army to fail in the Second Lebanon War. Later, Rabbi Laow, earlier the Chief Rabbi of Israel, described this phenomenon by comparing the two groups:

> It cannot be ignored that in the elite units of the IDF, such as the various reconnaissance units, the graduates of the religious Zionist educational institutions, partly occupy the place that was the domain of the sons of the Kibbutz movement in the past. This was evident both in the Second Lebanon War and in Cast Lead, in which more and

more of the soldiers in the elite units, are graduates of the Yeshivot Hesder and the pre-military academies. No doubt that patriotism and love of the land, along with the ultimate importance attached to the sacredness of life produced the fruit reaped. (quoted by Nachshoni 2009)

The religious-Zionist camp has a number of representatives in the new military elite. Major General Ya`akov Amidror was commander of the military academies during his service in the general staff and at present is head of the Council for National Security; Major General Yair Nave served as commander of the central command and today is the deputy chief of staff; Major General Elazar Stern was the chief educational officer and served as head of the Manpower Division in the General Staff; and Yoram Cohen, also a member of the religious-Zionist camp, is head of the General Security Service (Shabak). All these men are a part of the discourse presented in this article and serve as representatives of the conservative security community.

In short, the purpose of this article has not been to examine the opinions of senior military commanders, but, instead, the opinions of those striving to introduce their ideas into the military's discourse—the civilian leaders of the religious-Zionist camp, those individuals influencing the "acceptance" of defense reality. The purpose of this research was to learn how a security community is created from "below" and, even if it has not yet succeeded in promoting its members to senior ranks, the analysis of military demography enables scholars to predict the future character and doctrine of the military. As Cassidy explains, the strategic culture dealt with in this article will ultimately be translated into military culture and the day-to-day operative behavior related to the use of violence. "Military culture comprises the beliefs and attitudes within a military organization that shape its collective preferences towards the use of force. These attitudes can impede or foster innovation and adaptation" (Cassidy 2005:3).

At present, the majority of the senior command in the IDF belongs to the secular–liberal–global camp (Lebovitz 2010). However, according to current socio-demographic trends, future soldiers and commanders will increasingly emerge more and more from the religious-Zionist camp. In this article, an attempt is made at identifying the military doctrine that will likely be adopted at the opportune time. To the extent that this forecast becomes a reality, this will support the claim of the strategic culture school, namely that the composition of the combat forces has a greater impact on military doctrine than the objective security situation which the army is required to deal with.

Acknowledgments

I wish to thank the Joint Fund of the Samaria and Jordan Rift R&D Center, the Ariel University Center, and Professor David Wolf, Head of the Authority for R&D at the Ariel University Center, for granting me a research scholarship and other financial assistance that enabled me to complete this research. Thanks are also due to my devoted research assistants Eline Zehavi, Jonathan Blum, Assaf Lebovitz, Michal Vanchotzker, and Shoshana Luwisch-Omer. Many thanks to Miriam Kraus and Dr. Paul King for their assistance in editing this article. Above all, heartfelt thanks are due to the professional and intellectual supervision of Prof. Neovi Karakatsanis.

Notes

1. RMA is the process of introducing and enhancing technology within the military. It is a part of reshaping the military's nature as postmodern—for example, by waging swift campaigns with minimal casualties (Levy 2010c). Specifically, this is a part of the U.S. "quest for high-tech weapons systems and the comprehensive networking of these weapons using state-of-the art information technology" (Schrnig 2010:8).
2. In the international community this definition is subject to widespread subjective interpretations and sometimes also entails endangering soldiers' lives (See Barnidge 2011).
3. These matters were stated by the head of the branch for organizational psychology in the Department of Behavioral Sciences of the IDF, former psychology of the Central Command region, and psychologist for military organizational psychology of the Paratroop Brigade.
4. This procedure was adopted during the al-Aqsa Intifada. According to IDF soldiers, they would demand that the neighbor of a wanted terrorist knock on his door to tell him that the army had arrived to arrest him. This was done in order to prevent the suspect from opening fire on the IDF. On October 6, 2005, the Supreme Court ruled that this was unacceptable, endangering Palestinian civilians, even if the procedure reduced endangering the lives of soldiers (Shor 2008).
5. The Supreme Court determined a number of times that the path of the fence disproportionately harmed the life of Palestinians and compelled the army to make appropriate adjustments to its course (Khamaisi 2007).
6. This refers to the Supreme Court's decision to minimize the use of air power to liquidate through air power selected human targets who were about to perpetrate terrorist acts on the grounds that this violates the right of the terrorist suspect to claim his innocence through the legal process (Stahl 2010).
7. On March 29, 2002, the IDF launched Operation Defensive Shield in order to inflict damage on the Palestinian terrorist infrastructure and to stop the wave of terrorist attacks that had increased during this time. The Operation allowed the widespread entry of IDF ground forces into Palestinian urban centers, a military tactic that had been avoided by the IDF since the Oslo Accords.
8. See, for example, *The Limited Confrontation*, published by the Military Doctrine Division of the IDF (2001:4).
9. The writers are an infantry brigade commander and a military organizational psychologist of the Paratroop Brigade.

10. This was a slogan that was popular among the settlers, the religious Zionists, and the Israeli Right. See, for example, Segal (July 20, 2006).
11. Marine Corps Gazette, March 1995.
12. Reports and excerpts from these meetings were covered in *De Marker* [*Ha'aretz*] (September 6, 2006); *Ha'aretz* (September 10, 2006, and September 17, 2006).
13. The Winograd Commission included among its members the retired generals Menahem Einan and Haim Nadel.
14. This is in reference to civil social movements that led the Campaign for IDF withdrawal from southern Lebanon (Lebel 2011).

References

Adler, Emanuel and Michael Barnett, eds. 1998. *Security Communities*. Cambridge: Cambridge University Press.
Apple, Michael. 2004. "Creating Difference: Neo-Liberalism, Neo-Conservatism and the Politics of Educational Reform." *Educational Policy* 18(1):12–44.
Aronoff, Myron. 1999. "Wars as Catalysts of Political and Cultural Change." Pp. 37–56 in Edna Lumsky-Feder and Eyal. Ben-Ari, eds. *The Military and Militarism in Israeli Society*. Albany, NY: SUNY Press.
Avidor, Gideon. 2008. "Gunfire vs. Maneuvres or Maneuvres and Gunfire." *Sherion* 30:60–63.
Aviner, Shlomo. n.d. "The Soldier's Prayer." Retrieved January 13, 2011 (http://dev13.walla.co.il/?w=/1/1624906/632180/5/@@/media).
Avspenger, Neomi. 2011. "Checking Pre Military Academies." *Maarachot* 463:62–69.
Bauman, Zigmond. 1987. "The Left as the Counter Culture of Modernity." *Telos* 70:83–93.
Ben-Eliezer, Uri. 2001. "From a Nation in Uniform to a Post-Modern Army." *Tarbut Demokratit* 4:55–98.
Ben-Porat, Guy and Yuval Funny. 2007. 'Israeli Neo-conservatism: Rise and Fall?" *Israel Studies Forum* 22(1):3–25.
Bick, Etta. 2007. "Rabbis and Rulings: Insubordination in the Military and Israeli Democracy." *Journal of Church and State* 49(2):305–327.
Boin, Hart and Alexander McConnell. 2009. "Crisis Exploitation: Political and Policy Impacts of Framing Contests." *Journal of European Public Policy* 16(1):81–106.
Bracken, Paul and Alcala, Raoul. 1994. *Whither the RMA: Two Perspectives on Tomorrow's Army*. Carlisle Barracks, PA: Strategic Studies Institute, U.S. Army War College.
Burk, James. 1997. "Why Peacekeeping?" *Armed Forces and Society* 23(2):323–326.
Burk, James. 1998. *The Adaptive Military: Armed Forces in a Turbulent World*. New Brunswick, NJ: Transaction Publishers.
Cassidy, Robert. 2005. "The British Army and Counterinsurgency: The Salience of Military Culture." *Military Review* 85(3):53–59.
Chouchane, Samia. 2009. "The Judicialization of Israeli Military Ethics." *Bulletin du Centre de Recherche Francis de Jerusalem* 20:1–18.
Cohen, Stuart. 1993. "The Hesder Yeshivot in Israel: A Church-State Military Arrangement." *Journal of Church and State* 35(1):113–130.
Cohen, Stuart. 2000. "The Scroll or the Sword? Tensions between Judaism and Military Service in Israel." Pp. 254–273 in A. S. Cohen, ed. *Democratic Societies and their Armed Forces: Israel in Comparative Context*. London: Frank Cass.
Cohen, Stuart, A. 2005. "The Changing Jewish Discourse on Armed Conflict: Themes and Implications." *Terrorism and Political Violence* 17(3):353–370.

Cohen, Stuart. 2009. "The Futility of Operation Cast Lead." *Perspectives Papers* 68. Retrieved June 12, 2012 (http://www.biu.ac.il/SOC/besa/perspectives68.html).
Cohen, Stuart. 2007. "Tensions between Military Service and Jewish Orthodoxy in Israel: Implications Imagined and Real." *Israel Studies* 12(1):103–126.
Desmond, Jhon, Pierre McDonagh, and Stephanie O'donoho. 2000. "Counter Culture and Consumer Society." *Consumptions, Markets and Culture* 4(3):241–280.
Drory, Zeev. "Society Strength as a Base for Military Power: The State of Israel During the Early 1950s." Pp. 48–65 in Udi Lebel, ed. *Communicating Security: Civil-Military Relations in Israel*. London: Routledge.
Epstein, Alek. 2006. "Israeli-Palestinian Struggle Influence towards Former Russians Political Identity." *Israeli Social Issues* 2(1):94–115.
Everts, Philip and Pierangelo Isernia. 2005. "The War in Iraq." *Public Opinion Quarterly* 69(2):264–323.
Filc Dan and Udi Lebel Udi. 2005. "The Israeli Populist Radical Right: A New Phenomenon in a Comparative Perspective." *Mediterranean Politics* 10(1):85–97.
Freedman, Lawrence. 2006. *The Transformation of Strategic Affairs (Adelphi Papers)*. London: Routledge.
Gal, Reuven. 1986. *A Portrait of the Israeli Soldier*. Boulder, CO: Greenwood Press.
Gal, Reuven. 1990. *The Seventh War: The Influence of the Intifada on Israeli Society*. Tel Aviv: HaKibbutz Hameuhad.
Gordon, Shmuel. 1998. *The Vulture and the Snake: Counter Guerilla Air Warfare: The War in Southern Lebanon*. Ramat Gan: BESA Center for Strategic Studies, Bar Ilan University.
Gordon, Shmuel. 2002. "Spirit of the IDF—Background for a Broad Discussion." *Ma'arachot* 382:86–87.
Goulding, Christina. 1999. "Consumer Research, Interpretive Paradigms and Methodological Ambiguities." *European Journal of Marketing* 33(9–10):859–871.
Goulding, Christina. 2005. "Grounded Theory, Ethnography and Phenomenology: A Comparative Analysis of Three Qualitative Strategies for Marketing Research." *European Journal of Marketing* 39(3–4):294–308.
Gray, Colin. 1999. "Strategic Culture as Context: The First Generation of Theory Strikes Back." *Review of International Studies* 25(1):49–69.
Habermas, Jurgen. 1974. "The Public Sphere: An Encyclopedia Article." *New German Critique* 3:49–55.
Hankin, Yagil. 2006. "How to Win Small Wars." *Tchelet* 24:39–74.
Harel, Israel. 2009. "Personal Report." Channel 23 TV. February 26.
Hedley, Mark and Clark Sara. 2007. "The Microlevel Discourse of Social Movement Framing: Debating Antiwar Protests on a University Listserv." *Sociological Focus* 40(1):26–47.
Helman, Sara. 2001. "Citizenship Regime, Identity and Peace Protest in Israel." Pp. 295–320 in Eyal Ben-Ari, Daniel Maman, and Zeev Rosenhek, eds. *Military, State and Society in Israel: Theoretical and Comparative Perspectives*. New Brunswick: Transaction Publishers.
Hervieu-Leger, Damielle. 1990. "Religion and Modernity in the French Context: For a New Approach to Secularization." *Sociological Analysis* 51(8):815–825.
Higley, John And Pakulski, Jan. 2007. "Elite and Leadership Change in Liberal Democracies." *Comparative Sociology* 6(1–2):6–26.
Holsti, Ole. 1999. "A Widening Gap Between the US Military and Civilian Society? Some Further Evidence." *International Security* 23(3):5–43.
Horowitz, Dan. 1970. "Flexible Responsiveness and Military Strategy: The Case of the Israeli Army." *Policy Science* 1(1):191–205.
Horwitz Ely. 2007. *War of Culture*. Hebron: Mee'mek Hebron Pub. [Hebrew].

Huberman, Hagay. 2008. "The Sober Political Outlook of Dan Shomron." Channel 7 radio. February 27. Retrieved June 12, 2012 (http://www.inn.co.il/News/News.aspx/172158).

Idan, Effi and Pakar-Rinat Maya. 2000. "Limitation of the Use of Force in the West Bank During the Period of the Agreements." *Ma'arachot* 372:2–11.

Inbody, Donald. 2009. "Grand Army of the Republic or Grand Army of the Republicans? Political Party and Ideological Preferences of American Enlisted Personnel." Ph.D. Dissertation, University of Texas at Austin.

Inglehart, Robert. 2000. "Globalization and Postmodern Values." *The Washington Quarterly* 23(1):215–228.

Inglehart, Robert. 1990. *Culture Shift in Advanced Industrial Society.* Princeton, NJ: Princeton University.

The Institute of Democracy. 2005. *Civil-Military Relations in the Restricted Warfare.* Jerusalem: The Institute of Democracy.

Johnston, Hank. 1995. "A Methodology for Frame Analysis: From Discourse to Cognitive Schemata." Pp. 217–246 in Johnston Hank and Bert Klandermans, eds. *Social Movements and Culture.* Minneapolis: University of Minnesota Press.

Kaldir, Mary. 2003. *Global Civil Society: An Answer to War.* Cambridge: Polity Press.

Kasher, Asa. 2001. "Soldiers Conducting Non-Military Missions." *Tarbut Demokratit* 4:151–186.

Kasher, Asa and Amos Yadlin. 2005. "Assassination and Preventive Killing." *SAIS Review* 25(1):41–57.

Khamaisi, Rassem. 2007. "In The Shadow of the Separation Wall: Impeding the Right to the City and Shaping the Palestinian Spatial Environment in Jerusalem/al-Quds." Pp. 68–69 in Shlomo Hasson, ed. *Jerusalem in the Future: The Challenge of Transition.* Jerusalem: The Floersheimer Institute for Policy Studies, Publication No. 1/61.

Kier, Elizabeth. 1995. "Culture and Military Doctrine." *International Security* 19(4):65–93.

Kober, Avi. 1996. "A Paradigm of Crisis? Israel's Doctrine of Military Decision." Pp. 188–214 in Efraim Karsh, ed. *Between War and Peace: Dilemmas of Israeli Security.* London: Frank Cass.

Kober, Avi. 2006. "The Second Lebanon War." *Perspectives Paper* 22. BESA (Begin-Sadat Center for Strategic Studies).

Kober, Avi. 2011. "What Happened to Israeli Military Strategic Thought?" *Strategic Studies* 34(5):707–732.

Kremnizer, Mordevhay, ed. 2006. *Is Everything Legitimate in Coping with Terrorism?* Jerusalem: Israeli Institute of Democracy.

Laqueur, Walter. 1996. "Post Modern Terrorism." *Foreign Affairs* 75(5):25–34.

Lax, Ofra. 2005. "Where Do We Go from Here?" *B'sheva.* August 11. Retrieved February 23, 2011 (http://www.inn.co.il/Besheva/Article.aspx/4715).

Lebel, Udi. 2010. "'Casualty panic': Military Recruitment Models, Civil-Military Gap and their Implications for the Legitimacy of Military Loss." *Democracy and Security* 6(2):183–206.

Lebel, Udi. 2011. "Militarism versus Security? The Double-Bind of Israel's Culture of Bereavement and Hierarchy of Sensitivity to Loss." *Mediterranean Politics* 16(3):365–384.

Lebel, Udi. 2008. "The Disengagement as Elite Change Attempt in the Israel Military and Society." Pp. 207–232 in H. Misgav and U. Lebel, eds. *The Disengagement: Strategic Dialogue in Crisis.* Jerusalem: Carmel.

Lebovitz, Asaf . 2010. "The Political Process as a Vital Need: Liberal Discourse in Israel, Security Networks and Coping with the Notion of the Threat to Existence." *Politika* 20:97–122.

Leon, Nissim. 2009. "Religion, Class and Political Activism among Religious Zionism in Israel." *Democratic Culture* 11:105–144.
Levy, Yagil. 2007a. "The Embedded Military: Why Did the IDF Perform Effectively in Executing the Disengagement Plan?" *Security Studies* 16(3):382–408.
Levy, Yagil. 2007b. *From People's Army to Army of the Peripheries.* Jerusalem: Carmel.
Levy, Yagil. 2010. "How the Military's Social Composition Affects Political Protest: The Case of Israel." *Peace and Change* 35(1):123–145.
Lincoln, Yvonna and Guba Egon. 1985. *Naturalistic Inquiry.* Beverly Hills, CA: Sage.
Lord, Amnon. 2000. *Makor Rishon.* November 28, p. 7.
Lord, Amnon. 2003. "The Advisable Level of Terrorism." *Makor Rishon.* October 3. Retrieved June 12, 2011 (https://www.israpost.com/Community/articles/print.php?articleID=1173).
Lumsky-Feder, Edna and Eyal Ben-Ari. 2003. "From Nation in Uniform to Deferent Uniforms to a Nation." Pp. 255–286 in Majid Al-Haj and Uri Ben-Eliezer, eds. *In the Name of Security.* Haifa: Haifa University Press.
Luttwak, Edward. 1995. "Toward Post-Heroic Warfare." *Foreign Affairs* 74(3):109–122.
Melamed, Eliezer. n.d. "Rule of the Military and War." Beit El Yeshiva. Retrieved February 27, 2011 (http://yeshiva.org.il).
Melamed, Eliezer. 2008. "Military Service out of Religiosity." Beit El Yeshiva. January 27. Retrieved February 27, 2011 (http://www.yeshiva.org.il/midrash/shiur.asp?id=6721).
Merom, Gil. 1999. "Israel's National Security and the Myth of Exceptionalism." *Political Science* 114(3):409–434.
Merom, Gil. 2003. *How Democracies Lose Small Wars: State, Society and Failures of France in Algeria, Israel in Lebanon and the United States in Vietnam.* Cambridge: Cambridge University Press.
Meydani, Asaf. 2007. "Public Policy on Human Rights in Israel: The Perspective from a Local Military Court." *Democracy and Security* 3(3):279–299.
Mor, Ben. 2012. "Using Force to Save Face: The Performative Side of War." *Peace and Change* 37(1):95–121.
Morgan, Matthew. 2001. "Army Recruiting and the Civil-Military Gap." *Parameters* 154:101–117.
Moskos, Charles. 2000a. "Towards a Post-Modern Military: The United States as a Paradigm." Pp. 14–31 in Charles C. Moskos, John Allen Williams, and David R. Segal, eds. *The Postmodern Military: Armed Forces after the Cold War.* Oxford: Oxford University Press.
Moskos, Charles and James Burk. 1998. "The Post Modern Military." Pp. 163–182 in J. Burk, ed. *The Adaptive Military: Armed Forces in a Turbulent World.* Brunswick, NJ: Transaction Publishers.
Mozes, Haim. 2009. "From Religious Zionism to Post-Modern Religious Directions and Developments in Religious Zionism since the Assassination of Yitzhak Rabin." Ph.D. Dissertation, Bar-Ilan University.
Nachshoni, Kobi. 2009. "Rabbi Laow: We Cannot Ignore the Numbers of Religious Soldiers." Ynet. January 19. Retrieved on June 12, 2012 (http://www.ynet.co.il/articles/0,7340,L-658467,00.html).
Obsborne, Thomas. 2004. "On Mediators: Intellectuals and the Ideas Trade in the Knowledge Society." *Economy and Society* 33(4):430–447.
Pepper, Anchil. 2009. "The Chief Army Rabbi." *Haaretz.* November 15, p. 3.
Peres, Shimon. and Arye Naor. 1993. *The New Middle East.* NY: Henry Holt.

Peri, Yoram. 2001. "Civil-Military Relation in Israel in Crisis." Pp. 107–127 in Eyal Ben-Ari, Daniel Maman, and Zeev Rosenhek, - eds. *Military, State and Society in Israel: Theoretical and Comparative Perspectives*. New Brunswick, NJ: Transaction Publishers.

Peri, Yoram. 2007. "Intractable Conflict and the Media." *Israel Studies* 12(1):79–102.

Raveh, Saar and Maya Pakar-Rinat-. 2000. "To Be Victorious and Remain Human—Leadership Challenges in Limited Confrontation." *Ma'arachot* 385:20–25.

Ricks, Thomas. 1997. "The Widening Gap Between the Military and Society." *The Atlantic Monthly*. July 9. Retrieved June 12, 2012 (http://www.theatlantic.com/magazine/archive/1997/07/the-widening-gap-between-military-and-society/6158/).

Rosman-Stollman, E. 2008. "Mediating Structures and the Military: The Case of Religious Soldiers." *Armed Forces and Society* 34(4):615–638.

Rotenberg, Hagit. 2010. "Caution. Attorneys are Behind You." *B'sheva*. October 28, p. 38

Scheinold, Eliezer. 2010. "To Shake Off Self-Denial." *B'shev.* September 21. Retrieved February 14, 2011 (http://www.inn.co.il/Besheva/Article.aspx/6104/1).

Schrnig Niklas. 2010. *Robot Warriors: Why the Western Investment into Military Robots Might Backfire*. Frankfurt, Germany: Peace Research Institute.

Segal, Avi. 2006a. "Let the IDF Achieve Victory." *B'sheva*. July 20, p. 17.

Segal, Avi. 2006b. "On My Own Decision." *B'sheva*. September 7, p. 19.

Shafir, Gershon and Yoav Peled. 2002. *Being Israeli: The Dynamics of Multiple Citizenship*. Cambridge: Cambridge University Press.

Shamir-Donar, R. 2009. "IDF Language in the Space Between Simplicity and Complexity." *Ma'arachot* 423:48–53.

Shilo, Elazar. 2006. "To change a disk." *B'sheva*. September 2, p. 14.

Shilo, Elazar. 2011. "Luck Accompanies the Chief of Staff." *B'sheva*. February, 21. Retrieved February 14, 2011. (http://www.inn.co.il/Articles/Article.aspx/9357).

Shor, Eran. 2008. "Conflict, Terrorism, and the Socialization of Human Rights Norms: The Spiral Model Revisited." *Social Problems* 55(1):117–138.

Simionato, Reuben. 1991. "The Link Between Empirical Research, Epistemic Values and Psychological Practice." *Australian Psychologist* 26(2):123–127.

Singer, Peter. 2004. "War, Profits, and the Vacuum of Law: Privatized Military Firms and International Law." *Columbia Journal of Transnational Law* 44(2):36–68

Soffer, Gita., Lea Kassan, and Tama Shohat. 1993. "Family as 'Launching Pad.'" *Society and Welfare* 13(4):351–365.

Spector-Marzel, Gabriela. 2010. "Apparatuses of Choices and Narrative Identity." Pp. 63–96 in Lea Kasan and Lea Krumer-Nevo, eds. *Analysis in Qualitative Research*. Beer-Sheva: Ben Gurion University Press.

Stahl, Adam. 2010. "The Evolution of Israeli Targeted Operations." *Studies in Conflict and Terrorism* 33(2):111–133.

Stiltner, Ben. 1999. *Religion and the Common Good*. Oxford: Rowman and Littlefield.

Straus, Anselm and Corbin, Juliet. 1990. *Basics on Qualitative Research: Grounded Theory Producers and Teaching*. London: Sage.

Sultany, Nimer. 2007. "The Legacy of Justice Aharon Barak: A Critical Review." *Harvard International Law Journal* 48:83–92.

Teridman, Richard. 1985. *Discourse/Counter Discourse: The Theory and Practice of Resistance in Nineteen Century France*. New York: Cornell University Press.

Tschannen, Oliver. 1991. "The Secularization Paradigm: A Systematization." *Journal for the Scientific Study of Religion* 30(4):394–415.

Troper, Michele. 2000. "French Secularism, or Laicite." *Cardozo Law Review* 21(1):1267–1284.

Vaisse, Justin. 2010. *Why Neo-conservatism Still Matters?* Sidney, Australia: Lowy Institute for International Policy.

Van Creveld, Martin. 2004. *Defending Israel*. New York: Thomas Dunne Books.
Wagman, Yehuda. n.d. "The Security Conception of the IDF—From Conceptual Failure to Operational Failure." The Jewish Statesmanship Center for Strategic Planning. Retrieved May 21, 2012. (http://www.jsc1.org/?CategoryID=321&ArticleID=185).
Wagman, Yehuda. 2004. "The IDF's Achievements Wiped Out by the Conception." *Makor Rishon*. September 15, p. 21.
Wagman, Yehuda. 2002. "The Limited Confrontation Trap." *Nativ* 16(92):20–27.
Walter, Venessa. 1981. "From Counterculture to Subculture: An Episode in the History of Poverty." Pp. 103–134 in Leventman, Seymour ed. *Counterculture and Social Transformation: Essays on Negativistic Themes in Sociological Theory*. Illinois: Charles C. Thomas Publishers.
Weiss, Thomas and Katherine Campbell. 1991. "Military Humanitarians." *Survival* 33(5):51–465.
Weizan, Yossef. 2001. "Our Father Isaac from the Settlers: Lesson from 'And These Are the Generations.'" Retrieved March 21, 2011 (http://www.yeshiva.org.il).
Winograd Committee Report (for researching the 2006 Lebanon Campaign). Jerusalem, Israel: PM office.
Yadlin, Amos. 2004. "Combat Against Terror from the Air." Pp. 121–130 in A. Eden, ed. *Aspects of Terror and the Struggle against Terror (Series from University of the Air)*. Tel Aviv: Defence Ministry.
Zamir, Ytzhak. 2007. "The Judicial Elite." Pp. 137–156 in Ben-Raphael, Eliezer and Ytzhak Sternberg, eds. *New Israeli Elites*. Jerusalem: Bialik Institution.

Doing Army or Feeling Army? What Makes Women Feel Organizational Belonging in the Israeli Defence Forces?

Orlee Hauser
University of Wisconsin Oshkosh

Political and Military Sociology: An Annual Review 2012, Vol. 40: 59–95.

Army service signifies complete citizenship for Jewish-Israeli citizens. This article examines the participation of women in the Israeli Defence Forces with a focus on base placement and organizational belonging. Based on extensive field research and sixty-two open-ended interviews with women who have served in the IDF, I argue that women's army experience differs greatly, not only according to what position one holds in the army, but, more significantly, according to where one carries out her military service (closed base where one stays to sleep versus open base where one goes home to sleep). Since the military is closely associated with combat-type activity, women who serve in open bases and are removed from combat surroundings and conditions that resemble combat do not fully partake in the authentic military experience. One is left asking: Does army service carry a completely different set of meanings for them?

Discussing my research often gets tiresome. It seems that those who deal with the subject matter of women in the Israeli Defence Forces (IDF) are cursed with the need to explain, over and over again, that the media image of gender egalitarianism in the Israeli army is largely a myth. True, Israel stands apart from many other countries in that both men and women are drafted into the army. However, although most Jewish Israelis serve in the IDF and might appear to share a common army experience, conscription is not, in fact, universal, and the experiences of men and women are different. Although both men and women may hold career positions, when it comes to compulsory service, married women, pregnant women, mothers, and religious women are automatically exempted, resulting in a large discrepancy between the numbers of men and women serving in the army. In fact, due to the large numbers of religious women opting out of service, only 60% of Jewish women are drafted compared with 80% of Jewish men. Moreover, the length of obligatory service is different for men and women. Women are required to serve an army term of 24 months, whereas men are required to serve a term of 36 months (Cohen 1997b; Izraeli 1997; Sasson-Levy 2007; Weiss 1998; Wynne and Rudnick 1996). The majority of women do virtually no reserve army duty (though this has been changing in recent years), whereas men are expected to spend "a near life-time of active reserve" (Golan 1997:582). As Uta Klein contends, "All in all these aspects of different conscription policies show that what is called 'universal' conscription is selective rather than universal, when the female population is concerned" (2002:672).

Despite the discrepancy in male and female participation rates, the majority of Jewish women in Israel, similar to the majority of Jewish men, do serve in the IDF. However, this does not necessarily result in a uniformity of army experience. Women and men most often serve in very different positions in the military. The IDF is characterized by an extreme sexual division of labor; women are excluded from core combat positions, and one-third are relegated to clerical or administrative positions (Sasson-Levy 2007). Even in the area of combat, which is marked by a large growth in female soldiers and the opening of new combat roles for women, women soldiers' experiences remain distinct from those of men. Official data published by the office of the Advisor for Women's Issues suggest that the movement of women into combat roles is mostly symbolic, as most combat roles are still formally closed for women. Indeed, the majority of combat roles that were redefined as gender integrated are considered marginal to military functioning and hold less prestige (Rimalt 2007).

When discussing the differential status of male and female soldiers, differential role allocation is most often presented. Little attention is generally given to issues of base placement. Base placement is a bureaucratic issue that is considered of little relevance to the position of women and men in the military, let alone Israeli society.

Although issues of base placement are often considered trivial, I argue that base placement has a larger effect on differential gender status in Israel than military job allocation. Since they more often serve in combat positions and because of the misconception that girls prefer to be close to home, men more often than women serve in closed bases (in which soldiers stay to sleep) and women more often than men serve in open bases (in which soldiers return home to sleep).[1] Closed and open base experiences differ greatly from one another.

I argue that women's army experience suffers greatly due to being assigned a position on an open base. Indeed, many of the women who serve in open bases and whom I interviewed did not feel that they had really done what is considered army service. They pointed to the difference between simply "doing army" and "feeling army."[2] Those who "felt army" perceived themselves as having truly participated in the military organization; that is, they felt high levels of organizational belonging. Moreover, this gave them the feeling of having had the authentic army experience. Those who did not "feel army" often felt excluded from this national right of passage. Since the military is closely associated with combat-type activity, women who serve in open bases and are removed from combat surroundings and conditions that resemble combat (rough conditions, discipline, uniforms, etc.) do not fully partake in the authentic military experience. This article concentrates on the distinction between closed-base and open-base service and raises questions related to women's true participation in the military organization.

Gender, Organizations, and Culture

Participation in the military can take on many different forms and, as noted, army experiences are by no means uniform. This, of course, is not limited to militaries but is true of all organizations. Thus, it is fitting to begin with a brief discussion of organizations and, more specifically, what it means to participate in an organization.

Alvesson and Billing describe organizations as central economic institutions that take care of the production of goods and services and of a major part of the control and care of citizens (1997:5). While pointing out that organizational theory has largely ignored gender, they posit that organizations, as sites for human action, are central to the production of values, conceptions, and gender relations. Indeed, a large body of work discusses organizational culture, broadly defined as a set of meanings, ideas, and symbols that are shared by the members of a collective and which have evolved over time (Alvesson and Billing 1997:103). A structuralist perspective on organizations views an organization as a complex social unit in which many groups interact. These groups are defined by both their formal, functional connections and their informal connections. The relative power of each group and the ways in which the groups come into contact with each other shape the nature of the organization (Kanter 1981).

Organizational culture involves rituals, myths, stories, and legends as well as learned patterns of behavior by organization members. The definition of culture encompasses both values and feelings, as well as material aspects such as architecture and norms of dress (Alvesson and Billing 1997, Gherardi 1995, Strati 1992). Gherardi (1995) maintains that organizational cultures are strongly gendered and that organizational processes are themselves ways of organizing gender relations. She suggests that those following the gendered rules of a particular organization are often unaware of doing so. At the same time, failure to follow organizational rules may signify that an individual is not regarded as a full organizational member. This may be magnified by certain organizational practices which signal to members that their membership is not complete (Mills 1989). Simpson, et al. (1987) point out that women often have difficulty accessing informal networks, especially those that are rooted in male-centered extra-curricular activities. For instance, they found that things such as participating in lewd humor and intoxication were judged to be masculine prerogatives, yet may be necessary for success in supervisory roles as well as for acceptance by subordinates and colleagues. Indeed, organizational belonging may be dependent on involvement in both informal networks as well as officially sanctioned, but male-oriented, extra-curricular activities such as company sporting events and male-centered social clubs (Crompton and Jones 1984). Studies have shown that women have not been central to men's networks, especially the networks of the dominant coalitions of organizations, that is, the networks of those in power (Brass 1985; Rosen et al. 1981).

Noe (1988) points out that women are often excluded from complete participation in organizations, as they have few interactions with individuals who are in positions of power within them. He points out that women often have difficulty in cultivating mentor relationships owing to this limited contact with potential mentors. According to Ilgen and Youtz (1986), this may decrease the likelihood that women will receive support and cooperation from peers and subordinates. Thus, women's full acceptance in organizations is curtailed by the availability of mentors, who are more often available to men.

The motivating language of an organization may also be cast in terms of male-oriented metaphors. As Riley points out, "organizational political cultures are primarily male domains." She explains, "the language of political symbols—sports, military, 'who you blow'—does nothing to deny this perspective. The male language recreates the domination of male sectional interests in the political cultures" (1983:436). Thus, the language and symbolism of an organizational culture may also work to exclude women from complete membership.

Kanter (1977) analyzes how individuals are treated as tokens in a job environment in which their social category (such as sex or ethnicity) is under-represented. She posits that the typical behavior of women in organizations is most often a response to organizational situations in which women find themselves. Moreover, Kanter claims that the proportional representation of groups within organizations determines their relative status and power within the organization. Thus, if women's full participation in organizations is tied to their relative status and power, then it is also tied to their relative numbers; that is, in order for women to participate fully, they must be integrated proportionally into organizations at all levels. Although Kanter's claims have been supported by other studies,[3] I will demonstrate that this argument is only partly true and somewhat paradoxical when discussing women in the IDF.

Acker's (1990) groundbreaking work moved gender from the realm of the individual by suggesting that organizational structures themselves are gendered. She argues that these structures are embedded with assumptions about gender and gender roles. Abstract jobs and hierarchies "assume a disembodied and universal worker . . . [who is] actually a man; men's bodies, sexuality, and relationships to procreation and paid work are subsumed in the image of the worker . . . and pervade organizational processes."(1990:139). Acker uses this argument to explain why gender segregation is repeatedly reproduced and, in doing so, implies that integration is not a practical tool to lessen gender inequality. Britton (1997) adapts this theory which is used of gendered organizations and suggests that gendered organizations reproduce and sustain both gender roles and gender-based inequality. Britton (2000) takes this analysis a step further by asking what exactly is meant by saying that an organization is gendered. She argues that typical definitions of gendered organizations can be problematic when used to produce social and organizational change. She argues that context is critical and that gender can be more or less salient in different situations. Gender can "be deployed by organizations, by workers themselves, or both" in a variety of fashions (Britton 2000:423). She argues that the identification of the factors which make gender less salient in an organization is valuable for producing realistic and meaningful movement toward gender equality.

Kanter (1977) discusses the experiences of women who have integrated into previously male-dominated organizations in terms of tokenism, the marginal status of workers who are the minority in their workplace. Kanter, however, argues that tokenism is a problem of numbers and, therefore, the experiences of token women should become more positive as more women enter the organization. This argument, of course, stands in opposition to gendered organization theories. Today, scholars take issue with this gender-neutral analysis and posit that the negative experiences of women are a result of their positions as social minorities as opposed to numerical minorities. Thus, work experiences are determined by the status of the minority group in society and not by relative numbers (Williams 1992; Yoder 1991; Zimmer 1988). This may explain why the movement of women into closed bases has done little to change the status of women in the IDF.

Tying together the examination of the military as a gendered institution that creates gendered behavior is the remarkable work of West and Zimmerman, in which they argue that gender is the product of social interactions. They argue that gender is a "situated doing," not a property of individuals, but rather "a feature of social situations: both as an outcome of and a rational for various social arrangements and as a means of legitimating one of the most fundamental divisions of society" (1987:126). In the highly gendered institution of the military, army life and positions provide a great deal of opportunities that reinforce traditional gender behavior patterns and, more importantly, use biology as a means for membership sorting (see Goffman 1977:330). Gender is, indeed, constructed and sustained through social performances (Butler 1990; Howard and Hollander 1997) for which the military provides an optimal stage.

Acker (1992) points out that simply knowing which gender category one belongs to is not necessarily an adequate guide as to what is appropriate male and female behavior. Rather, what is acceptable gendered behavior is dependent on the structure of the institution one is participating in. Although the IDF neatly places female and male soldiers into groups that adhere to their needs, soldiers actively construct personas that are appropriately gendered for the institutional setting of the military.

Military Culture and the Gendered Nature of the Military

Military culture is distinctive and differs from other organizations. The military values qualities such as honor, courage, discipline, and commitment and imposes these ideals on service members who are both on and off duty. Moreover, the military has clearly defined roles and statuses, holds tight to a hierarchical structure, and places a great deal of emphasis on the virtue of obedience (This is in contrast to other organizational cultures where roles and status are more ambiguous and where rules of conduct are implied yet not clearly stated.). Unlike other organizations, the military affords very little room for individual autonomy (as a sense of individuality may become a liability in times of conflict). This results in an emphasis on common objectives and unit cohesion (Coll et al. 2011; Exum, Coll, and Weiss 2011; Hooker 2003; Levy 2007).

Embedded in military culture is the prominence of the "cult of masculinity." The military is a masculine institution by nature and, in fact, as Segal notes, the military may be "the most prototypically masculine of all social institutions" (1995:758). Military culture honors traits that are associated with combat, especially those which are traditionally deemed to be masculine: physical strength, force, aggressiveness, and so on. Morgan writes: "Despite far-reaching political, social, and technological changes, the warrior still seems to be a key symbol of masculinity" (1994:165). Indeed, women's participation in the military has often been fraught with hurdles due to anti-female attitudes embedded in military culture. This often leads to feelings of marginalization and even harassment and abuse (Burke 2004).

Herbert argues that not only is masculinity in the military rewarded, but it is also the primary construct around which socialization into soldiering takes place (1998). Furthermore, contrasting hegemonic masculinity with traditional femininity not only differentiates between masculine and feminine army roles but also reinforces the perception of the female as the weaker sex and the male as the soldier protector. She argues that "by requiring women to maintain a degree of femininity, perceptions of masculinity remain intact" (Herbert 1998:10). Carreiras adds to this, pointing out that "hegemonic definitions of military conflate with hegemonic masculine culture and ideology" (2006:40). Thus, the military not only reflects notions of masculinity but also acts as "a source of normative conceptions of gender" (2006:40), producing and then reproducing these norms.

Enloe argues that allowing women entrance into the military core "would throw into confusion *all* men's certainty about their male identity and thus about their claim to privilege in the social order" (1983:15, emphasis in original). When present as soldiers, women's army roles are often meant to reinforce masculinity by providing reminders of femininity. For instance, women are viewed by the IDF as "civilizing forces" and are expected to behave as such; that is, women's presence in the army is seen to have a civilizing effect on male soldiers' behavior. Moreover, women provide "symbolic touches of home" and are encouraged to demonstrate their femininity as well as the nurturing aspects of their personalities (Berkovitch 1997; Izraeli 1997; Silverbaum 1996).

Research Methodology

Initially, the focus of my research was not on base placement and organizational belonging, but on the integration and promotion of women in the IDF in terms of women's official ranks and positions. As I began searching for respondents, I found that many women felt that they were not potential interviewees for me, as they did not serve on closed bases. These women assumed that what I meant when I said that I wanted to talk to women about their army experiences was, in fact, that I only wanted to speak to women who served in closed bases or in combat-type positions. The women were, of course, mistaken, yet this misunderstanding revealed a great deal concerning women's perceptions of army service as it relates to base placement. Eventually, this led to the shifting of the focus of my research to organizational belonging, and I began to emphasize the base placement of my interviewees rather than simply concentrating on their official positions and military ranks.

I conducted open-ended interviews with 62 Jewish-Israeli women. Respondents ranged in age from 18 to 31, the majority being between the ages of 23 and 28. My sample varied greatly in terms of ethnicity and included women from many backgrounds: Polish, Romanian, Iraqi, Moroccan, Egyptian, German, Yemenite, Turkish, Russian, Indian, South American, and others. Respondents' cities of residence were also varied and included major cities such as Haifa, Tel Aviv, and BeerSheva and their surrounding areas as well as peripheral cities that were somewhat more remote. My sample consisted of both women who were drafted into service and those who chose to volunteer (as they were not drafted due to medical/physical difficulties). The majority of my interviewees came from the upper working class and lower- to mid-upper class backgrounds. My sample was, therefore, reflective of the secular and semi-religious Jewish-Israeli population and its diversity (See appendix A for a complete listing of respondents' age, ethnic background, base placement, military position, etc.).

Interviews were conducted in Hebrew and were semi-structured in format. Respondents were asked a series of questions pertaining to their army experiences. I explored the same group of central themes with respondents while allowing for flexibility in terms of probing any comments that seemed especially interesting. Interviews took place in respondents' homes, in my home, in cafes, and often on trains. Interviews ranged in time from as short as 15 minutes to as long as an hour and a half. The average length of the interviews was 45–50 minutes. With the exception of two interviews in which respondents requested not to be recorded, the interviews were tape-recorded and later transcribed and translated verbatim. The data were then coded into themes such as proximity to combat, tokenism, and open-base service.

My sample was obtained by approaching both women known to me through family and friends as well as strangers and simply requesting an interview. Often informants referred me to others. Thus, I used a snowball sampling technique that consisted of a number of small snowball groups. Approximately one quarter of respondents were still serving in the IDF during the time of the interview. Many of my interviews were carried out with soldiers whom I met on the train. These women, who were most often traveling from their bases to their homes, were usually quite eager to be interviewed, as it helped them pass the time on what seemed to them to be a rather long commute. The function of interviewing women on the train was twofold. First, I found this a good venue for interviewing women who were currently serving in the IDF. The train ride also provided an available time frame and a comfortable (if not quiet), non-threatening space for me to carry out interviews. Second, since soldiers serving on closed bases are more likely to be found taking the train than women who serve on open bases closer to their homes, I used train interviews as a means of oversampling women serving on closed bases. Since the majority of women in the IDF serve on open bases, had I not used strategies to oversample women serving on closed bases, I would not have obtained a sample that allowed me to compare these two populations.

In addition to interviews, I conducted two months of field research on six army bases throughout Israel. The base sample consisted of both open and closed bases as well as both large and small bases (three large bases and three small bases). I conducted this field research by volunteering for the IDF through a program set up for both Israeli citizens and tourists who wanted to spend a period of time working for the army. The program encompasses people from various countries and religious backgrounds (approximately half of the volunteers identified as Jewish and the other half identified as Christian) and can vary in time period from as little as one week to as long as desired (Indeed, many of the volunteers had been there for more than one year.). During the volunteer period, volunteers eat with soldiers in the dining hall, socialize with soldiers during both the workday and evening, and sleep in soldiers' barracks.

My knowledge of Hebrew was especially helpful during my field work period. Whereas other volunteers were sometimes treated as outsiders, I was often mistaken for a regular soldier. When other volunteers were taken on sightseeing trips, I would find an excuse to remain alone on the base and make friends with the soldiers. By these means, I began to fit in with the soldiers on the base. I was invited to chat over refreshments in the offices and to both male and female soldiers' rooms to smoke water pipes (which is actually prohibited by the IDF). I often sat with them at mealtime and drank coffee with them during my breaks. Each evening, I would privately write down my field notes. If something especially interesting occurred during the day, I would often run to the bathroom and write down my observations. I also utilized the army environment for securing interviews from the women serving on the base. In fact, these interviews proved to be the most interesting and often the most relevant to my research.

Throughout my field research, I attempted to vary my physical location and my army jobs as much as possible. When I was finished with my job for the day (jobs were allocated by the soldiers in charge of the volunteers), I would often seek out other jobs in order to maximize the number of soldiers whom I met as well as the number of job settings that I observed. Through this strategy, I was able to participate in many capacities, including kitchen work, sorting and packing medical supplies (for both army and public use), laundry and uniform distribution, bakery work, gas mask inspection, food distribution services (for soldiers serving in the occupied territories), cooking, and cleaning.

I often found my way into other job settings by talking with soldiers who worked in them and by finding excuses to visit. I visited the infirmary and entered offices in order to share in their snacks or help with volunteer paperwork. I requested tours from soldiers who were pleased to show me their workstations, and, thus, I had access to army tanks, guard stations, and so on. During all these visits, I identified myself as a volunteer who was also carrying out research. Thus, although I may have found excuses to enter offices and workstations, once there, my role as a researcher was made clear. I also informed the IDF of my presence as a researcher/volunteer by relaying this information to the IDF branch that was responsible for foreign volunteers as well as their sister organization in Canada through which I entered the volunteer program. Thus, the IDF was aware of my presence. In fact, several officers volunteered to find me respondents! Since my research mostly concentrated on soldiers' feelings and not on the details of their work or on military tactics, I did not require official permission from the IDF in order to carry out my research.

Special Circumstances: The Impact of Doing Research during the Al-Aqsa Intifada

My research took place at the height of the al-Aqsa Intifada, the second Palestinian uprising against Israel's military and civilian population. During the period of my research, terrorist attacks against Israeli civilians took place at alarming rates, at times averaging one attack per day. Concurrently, IDF operations in the occupied territories also increased to a great extent, resulting in many deaths and much suffering for those on both sides of the existing conflict. Thus, the Intifada created special circumstances for Israeli society, for the IDF, and, thus, for my research. First, the security situation in Israel was heightened, and many soldiers who served in non-combat positions were placed in situations in which they were expected to perform semi-combat duties. For instance, soldiers whose only experience with weapons was from their few weeks in basic training often found themselves having to carry weapons. Technicians who served in open bases and had little combat training were often placed on call for repair duty in the occupied territories. Should military equipment break down, these soldiers would then be transferred to the territories to do repairs and, thus, were required to be armed. During the period of being on call, these soldiers were responsible for their weapons and were forced to keep them on their bodies at all times. This had the effect of exaggerating the combat environment, as it created the impression that there were more combat soldiers than there actually were. Moreover, soldiers, especially armed soldiers, were expected to represent security and calm, as if their very presence would somehow prevent an attack. Thus, soldiers who did not have positions associated with combat were thrown into the soldier role, corresponding to the myth that most soldiers serve in combat positions when, in reality, only a minority (20% of male soldiers, 2.5% of female soldiers do [Klein 2002; Sasson-Levy 2007]).

The second major impact of the Intifada on my research resulted from the draft. During my research, there were several large draft calls for reserve duty. These drafts, considered as emergency drafts by the IDF, required soldiers to leave at a moment's notice and serve extra time beyond the month of reserve duty already expected of them. Thus, the Intifada blurred boundaries between military and civilian spheres in

Israel and further cemented the military firmly at the center of Israeli culture. The general impact of the Intifada, then, was to magnify already existent gender roles in the IDF as well as to reinforce the emphasis and prestige placed on combat roles due to the false characterization of the military as being primarily a vehicle for combat.

"Doing Army"/"Feeling Army"

Although the main differentiating point between closed-base and open-base placement pertains to where one sleeps (in closed bases, soldiers stay on base to sleep, whereas in open bases, soldiers return home every day), this simple distinction has great implications. A closed base provides an army experience that allows women access to the organizational culture of the army, albeit an overwhelmingly masculine culture, and enables them to relate to what is generally considered the common Israeli army experience. An open base does not provide this aspect of "feeling army" to the same degree. In addition, women who serve in close proximity to combat, use weapons, or have high degrees of army discipline during their service are more likely to relate to what is commonly thought of as the army experience and more likely to feel that they have participated in the IDF in a meaningful way. Many women use the term *lehargish tzava*, literally translated as "to feel army," to encompass this idea of feeling that one is serving in a way which reflects general army service and allows one to participate in the shared Israeli army experience. It seems that *laasot tzava* (doing army) and *lehargish tzava* (feeling army) are not one and the same.

A Citizen's Rite of Passage

Military service signifies true citizenship for Jewish Israelis. It is deemed a right of passage for Jewish-Israeli youth, and completion of the army is symbolic of complete citizenship. In fact, the distinction between those who possess a service record and those who do not have one has become a social boundary within the Jewish-Israeli population. Those who have served or are serving in the military benefit from social esteem while people who are unable to document their military record or prove their discharge on the grounds of physical illness are often marginalized (Cohen 1995). This is because military service is perceived as "the fundamental expression of the individual's commitment to the state" (Sasson-Levy 2002:359). Military service is seen as defining who is a patriot and to what extent. As Sasson-Levy (2002) explains: "military service and the position one holds during this period shape a hierarchy of belonging and loyalty to the state" (2002:360). Those who do not serve, or who do not display socially sanctioned reasons for not having served (e.g., physical illness), are often perceived to be unpatriotic and/or social outcasts (This has been changing, as the prestige of the military has fallen, and the number of conscientious objectors has risen. Israel has been adopting attributes of modern military professionalism that have been, up until now, associated only with other modern military bodies. The IDF has become, over recent years, more selective in its recruitment and has focused more attention on creating career soldiers (Cohen 1995). This has slightly weakened the strength of the stigma placed on those who do not serve.).

David Ben-Gurion, Israel's first prime minister and minister of defense, intended the armed forces to be instruments of cohesion for the new Jewish state, and insisted that the IDF consist primarily of citizen-soldiers, rather than professional troops. It was to be (and is considered today) an instrument of social integration and assimilation for Israeli Jews (Azaryahu 1999; Berkovitch 1997; Cohen 1997a, 1999; Okun 1997). Thus, women's exclusion from army service, or pivotal army roles, is highly symbolic as a measure of their inclusion in Jewish-Israeli society—women who do not participate fully are not "complete citizens." Horowitz and Kimmerling argue that contributing to the country's security represents a reward and "defines the extent to which an individual is 'in' the social-evaluative system of Israel" (1974:265). Indeed, the majority of Jewish Israelis take for granted their invitation to participate in army service and, with it, army culture. Many of my respondents explained that they felt it was important for them to do army service in order to fit into society and that not doing army service would result in people looking down on them:

> I felt that it was something that everyone does and if I don't do it then people will always see me in a bad way...and I wanted to be like everyone. It didn't suit me to be the exception. (Respondent # 10)
>
> It's a sort of education procedure . . . of society in Israel. . . . You know that it's a procedure like that, that you're going to kindergarten, then to grade school, then junior high, high school and straight to the army. (Respondent # 6)
>
> It's me, it's my parents, it's my brother . . . everyone I know. I don't know people who didn't serve in the IDF. (Respondent # 21)

Many respondents felt that army service confirmed their identity as members of Israeli society and that had they not participated they would have felt left out.

> Whoever doesn't do army, when you talk about all sorts of concepts that they don't understand, then they feel like they don't belong. (Respondent # 28)

Interestingly, although many respondents pointed out that the army is something that "everyone does," many mentioned that they did not feel as if they themselves had had a real army experience; that is, their participation in Israel's military organization was limited—they "did army" but they did not "feel army." This feeling was mostly prevalent among women who served on open bases.

Approximately half of my respondents served oin open bases during their service. Several of these women did so within a civilian army frame; that is, they served on a base that was run primarily by civilians and where the soldiers present were a minority. Examples of positions found on civilian bases include soldier teachers who work within the regular education system (often with new immigrants or economically deprived populations), clerical work in civilian factories that deal primarily with military needs, and positions in the Nachal brigade (Youth Pioneer Fighting Brigade), a brigade that has in the past required soldiers to work on kibbutzes and new settlements for either part or all of their army service. Some of these women reported that the level of discipline was high on their bases (soldiers were expected to wear uniforms in an appropriate fashion, attend morning parades, etc.), many others reported a complete lack of army discipline, and some were not required to wear uniforms as a part of their service. These women reported not having felt that they were participating in army service in a meaningful way. While some felt that their work was useful or important, none felt that they had really experienced army.

> No, it was civilian. It's a civilian factory. Everyone wears regular clothes. Regular people, like, not soldiers . . . only I was a soldier. . . . No one cared what. With uniform, without uniform. No one was interested. (Respondent # 54)
>
> Where I was, because it was actually civilian, so I had absolute freedom. Like that, I didn't feel the army as army. That is, the discipline of the army and things like that . . . (Respondent # 40)
>
> There no, we were together with regular civilians. . . . Not in the army then. So she [the commander] was our army link. For instance, we had to always wear uniform. . . . But the [school] principal . . . at first told us: what is that green thing? Take it off. And we didn't like it that much [anyway] so many didn't wear uniform. (Respondent # 49)

A cohesive organizational culture requires that an organization have a clear set of norms and expectations and includes shared heroes, stories, and rituals which promote bonding among the organization's members. The members of an organization must have a common history or a shared experience of some sort in order for a culture to develop (Schein 1990; Snider 1999). Obviously, civilian frames do not provide access to military culture. The women serving in civilian frames have little contact with others in the military (making bonding with other soldiers difficult), limited military discipline (which often takes the form of rituals), and very little knowledge of army terminology. One respondent (Respondent # 7) reported: "The ranks of the IDF, I don't know! . . . [names several army ranks randomly] . . . I don't recognize these."

Other respondents reported not having done "real" army service, as there were no kitchen or guard duties to do at their bases. According to respondents who served in closed bases, the most often hated rites of doing kitchen duty and/or guard duty served as bonding elements and helped them identify as soldiers. Morning flag-raising ceremonies also served this purpose, as they were daily reminders of military culture. In fact, during my volunteer service, we were required to attend morning flag raising in order to give us the feeling that we were actually in the army (when, in fact, what we were doing would best be described as "military tourism"). Open bases were less likely to require women to perform these duties and participate in these rituals, and open bases run by civilians (civilian bases as outlined earlier) almost never did.

Closed bases are centers for military culture and often even form subcultures that are specific to the army unit or to the base itself. Several respondents serving in closed bases reported that their base had a language of its own which outsiders could not understand. As one respondent (Respondent # 18) told me, "There are ways of talking that they only talk at my base." The fact that closed bases promote feelings of having completed "real" service was not lost on any of my respondents. Nearly all of the women interviewed, regardless of where they served, gave the same answer when asked about the differences between open and closed bases: On closed bases, you "feel army" more. Many respondents said that they would recommend to others that they serve on a closed base and often had others recommend this to them.

> I said: I want to serve far from home. I want to feel what army is. I understood that whoever serves far from home, he feels what army is, sees what it is . . . (Respondent # 61)
>
> And my mother *doesn't* want me to be at home every day. She wants me to be far in order for me to feel army. Because to be at home every day is not—army is to sleep outside in a base and that way you feel more in the army. (Respondent # 37)

All but a few of my respondents had requested closed bases, though not all had their requests granted. Most interesting were four of the women interviewed who were serving on an open base, yet slept in army barracks, as the base location was far from their homes. Thus, what was an open base for their coworkers became a closed base for them. Due to the common Israeli belief that female soldiers prefer to be close to their homes and parents, these women were perceived by their coworkers and commander as having been dealt a bad hand. However, they themselves felt that they were lucky to serve at a base far from home, and only one was attempting to be transferred to an open base closer to home (in order to be closer to her boyfriend). As one of these women said:

> People come here at eight, do their work, at five they go home. Just like [civilian] work. And that's what I didn't want the most. . . . There are many bases close to home, many. But I didn't want [that]. I wanted to feel army, not [civilian] work. . . . I want to feel army. To tell my kids: I did army. . . . To feel army. . . . Because I sleep here, I feel it more. (Respondent # 35)

One of these women actually had a home in a nearby city but chose to sleep at the base in order to experience army culture. She explained:

> I also sleep here by choice. . . . My mother doesn't want it a bit. She wants me to come home every day. She also doesn't understand why I stay here, like most people. But in my opinion, it's more of an experience. It's more the atmosphere of being far from home. It's everyone [serving on] a closed base. . . . it's really an experience and I would want to go through that. (Respondent # 36)

It seems that much of "feeling army" is linked to spending evenings in the base environment and socializing with other soldiers after hours. Indeed, it is the army "atmosphere" that is most often mentioned by respondents who served on closed bases when they speak of feeling what they termed "the army frame." Seldom is there any mention of army position or rank as a vehicle for "feeling army" (with certain exceptions regarding female officers).

Many of my respondents serving in civilian frames or in open bases reported feeling cheated by their army experience, or lack thereof. Although often satisfied by their army positions in terms of the jobs they had been given, they expressed regret over not identifying with the common army experience. One respondent explained:

> I didn't connect with a civilian base at all. Because it's not really—I don't know, it's not the point of the army in my opinion. . . . I didn't experience the 100% in my opinion. In a closed base I think I could have experienced more. (Respondent # 55)

When asked about the difference between her army experience and that of others, one woman (Respondent # 14) answered, "That they know what army is, and I don't. Really! They would be able to tell you what a base is, what a unit is. I haven't a clue!" She continued by expressing regret that she did not share in the army experience, "because it's an experience that is really shared [by] everyone here and I don't know what they're talking about when they talk about that." For this woman as well as other respondents, serving in the IDF, in and of itself, was not sufficient to provide feelings of belonging and identification with Israeli society in terms of army culture. Considering that army service signifies "true" citizenship for Israelis, one may question whether these women have truly experienced this rite of passage.

The Myth of Military Service

On discussion of military in Israel and elsewhere, certain images emerge as being central to army service. The military is most often associated with weapons, borders, and combat. In the IDF, combat roles are among the most esteemed positions, and this prestige is transferable to civilian life. While white-collar military roles are granted high status, the highest status is reserved for soldiers serving in combat units (Y. Levy 1998; Sasson-Levy 2002). As Edna Levy contends, "combat soldiering is not simply another job in the IDF, but is conceived of as a key to entry into the collective. It is the strongest version of the link between army service and national belonging" (1998:87).

Combat missions, however, play only a small part in the operations of the IDF. As previously mentioned, only 20% of male soldiers in the IDF are considered combat soldiers, and only 2 ½% of female soldiers are considered as holding combat positions (Klein 2002; Sasson-Levy 2007). Since most soldiers are not directly linked to combat, the notion that army experience is regularly connected to weapons and fighting is largely a myth. Still, there is an overwhelming conception in Israeli society that army service is somehow linked to being in direct contact with combat. Just as prestige is connected to combat positions, so also having had a "real" army experience is connected to having had contact with combat. The closer one's proximity to combat, the greater the prestige of the position and the more authentic the army experience. Since women serving in the IDF serve mostly in peripheral positions, their army experiences are often highly removed from the combat frame.

Many of the women whom I interviewed and others whom I met during my field research remarked that it would not be worth my time to interview them, as they did not serve in combat, in close proximity to combat, or in combat-type positions (such as combat instructors). The extent to which these women perceived themselves as having carried out "real" army service corresponded to their involvement in combat-type roles. Just over 20% of my sample had served in close proximity to combat or in combat-type positions during their service. Others went through combat-type training during their army courses (which are generally held on closed bases). For many women who served on open bases (especially those who served in lower-status positions that do not require courses), contact with combat-type activities was limited to basic training. The less contact that respondents had with combat, the less they perceived themselves to be "real" soldiers. As one respondent (Respondent #4) articulated: "So my army experience is really, if you mean using tools of war and such, it's basically from basic training." Another respondent who spent part of her service in a civilian frame further explained the link between "feeling army" and combat:

> It's like you're not in the army. . . . Sure, you're not in—do you have something that is characteristic of the army? You don't have to wear uniform; you're not told what to do . . no one checks. You don't have orders. You don't carry a weapon. There is nothing that is connected. (Respondent # 8)

On the other hand, women who carried weapons or who reported feeling that discipline was high in their base were more likely to report having "felt army." Those respondents who served in close proximity to combat were the most likely to report "feeling army." In fact, many of the women in my sample who served in administrative and clerical positions in bases and who were in close proximity to combat considered themselves to be very similar to combat soldiers and used the word *kravi* (meaning combat soldier) to describe their army positions. Women who engaged in a great deal of physical activity as a part of combat training (mainly combat instructors) also considered themselves to be combat soldiers in spite of the fact that they were prohibited from engaging in actual combat and battle.

The majority of the respondents who considered themselves to be in combat-type positions served in bases where women were in the minority. This, of course, is not surprising considering the fact that the IDF excludes women from the majority of combat positions. Thus, "feeling army" is something that is closely linked with the male army domain. This point was not lost on my respondents. For instance, when I asked what she meant when she said, "feeling army," one woman responded:

Not to be in some base where I'm at home every day and it's like a workplace but more to feel, to be once every week or two at home, to be with soldiers, to be in a battalion of fighters, of very few girls.(Respondent # 19)

Many argue that the IDF, not unlike other militaries, is a masculine institution by nature. Congruent with the myth of military service, the dominant and prestigious aspects of military are those that are associated with combat. Moreover, the traits that are associated with combat are traditionally deemed to be masculine, such as physical strength, force, and aggressiveness, are most highly valued. Indeed, the emphasis placed by my respondents on combat-type activity and combat proximity as a means of "feeling army" lends support to Klein's argument that, although Jewish women are conscripted into the IDF, the military is the "main force in shaping *male* identity" and "military service can be understood as a rite of passage to *male* adulthood" (2002:671; emphases in original).

It seems that in order for a woman to "feel army" to the highest level, she should remain in the gender minority. The masculine nature of military organizations creates this paradoxical situation that would not occur if the military organization itself were gender neutral. This does not mesh well with Kanter's theory of proportional representation and tokenism which suggests that when more women move into a male-dominated organization, the treatment of women within that organization, especially those in token positions, will change (1977). Indeed, Kanter links the position of women in the organization to relative numbers and suggests that "as proportions begin to shift, so do social experiences" (1977:207). Following Kanter's arguments, it is clear that in order for women to fully participate in the military organization, they should achieve equality in terms of numbers in all of its areas. However, the proportional integration of women into an army unit would most likely change the culture and status of the unit. Since the military can be seen as the epitome of masculine institutions, gender neutrality would change its nature to the extent that it would no longer be considered "typical military" and, consequently, those participating in it would "feel army" to a lesser extent. Thus, although the integration of women into army units (as in the "professional revolution" after the 1973 war) raises women's status and power within the unit itself, it lowers women's feelings of having truly participated in the country's military (As is the case with many organizations, the integration of women into a unit may also serve to lower the overall status of the unit itself.). It seems that for women soldiers, there is no way to win.

Uniforms

Wearing a uniform is often regarded as synonymous with serving in the military. When Israeli youth first enlist in the military, their parents often take pictures of them in their uniforms in order to mark their rite of passage into army service (My fellow volunteers, in fact, took many pictures of themselves in uniform and made many comments, such as "Now I'm a real soldier!"). Donning military apparel is symbolic of belonging to the military organization. The majority of my respondents at one point during the interview reported (without being asked) on whether or not they wore military uniform during their service. Respondents associated wearing a uniform with the army, and those respondents who did not wear uniforms at certain points or throughout their service (approximately 8% of my respondents) reported this fact to me immediately and in a manner which suggested that this lack of having worn a uniform negated the very fact that they had served at all. They felt that they had carried out some sort of service for the country, but it wasn't exactly "real" army service. This is not surprising when one considers the role of uniforms as communicating inclusion in the military organization. In fact, the term "in uniform," in many countries, is often used to refer to soldiers. Furthermore, uniforms in the military are used to communicate a soldier's rank and status. This is done through the placement on the uniform of symbols of rank, units, and courses passed which become mandatory parts of the uniform itself. As such, uniforms do not only signify belonging, but also specify exactly where one belongs and to what degree.

Several respondents reported having had discipline issues and trials surrounding issues of how they were wearing their uniforms: missing dog tags, inappropriate footwear, wearing their hair down, and so on. Women who were required to wear their uniforms properly at all times were more likely to report "feeling army" than those who were not obligated to wear a uniform or who were allowed to let this matter slide. Thus, uniform issues overlap with those of discipline, and rules and structure become a source for organizational belonging. It is interesting to note that the only exceptions to this were those women who served in close proximity to combat. In these bases, both discipline and uniform rules were relaxed. Letting the uniform matter slide includes things such as wearing hair down, wearing inappropriate footwear, or wearing only a T-shirt. One woman even reported having worn sweat pants instead of her uniform pants. This is because women on closed bases had other means of "feeling army," and so, the relaxing of uniform issues had little effect on their feelings of organizational belonging.

Often, wearing a uniform made respondents feel that they belonged to a larger organization and that they had much in common with other soldiers. One woman explained:

> Like [my sister] says, everyone wears green, everyone has the same status. You don't know the person in his private life, like how he behaves, where he goes out, who his friends are.... Everyone is at the same level and everyone simply behaves the same. (Respondent # 28)

Though most respondents recognized that there are status differences within the IDF, yet many, nevertheless, shared the feeling that soldiers are in some ways all the same. The uniform, after all, signifies membership in the IDF and restricts the demonstration of individuality. A good example of this is the IDF rule that prohibits soldiers wearing uniforms from discussing politics. This rule is based on the notion that the personal opinions of uniformed soldiers may be mistaken for those held by the IDF. One officer explained to me that she could answer my question related to Israel's security situation only if she removed her shirt! I remember wondering at the time how one would feel as a soldier who did not serve in uniform while overhearing this conversation. Would their ability to voice their political opinions lessen their feelings of participating in the military as a "real" soldier? That is, would their exemption from this rule lessen their feelings of organizational belonging?

Several respondents reported that wearing a uniform made them feel as if they were different people and reinforced their identity as soldiers. One respondent explained:

> You wear [a] uniform and that's it, you're seen as a female soldier. You're not a girl anymore. They don't call you "girl" on the street, [they call you] "female soldier." (Respondent # 36)

Other respondents felt that wearing a uniform gave them a sense of duty toward the IDF. One woman (Respondent # 34) noted, "the moment that I have a uniform on, I have to give 200%, not 100% of myself." These feelings were magnified by the security situation in Israel during the period of my research. At the height of the Intifada, several respondents reported being looked to as security people on buses and trains. They were taught by their commanders that "someone in uniform gives security to civilians" and that a uniformed soldier has a calming effect on civilians in public places. However, these same soldiers do not carry weapons. It is the uniform alone that reminds civilians of combat and calms their fears of terrorist attacks. One soldier told a story that exemplifies this notion:

> Also when I don't carry a weapon, the fact that I have a uniform, so people already look at me a bit. . . . I was in a bus, I got on a bus, I wasn't with a weapon, I was a *Mashakit Cheenooch* [a position that deals with army education], I had a pen in my pocket [not a weapon]. . . and this girl in high school comes to me and says to me in all seriousness, she looks at me: "eh, keep an eye out, look at what's going on." So what can I tell her: Listen sweetheart, I don't have a clue what [to do in event of a terrorist attack]? . . . I need to let her feel that there are soldiers and they'll protect her and everything is ok. . . . I told her: "there's no problem" and like that so she sat calmly on the bus. (Respondent # 34)

Having others perceive one as a "real" soldier, linked to combat, who can protect the citizenry in case of attack, magnifies the extent that one "feels army." Thus, wearing uniforms increases the likelihood of feeling organizational belonging.

Implications of Different Bases on Confidence and Networking

The non-uniformity of army experiences not only creates different perceptions of whether real army service has taken place, but also has an impact on the experiences and skills that women have and develop during their army service. If "doing army" has different meanings for women serving on closed and open bases, it follows that women serving on different types of bases also differ in terms of what they feel they get out of the army. Women serving on closed bases more often reported having developed a sense of confidence, independence, maturity, social skills, and networking ability during their service. Overall, they were more likely to have reported having positive army experiences. Women serving on open bases were less likely to report changes in their lives, and more often reported that their army experiences were negative and/or had negatively affected their lives. Of five respondents who reported that the army had absolutely no positive influence on their lives, four served on open bases.

Confidence and Independence

The widespread belief in the indispensability of the Israeli army to the nation affects Israeli perceptions of men and women in that men, who are deemed essential to the army, are deemed to be more essential to society than are women. The secondary roles that women play in the IDF reinforce cultural conceptualizations of women as weak and vulnerable, and in need of protection by men (Golan 1997; Sered 2000). The distinctions between women's and men's roles and locations in the IDF symbolize the perceived worth and abilities of women in comparison to men in Israeli society. It is not surprising, then, that my respondents who served on closed bases, which are more traditionally masculine army environments, were more likely to report a rise in personal confidence and feelings of independence than those who served on open bases. Closed bases provide more of an army-type atmosphere and allow access to army culture. As noted, closed bases generally contain more male soldiers than do open bases. This is especially true for bases that are in close proximity to combat. Women serving on these closed bases are closer to "serving just like men" than are women serving on open bases. Several respondents serving on closed bases even mentioned that they almost felt as if they were combat soldiers as a result of their confinement to the base and infrequent visits home. Hence, proximity to male army culture seemed to be positively correlated with women's self-esteem and sense of independence.

Approximately half of my sample consisted of women who had served (or were serving) on closed bases; 10% had served on both open and closed bases throughout their service; and the remaining 40% had served on open bases. In general, those serving on closed bases were far more likely to report having had a positive army experience than those serving on open bases. The majority of women serving on closed bases indicated that they had attained greater levels of confidence through their army service. This was indicated through statements depicting their feeling stronger, more secure with their abilities, and so on. Almost 30% of my respondents claimed outright that their army service had resulted in an increase in their confidence levels. Of these 30%, just over half had served on closed bases, whereas the other half had served on open bases. However, this number does not convey an accurate picture. Of the women in open bases who felt that there was an increase in their confidence levels due to army service, more than one-third had spent a great deal of their army service in closed bases carrying out courses and indicated during interviews that it was this time which was most important in the formation of their confidence. Of the remaining women in this category, several noted that the increase in their confidence came solely from their weeks in basic army training. They stated that these few weeks at the onset of their service spent in a closed-base environment played a larger role in the formation of their new confidence than their entire service. One respondent related:

> I went to basic training in fear and I came back, I remember, the same week that I came back from basic training I already had confidence. They gave us a great deal of confidence there. (Respondent # 60)

Another respondent explained to me that basic training was the first thing that resulted in her increase in confidence. She compared her basic training with her service on an open base:

> It was harder for me than in the base during basic training. The basic training was also in a closed base, we slept there.... It was also physical and spiritual and it was, for me, it was the hardest part. Because it was also the beginning. The beginning of what the army is. So it's something that I'll remember more than [the rest of] my service.... There are sometimes short moments that you remember. (Respondent # 55)

It is noteworthy that the women in open bases who reported an increase in confidence levels were almost exclusively in high-status positions (such as officer); whereas those in closed bases who reported an increase were in both high- and low-status positions. This is not surprising in light of the link between organizational belonging and confidence.

Respondents often expressed feelings of pride that they had developed by serving in the country's military, thus contributing to the nation's security. This pride was associated with what was thought of as the "typical" army experience which, as discussed in the previous section, included wearing uniforms, carrying weapons, sleeping at bases, and so on. At the same time, respondents explained to me that serving in an open base was very similar to regular work, removed from an army-type atmosphere. Indeed, even when an open base is rich in army-type atmosphere, those who serve there are only there for half of their day. Respondents explained:

> And at home you're like, you're in the army and you're not in the army. That is, you also have your civilian, private life that is the afternoon when you come home. Whoever has a closed base, she doesn't have a private, civilian life... you're inside an army frame, not outside. (Respondent # 53)
>
> It was like going to work at eight and coming home at three. I had civilian life in every way in the afternoon. I would dress regularly and I'd go and do whatever I want however I wanted. (Respondent # 42)

It seems then that serving in an open base is like being only half in the army. The "army lifestyle" seemed to have a greater impact on respondents than the positions that they held. If army service is a source of pride and confidence for women, it follows that women who live a half army/half civilian lifestyle feel this pride only half the time. It is no wonder, then, that only closed bases are associated with an increase in confidence. Several women also suggested that their increase in confidence was a result of being one of a few women among many men, which resulted in a great deal of male attention as well as feelings of pride at having been chosen to be in this male-dominated environment. As one woman (Respondent # 29) explained: "You felt that you're doing something important because not every girl ends up there and not every [female] person that wants gets there."

As previously noted, the majority of my respondents reported having requested to serve on closed bases. Interestingly, these women perceived themselves to be in the minority and believed that, in general, women most often request to serve on open bases close to home. Indeed, during my research, I heard many people speak of the "fact" that female soldiers find being far from home far more difficult than male soldiers do. It is a common perception that girls are more emotionally and physically fragile than boys and that the army should attempt, wherever possible, to keep them close to home and family. This is precisely what the majority of women in my study did not want. Many mentioned that they wanted to serve far from home in order to develop responsibility and independence. Ironically, most of the few respondents who did not ask to serve in closed bases, and who were placed far from home against their wishes, felt that the independence which they developed during their service was worth the sacrifice of the comforts of home and family, and they were thankful that their requests to be placed in open bases were not granted.

Networking Ability

Juliet Pope, in her discussion of Na'amat (the largest women's organization in Israel), notes the role of the military in career structuring in Israel. She points out that "for Jewish males, the IDF can provide training opportunities, work experience, and access to professional contacts which constitute a form of 'old boys' network'" (1993:230). She explains that Na'amat has focused on extending these benefits to women by fighting against legislation that made it less difficult for women to exempt themselves from service and by campaigning for women to carry arms in the Civil Guard. Na'amat acknowledges that military service is considered a "calling card" when seeking paid employment and that women cannot expect equal rights in a society if they do not have equal responsibilities

(Pope 1993). Truly, the exclusion of women from combat service (arguably the most important military function) restricts women's military employment to low-status positions and results in frequent assignments to open bases. This may have the effect of impeding women's chances of advancement in their subsequent civilian careers.

Placing women on open bases blocks their accumulation of what Pierre Bourdieu (1986) refers to as social and symbolic capital. Military experience becomes key to entry into Israeli society, politics, and job markets (Linn 1996; Fisch 2004). Izraeli (1997) builds on this argument, and contends that, since female soldiers acquire less symbolic capital (prestige, celebrity, reputation, etc.) during army service, they accumulate fewer advantages in civilian life. She points out that, since female soldiers are generally not required to carry out reserve duty, they also acquire less social capital (network relations, strongly bonded relationships, etc.) and are, thus, limited in their networking capacities in terms of the civilian paid labor market. This same argument can be made with regard to open bases. Low levels of organizational belonging do not facilitate networking.

Although networking contacts are difficult to measure, respondents shared with me their experiences of bonding and friendship. Women who had served on closed bases were more likely to report having bonded strongly with others on the base than were women who had served on open bases. None of the women who had served on both open and closed bases during their service reported having bonded with their coworkers. This may be explained by the fact that they had to change locations mid-service and serve with new coworkers. Thus, women who served on both open and closed bases were the most disadvantaged in terms of making contacts and friends during their army service.

It was generally accepted by most respondents (regardless of where and on which type of base they served) that in closed bases, friendship bonds are stronger, because people spend a great deal of time together. As respondents noted:

> In some way it's all the same because it's army, on the other hand you know people the best in the world because you're with them twenty-four hours a day. (Respondent # 25)
> ... I think that in an open base there aren't really [bonded] relations like those. ... and I think that in regiments that are more combat oriented ... let's say in a regiment of paratroopers or in a regiment of combat ... the relations are much more uniting. (Respondent # 5)

The majority of my respondents shared the notion that bases which are in close proximity to combat are more strongly bonded than others. What was not generally commented on, but did emerge during my research, was the idea that different bases and positions allowed not only different degrees of networking but also different *kinds* of network contacts. Women serving on bases where work was segregated according to sex (something that is more common on open bases but occurs on closed bases as well) did not have an opportunity to meet, bond, and network with members of the opposite sex. This limited women serving in female-dominated positions to networking with other women who were most often either of the same rank or slightly higher. Thus, women who serve in all-female environments have little access to high-ranking army officials and other powerful people in Israel's male-dominated society. Moreover, the condition of "army distance" is much stronger in open bases than on closed bases. "Distance" refers to more formal relations between members of different ranks and regulates behavior according to army hierarchy. Those in lower ranks must maintain a distance from those in higher ranks and may not become too friendly with them, argue with them, or in extreme cases (such as during basic training), even look them in the eye. Distance is highest during basic training and declines as army service progresses. Open bases are more likely to be stringent with distance regulations than are closed bases where close living relations allow for greater bonding. One respondent explains this well:

> But in a closed base there's less "distance". Much less . . . there's more closeness because you *live* with people. So it doesn't really matter if a person is an officer or a cook . . . officers and cooks are good friends. . . . Ask boys, they'll say . . . in bases that are combat, that is with combat soldiers there isn't anything like "distance" at all! At all. . . . So again, it's according to ranks. If the base is open then the relations are distant as well. . . . In a . . . closed base the relations are more close. In a base where one [person] is dependent on another [person] like in a war, then the relations are the closest. (Respondent # 9)

Concluding Remarks

Research on organizational belonging is commonly situated in the study of the workplace organization. As such, data on absenteeism, turnover rates, and so on are often the basis of measurement and analysis. This research studies organizational belonging in a setting in which these have little value as measurements. Indeed, it is an examination of what it really means to participate in an organization when physical participation is not voluntary. Soldiers most often have no choice but to carry out their assigned positions and duties. Still, there is a clear difference between true commitment and simply going through the motions. True commitment involves high levels of organizational belonging—what my respondents referred to as "feeling army."

Using the IDF as an example of a large organization, I found that base placement is more significant in determining organizational belonging than are military position and rank. Being placed at a closed base is more beneficial to a soldier than being placed at an open base in terms of networking ability, development of confidence and independence, and, most importantly, in the development of one's sense of identity as a member of the military. This is especially important in societies in which military involvement is closely linked with one's sense of national belonging and citizenship.

Tyler (1999) argues that the formal structure of an organization and its informal organizational culture play a large role in shaping an individual's identity. In the case of the IDF, the formal structure takes the shape of base placement, and the identity under question is that of being a "real" soldier who "feels army" versus being a soldier who simply "does army." Individuals who believe that the organization has provided them with a measure of status and a sense of favorable self-worth are most likely to become committed to the organization and to feel high levels of organizational belonging. Thus, soldiers who have been placed, by the formal structure, on closed bases are more likely to "feel army" than others.

The roles of official status and rank in shaping organizational belonging are significant but limited. Unofficial status and work context play a larger role in creating a sense of belonging for women soldiers in the IDF. This is significant, as the IDF provides an example in which there is a great deal of occupational gender segregation. Many scholars contend that if most positions within the paid labor market were shared by equal numbers of men and women, then gender inequality would be far more difficult to sustain. Kanter's (1977) theory of proportional representation is a leading example of such analysis. My research, however, suggests that the picture is somewhat different when the organization in question is extremely masculine in nature. In order to create real change, not only must there be a movement of women into male-dominated positions, but there must also be a change in the underlying structure of the organization and the mentality of its members. In the case of the IDF, in order to stimulate real progress toward gender equality, there must be a change in the actual structure of the military as well as the culture. Thus, in line with the positions taken by scholars such as Acker and Britton, I contend that not only should the numerical male domination of the military be challenged, but its ideological male domination must be confronted as well.

When I began my research, I planned to examine the impact of the promotion and integration of women into the IDF. However, once I began my interviews, it struck me that many of my respondents were apologizing for not being able to present me with what they perceived as the typical army experience. The majority of these apologetic women served on open bases. I was told over and over again that my interviews would be more interesting and accurate in terms of the army experience if I interviewed mainly women who had served on closed bases. Although the IDF will not provide recent statistics concerning where most women conscripts carry out their service, it is clear from an examination of women's positions within the IDF and the military's exclusion of women from most combat positions that the majority of women in Israel serve on open bases. This then raises a key question. If the things that make people "feel army" are those which are most strongly associated with closed bases (combat, weapons, discipline, uniforms, etc.), then do most Jewish-Israeli women share in the country's collective army experience? Does army service carry a completely different set of meanings for them? How important is the difference between "doing army" and "feeling army"?

Notes

1. Unfortunately, the IDF will not disclose the percentages of women and men serving on closed and open bases, as they deem the release of this information to be a security threat.
2. The terms "feeling army" (*lhargish tzava*) and "doing army" (*laasot tzava*) were used by almost every respondent without interview prompting.
3. For examples, see Izraeli (1983, 1984); Chambliss and Uggen (2000).

References

Acker, Joan. 1990. "Hierarchies, Jobs, Bodies: A Theory of Gendered Organizations." *Gender & Society* 4(2): 139–158.

Acker, Joan. 1992. "From Sex Roles to Gendered Institutions." *Contemporary Sociology* 21(5): 565–569.

Alvesson, Mats and Yvonne Billing. 1997. *Understanding Gender and Organizations*. London: Sage.

Azaryahu, Moaz. 1999. "The Independence Day Military Parade: A Political History of a Patriotic Ritual." Pp. 89–116 in Lomsky-Feder and Ben-Ari, eds. *The Military and Militarism in Israeli Society*. Albany: State University of New York Press.

Berkovitch, Nitza. 1997. "Motherhood as a National Mission: The Construction of Womanhood in the Legal Discourse in Israel." *Women's Studies International Forum* 20(5–6): 605–619.

Bourdieu, Pierre. 1986. "The Forms of Capital." Pp. 241–258 in J. Richardson, ed. *Handbook of Theory and Research for the Sociology of Education*. New York: Greenwood.

Brass, Daniel. 1985. "Men's and Women's Networks: A Study of Interaction Patterns and Influence in an Organization." *Academy of Management Journal* 28(2): 327–343.

Britton, Dana M. 1997. "Gendered Organizational Logic: Policy and Practice in Men's and Women's Prisons." *Gender & Society* 11(6): 796–818.
Britton, Dana M. 2000. "The Epistemology of the Gendered Organization." *Gender & Society* 14(3): 418–434.
Burke, Carol. 2004. *Camp All-American, Honoi Jane, and the High and Tight: Gender, Folklore, and Changing Military Culture*. Boston: Beacon Press.
Butler, Judith. 1990. *Gender Trouble: Feminism and the Subversion of Identity*. New York: Routledge.
Carreiras. Helena. 2006. *Gender and the Military: Women in the Armed Forces of Western Democracies*. New York: Routledge.
Chambliss, Elizabeth and Christopher Uggen. 2000. "Men and Women of Elite Law Firms: Reevaluating Kanter's Legacy." *Law and Social Inquiry* 25(1): 41–68.
Cohen, Stuart A. 1995. "The Israel Defense Forces (IDF): From a 'People's Army' to a 'Professional Military'--Causes and Implications." *Armed Forces and Society* 21(2): 237–254.
Cohen, Stuart A. 1997a. "Military Service in Israel: No Longer a Cohesive Force?" *Jewish Journal of Sociology* 39(1–2): 5–23.
Cohen, Stuart A. 1997b. "Towards a New Portrait of the (New) Israeli Soldier." *Israel Affairs* 3(3–4): 77–114.
Cohen, Stuart A. 1999. "From Integration to Segregation: The Role of Religion in the IDF." *Armed Forces and Society* 25(3): 387–405.
Coll, Jose E., Eugenia L. Weiss and Jeffrey S. Yarvis. 2011. "No One Leaves Unchanged: Insights for Civilian Mental Health Care Professionals into the Military Experience and Culture." *Social Work in Health Care* 50(7): 487–500.
Crompton, Rosemary and Gareth Jones. 1984. *White Collar Proletariat*. London: Macmillan.
Enloe, Cynthia H. 1983. *Does Khaki Become You? The Militarisation of Women's Lives*. London: Pluto Press.
Exum, Herbert, Jose E. Coll and Eugenia. L. Weiss. 2011. *A Civilian Counselor's Primer for Counseling Veterans 2nd edition*. Deerpark, NY: Linus Publications.
Fisch, Michael. 2004. "Resistance in the IDF and the Emergence of the Gay Community: An Instance of Social Transformation in Israel." *Israel Studies Forum* 19(2): 108–126.
Gherardi, Silvia. 1995. *Gender, Symbolism and Organizational Cultures*. London: Sage.
Goffman, Erving. 1977. "The Arrangement between the Sexes." *Theory and Society* 4(3): 301–331.
Golan, Galia. 1997. "Militarization and Gender: The Israeli Experience." *Women's Studies International Forum* 20(5–6): 581–586.
Herbert, Melissa. S. 1998. *Camouflage Isn't Only For Combat: Gender, Sexuality, and Women in the Military*. New York: New York University Press.
Hooker, Richard D. 2003. "Soldiers of the State: Reconsidering American Civil-Military Relations." *Parameters, U.S. Army War College Quarterly* 33(4): 4–18.
Horowitz, Dan and Baruch Kimmerling. 1974. "Some Social Implications of Military Service and the Reserves System in Israel." *European Journal of Sociology* 15(2): 262–276.
Howard, Judith and Jocelyn. Hollander. 1997. *Gendered Situations, Gendered Selves*. Thousand Oaks: Sage.
Ilgen, Daniel. R. and Margaret A. Youtz. 1986. "Factors Affecting the Evaluation and Development of Minorities in Organizations." Pp. 307–337 in K. M. Rowland and G. R. Ferris, eds. *Research in Personnel and Human Resource Management*. Greenwich: CT: JAI Press.

Izraeli, Dafna. 1983. "Sex Effects or Structural Effects? An Empirical Test of Kanter's Theory of Proportions." *Social Forces* 62(1): 153–165.

Izraeli, Dafna. 1984. "The Attitudinal Effects of Gender Mix in Union Committees." *Industrial and Labor Relations Review* 37(2): 212–221.

Izraeli, Dafna. 1997. "Gendering Military Service in the Israel Defense Forces." *Israel Social Science Research* 12(1): 129–166.

Kanter, Rosabeth M. 1977. *Men and Women of the Corporation*. New York: Basic Books.

Kanter, Rosabeth M. 1981. "Women and the Structure of Organizations: Explorations in Theory and Behavior." Pp. 395–424 in Oscar Grusky and George Armitage Miller, eds. *The Sociology of Organizations: Basic Studies*, 2nd ed. New York: Free Press.

Klein, Uta. 2002. "The Gender Perspective of Civil-Military Relations in Israeli Society." *Current Sociology* 50(5): 669–686.

Levy, Edna. 1998. "Heroes and Helpmates: Militarism, Gender and National Belonging in Israel." Unpublished Ph.D. dissertation, University of California, Irvine.

Levy, Yagil. 1998. "Militarizing Inequality: A Conceptual Framework." *Theory and Society* 27(6): 873–904.

Levy, Yagil. 2007. "The Right to Fight: A Conceptual Framework for the Analysis of Recruitment Policy toward Gays and Lesbians." *Armed Forces and Society* 33(2): 186–202.

Linn, Ruth. 1996. *Conscience at War: the Israeli Soldier as a Moral Critic*. Albany: State University of New York Press.

Mills, Albert J. 1989. "Gender, Sexuality and Organization Theory." Pp. 29–44 in Jeff Hearn, Deborah L. Sheppard, Peta Tancred-Sheriff, and Gibson Burrell, eds. *The Sexuality of Organization*. London: Sage.

Morgan, David H. J. 1994. "Theater of War: Combat, the Military, and Masculinities." Pp 165–181 in Harry Brod and Michael Kaufman, eds. *Theorizing Masculinities*. Thousand Oaks, CA: Sage.

Noe, Raymond A. 1988. "Women and Mentoring: A Review and Research Agenda." *The Academy of Management Review* 13(1): 65–78.

Okun, Barbara S. 1997. "Innovation and Adaptation in Fertility Transition: Jewish Immigrants to Israel from Muslim North Africa & The Middle East." *Population Studies* 51(3): 317–335.

Pope, Juliet J. 1993. "Conflict of Interests: A Case Study of Na'amat." Pp 225–233 in Barbara Swirski and Marilyn Safir, eds. *Calling the Equality Bluff: Women in Israel*. New York: Teachers College Press.

Riley, Patricia. 1983. "A Structurationist Account of Political Culture." *Administrative Science Quarterly* 28(3): 414–437.

Rimalt, Noya. 2007. "Women in the Sphere of Masculinity: The Double-Edged Sword of Women's Integration in the Military." *Duke Journal of Gender Law & Policy* 14: 1097–1119.

Rosen, Benson, Mary Ellen Templeton and Karen Kirchline. 1981. "First Few Years on the Job: Women in Management." *Business Horizons* 24(12): 26–29.

Sasson-Levy, Orna. 2002. "Constructing Identities at the Margins: Masculinities and Citizenship in the Israeli Army." *The Sociological Quarterly* 43(3): 357–383.

Sasson-Levy, Orna. 2007. "Contradictory Consequences of Mandatory Conscription: The Case of Women Secretaries in the Israeli Military." *Gender & Society* 21(4): 481–507.

Schein, Edgar. 1990. "Organizational Culture." *American Psychologist*, February: 110.

Segal, Mady. W. 1995. "Women's Military Roles Cross-nationally: Past, Present, and Future." *Gender and Society* 9(6): 757–775.

Sered, Susan. 2000. *What Makes Women Sick?: Maternity, Modesty, and Militarism in Israeli Society.* Hanover: Brandeis University Press.

Silverbaum, Judith. 1996. *Women in the Army. Women in Israel: Information and Analysis.* Jerusalem: Women's Network and The Inner Wheel.

Simpson, Suzanne, Michael McCarrey and Henry P. Edwards. 1987. "Relationship of Supervisors' Sex-Role Stereotypes to Performance Evaluation of Male and Female Subordinates in Non-traditional Jobs." *Canadian Journal of Administrative Sciences* 4(1): 15–30.

Snider, Don M. 1999. "The Future of American Military Culture: An Uninformed Debate on Military Culture." *Orbis* 43(1): 11–26.

Strati, Antonio. 1992. "Organizational Culture." Pp. 578–584 in Gyorgy Szell, ed. *Concise Encyclopedia of Participation and Comanagement.* Berlin: de Gruyter.

Tyler, Tom R. 1999. "Why People Cooperate With Organizations: An Identity-Based Perspective." Pp. 201–246 in Robert I. Sutton and Barry M. Staw, eds. *Research in Organizational Behavior: An Annual Series of Analytical Essays and Critical Reviews* vol. 21. Greenwich, CT: JAI Press.

Weiss, Meira. 1998. "Engendering the Gulf War: Israeli Nurses and the Discourse of Soldiering." *Journal of Contemporary Ethnography* 27(2): 197–218.

West, Candace and Don H. Zimmerman. 1987. "Doing Gender." *Gender and Society* 1(2): 125–151.

Williams, Christine L. 1992. "The Glass Escalator: Hidden Advantages for Men in the 'Female' Professions." *Social Problems* 39(3): 253–267.

Wynne, Cynthia, and Judith Rudnick. 1996. "The Position of Women in Israeli Law." *Women in Israel: Information and Analysis.* Jerusalem: Women's Network and The Inner Wheel.

Yoder, Janice. D. 1991. "Rethinking Tokenism: Looking Beyond Numbers." *Gender & Society* 5(2): 178–192.

Zimmer, Lynn. E. 1988. "Tokenism and Women in the Workplace: The Limits of Gender-neutral Theory." *Social Problems* 35(1): 64–77.

Appendix A—Respondents

All interviews were carried out in 2002. Any respondent whose year of enlistment was 2000 or after was still serving at the time of the interview.

Bases: C=closed, O=open, OMM=open with mostly male soldiers, B=both, B-C=both but mainly closed, B-O=both but mainly open, OT=other, OT-C=other but mainly closed, OT-O=other but mainly open.

Other Abbreviations: I=Individual interview (respondent interviewed alone), J=Joint interview (respondent interviewed with one other person), MC=Mashalit Cheenooch, MH=Mashakeet Hora-ah, ARO=Academic Reservist Officer, CI=Combat Instructor, SC=Signal Corps.

fh=friend's home, ab=army base

E=Egyptian, H=Hungarian, G=German, M=Moroccan, P=Polish, R=Russian, Rom=Romanian, T=Turkish Y=Yugoslavian.

Closed Bases (and both open and closed)

#	Military Rank	Position	Base	Year Enlisted	Place of Interview	I or J	Interview Length	Age	Ethnic Background
1	Sergeant	Instructor – SC	C	1994	her home	I	50 min.	26	R
2	Lieutenant	MC / Officer	C	1994	her home	I	40 min.	26	P
3	Sergeant	CI / Mashakit Milluim	B	1993	fh	I	45 min.	27	Iraqi + T
4	Sergeant	MC	C	1991	university	I	50 min.	29	R + P
5	Sergeant	Dental Assistant	C	1996	my home	I	30 min.	24	Cyprus + R
6	Sergeant	Equipment	C	1997	my home	I	50 min.	23	M
7	Sergeant	Nachal	OT	1995	fh	J	1 hour 20 min.	25	P
8	Sergeant	Nachal – Pkida	OT-C	1990	fh	I	45 min.	31	Argentinean
9	Sergeant	Military Police	C	1990	fh	J	1 hour 15 min.	28	T + Italian
10	Sergeant	Pkida	C	1995	fh	I	1 hour	25	G + P
11	Sergeant	Finance Administrator	C	1996	her home	I	1 hour 30 min.	24	G + P
12	Sergeant	Equipment	C	1992	her home	I	35 min.	28	P
13	Sergeant	Commander (Makit Banim)	C	1991	her home	I	1 hour 5 min.	29	Tunisian
14	Sergeant	Nachal	OT	1990	her home	I	45 min.	30	Y + Rom
15	Sergeant	CI	C	2000	cafe	I	1 hour 10 min.	19	M + P
16	Sergeant	Combat/Radar	C	1995	my home	I	40 min.	25	Latvian + P
17	Sergeant	Intelligence	C	1999	her home	I	1hour 15 min.	21	E + Rom
18	Sergeant	Computer Tech	C	2000	my home	J	1 hour 10 min.	20	Iraqi + P + R

Doing Army or Feeling Army? 93

19	Sergeant	Human Resources Coordinator	C	1992	her home	I	35 min.	28	Rom
20	Sergeant	MH	C	1997	university	I	40 min.	23	R + Rom
21	Sergeant	Psychometric Examiner	C	1993	her home	I	1 hour 10 min.	27	P + Ukrainian + Czech
22	Sergeant	Enlistment Coordinator	B	1994	mall cafe	I	1 hour 5 min.	26	E + Czech
23	Sergeant	Pkida	B-C	1994	fh	I	40 min.	26	R
24	Sergeant	Intelligence	C	1999	mall cafe	I	1 hour 20 min.	21	Yemenite and Iraqi
25	Corporal	CI	C	2001	train	J	40 min.	19	Rom + Iraqi
26	Corporal	CI	C	2001	train	J	40 min.	19	M + Tunisian
27	Sergeant	Intelligence – Pkida	B	1997	mall cafe	J	1 hour 5 min.	23	Yemenite
28	Sergeant	Intelligence	B-C	1997	mall cafe	J	1 hour 5 min.	23	Yemenite
29	Sergeant	MC	C	1992	her home	I	1 hour	28	Iraqi + G
30	Sergeant	CI	C	2000	train	J	45 min.	20	English + G
31	Second Lieutenant	MH / Radar Officer	B	2001	train	J	1 hour	19	Iranian + M
32	Second Lieutenant	Intelligence Officer	B	2001	train	J	1 hour	19	Yemenite
33	Sergeant	SC	C	1995	her home	I	45 min.	25	Greek + P
34	Corporal	MC	B	2001	ab	I	50 min.	19	Lithuanian + Moldavian

(Continued)

Closed Bases (and both open and closed) (Continued)

#	Military Rank	Position	Base	Year Enlisted	Place of Interview	I or J	Interview Length	Age	Ethnic Background
35	Private	Armory	C	2002	ab	I	40 min.	18	R
36	Corporal	Armory	C	2001	ab	I	30 min.	19	Yemenite + Libyan
37	Private	Armory	C	2002	ab	I	25 min.	18	Algerian
38	Private	Armory	C	2002	ab	I	35 min.	18	R

Open Bases

#	Military Rank	Position	Base	Year Enlisted	Place of Interview	I or J	Interview Length	Age	Ethnic Background
39	Sergeant	Mashakit Tash	O	1994	cafe	I	45 min.	26	Argentinean
40	Sergeant	Pkida	OMM	1989	her car	I	35 min.	31	R
41	Sergeant	Pkida	O	1993	fh	I	38 min.	27	Syrian + Iraqi
42	Sergeant	Intelligence	O	1991	her home	I	30 min.	29	Rom + E
43	Sergeant	Pkida	O	1992	fh	J	1 hour 20 min.	28	P
44	Sergeant	Pkida	O	1991	her home	J	1 hour 15 min.	29	T + P
45	Sergeant	Intelligence	O	2000	cafe	I	50 min.	20	Swiss + H
46	Lieutenant	Law Officer	O	1999	cafe	I	45 min.	21	Latvian + P
47	Sergeant	Psychometric Examiner	O	1996	university	I	1 hour 5 min.	24	R + Austrian
48	Sergeant	Intelligence	O	2000	mall cafe	I	40 min.	20	Yemenite
49	Sergeant	Soldier/Teacher	OT-O	1990	cafe	I	40 min.	27	P + R
50	Sergeant	Intelligence	O	1996	her home	I	40 min.	24	Rom + P

51	Sergeant	Computer Tech	O	2000	my home	J	1 hour 10 min.	20	M
52	Sergeant	Mashakit Tash	O	1997	university	J	1 hour 15 min.	23	R
53	Sergeant	Mashakit Tash	O	1997	university	J	1 hour 15 min.	23	Rom + P
54	Lieutenant	ARO	O	1991	her home	I	1 hour	29	E + Czech
55	Sergeant	Pkida	O	1997	cafeteria	I	40 min.	23	Rom
56	Sergeant	Selection Examiner	O	1994	park	I	20 min.	26	Iraqi
57	Private	Health Inspector	O	2002	train	I	20 min.	18	Brazilian
58	Corporal	Intelligence	O	2001	train	J	45 min.	19	Indian
59	Sergeant	Pkida	O	1995	her home	I	50 min.	25	M + G
60	Sergeant	Intelligence	O	1991	her home	I	1 hour	29	T
61	Lieutenant	Officer (Undisclosed)	OMM	1994	her home	I	1 hour 15 min.	26	P + G
62	Sergeant	Soldier/teacher	OT-O	1993	her home	I	1 hour	30	Iraqi + G

Glossary

Cheenooch=Education

Hora-ah=Instruction

Mashakit=Commander who is not an officer

Mashakit Tash=A position which is akin to that of a social worker

Milluim=Reserve duty

Nachal=Pioneer Youth in Combat Division

Pkida=Clerk/secretary

Reconsidering the Defense–Growth Relationship: Evidence from the Islamic Republic of Iran

Bruce D. McDonald, III
Indiana University South Bend

Political and Military Sociology: An Annual Review 2012, Vol. 40: 97–117.

Recent literature has failed to reach a consensus on how best to model the defense–growth relationship. Although several attempts have been made to solve the problem by the theoretical comparison of models, empirical attempts at comparison have been largely restricted to the United States. Given the recent criticism of the Feder–Ram model, this article uses Iranian data to compare the performance of the Feder–Ram and augmented Solow models in the context of a growing, yet heavily militarized, economy. The results indicate that the improved ability of the augmented Solow model to explain economic growth can better account for the effects of an increase in defense expenditures.

Introduction

Despite the significant attention paid within the literature to the relationship between defense spending and economic growth, commonly referred to as either the *defense–growth relationship* or the *defense–growth nexus*, a meaningful consensus has failed to be reached as to whether defense expenditures hinder growth or promote it (McDonald and Eger 2010; McDonald 2011). The failure of a dominate framework that emerges by which the relationship could be investigated further complicates the problem (Atesoglu 2009; de Groot 2011; Heo 2010), leading many to believe that work on the relationship produces as many questions as it does answers (Atesoglu 2009; Chan 1985; McDonald and Eger 2010).

Ultimately, this failure has led the mainstream growth literature to conclude that the defense sector is not a significant factor in the explanation of economic growth (Dunne et al. 2005).

Regardless of the problems facing the defense–growth relationship, the issue of how a nation's defense expenditures affect its overall economic growth has been an area of concern and contention to both academics and politicians for some time (Aizenman and Glick 2006; Ali 2011; Mintz and Huang 1990). To explore the defense–growth relationship, two dominant approaches have been used: a Feder–Ram-based approach and an augmented Solow approach.[1] Although the Feder–Ram approach has been accepted with widespread use, the augmented Solow approach touts an unparalleled theoretical literature. Several recent works have attempted to solve the problem by theoretically comparing these models, but the empirical attempts of comparison have been largely restricted to the United States. An American-based comparison certainly provides useful results for those wanting to understand and explain the defense–growth relationship in the United States. However, is the comparison useful for understanding the relationship elsewhere? During 2007, world defense expenditures totaled $1.339 trillion, of which the United States accounted for $547 billion (about 45%) (Stockholm International Peace Research Institute 2008). During the same time, world GDP was $53.352 trillion, of which the United States accounted for $13.794 trillion (about 26%) (International Monetary Fund 2008). Given the dominance of the United States in the world market, international inference from past comparisons is limited.

A clear understanding of the defense–growth relationship around the globe still holds some interest, given the uncertainty of the effects of the remaining $792 billion in global expenditures. More compelling for the need to understand the defense–growth relationship in other countries is the rate at which defense expenditures are increasing. From 1998 to 2007, global defense expenditures increased by 45%, the fastest rate of increase since World War II. Given the War on Terrorism, regional instability, and the standoff between the Islamic Republic of Iran and the United States, the defense–growth relationship in the Middle East is of particular interest. When excluding the United States from analysis, from 1998 to 2007, the Middle East witnessed the highest regional growth of defense expenditures, increasing by 62% from $56.5 billion to $91.5 billion (Stockholm International Peace Research Institute 2008). In this article, the literature on modeling the defense–growth relationship is advanced through an empirical comparison of the Feder–Ram and augmented Solow models. Using Iranian data from 1960 to 2006, both approaches are employed to demonstrate their use in explaining how increases in defense expenditures influence economic growth in the context of a highly militarized, non-Western economy.

As the article demonstrates, the reliance on the Feder–Ram model to explain the defense–growth relationship is misguided. Despite being the dominant model for the past twenty years, this model suffers from several problems, including the inability to deal with the delayed effects of defense expenditures and the absence of a strong theoretical reasoning as to why the model should work. As a replacement model, this article recommends the augmented Solow model. Though simple in design, a Solow-based approach to economic growth has been shown to successfully explain variations in the rate of economic growth across the globe (Barro 1990). When applied to the defense–growth relationship, not only is the model able to overcome the failings of the Feder–Ram approach, but it is also able to make use of the extensive literature on neoclassical economics in clarifying the cause and direction of the relationship. While comparing the ability of both models to explain the economic growth in Iran, this article shows that the augmented Solow model is clearly superior not only in terms of its ability to explain economic performance, but also in terms of the clarity in direction and significance of the defense–growth relationship. As shown by the estimates of the augmented Solow model, defense expenditures produce a positive effect on Iranian economic performance.

The Defense–Growth Relationship

Beginning with the pioneering work of Hitch and McKean (1960), defense economics has been an area of interest and an issue of academic focus since the commencement of the 1960s. The escalation, and later the conclusion, of the Cold War brought greater interest to the issue, leading to a controversy of whether an expansion of the defense sector would lead to an increase in economic growth or impede growth. From this literature, at least three channels through which defense expenditures can influence the economic growth of a state can be observed.[2] The first channel is through the defense sector's investment in technological research and development. In addition to being charged with overseeing issues of national security, the defense sector is charged with the development of new weapons technology, often including heavy industry (Gold 1990). Although the research interests of the defense sector are largely militarily related weapons, development and production have often led to technological innovations that have public uses (Adams and Gold 1987;

Phillips 1983). Similar to private sector innovations, the spillover effect from defense technology contributes to the total factor of productivity of the economy as a whole. Although not directly usable within the private sector, weapons development and production have often led to technological innovations that have public uses (Trebilcock 1969). The development of the atom bomb during World War II, for instance, led to the development and application of nuclear technology and energy production. Other examples include innovations in transportation, nuclear power, and computers that have been adopted by the private sector as a means of maximizing employee and firm efficiency.

The second channel through which military expenditures can influence growth is through the tax burden created by increased defense expenditures (Chan 1987; Heo 2010). An increase in defense expenditures creates a budgetary trade-off because expenditures can only be financed by creating new taxes, by increasing the budgetary deficit, or by issuing additional money (Chan 1985; DeGrasse 1983; Ward and Davis 1992). Following a Keynesian school of thought, Carroll (2006) argues that different modes of financing produce different economic effects, with defense expenditures being funded through taxation, restricting growth by lowering the expected after-tax return on capital and reducing the flow of savings available to finance capital formation. Conversely, expenditures funded through deficit financing produce a positive, accelerator effect by which government output is expanded, increasing employment and stimulating consumer demand, resulting in an encouragement of investment. Historically, nations have relied on increased taxation to finance defense expenditures, leading Carroll (2006) to conclude that defense expenditures are more likely to restrain growth than promote it.

The third channel occurs by crowding out investment from areas that might be considered more productive (Heo and Eger 2005; Knight et al. 1996; Mintz and Huang 1990). Financial resources are limited, forcing the defense sector and private investors to compete for the available capital. According to Knight, Loayza, and Villanueva (1996), crowding-out occurs due to the lower return on fixed capital, reducing the investment available to finance capital formation in the private economy. As defense expenditures increase, the capital available for private investment declines, forcing the choice of investing in either the defense or private sectors (Russett 1969). Defense expenditures may also affect growth through their influence on the efficiency of resource allocation (Knight et al. 1996). The private sector is guided by a market economy, but the defense sector does not face similar dynamics. Demonstrating the inefficiency of resource allocation, Ward and Davis (1992) show that defense expenditures can limit growth by moving resources away from the private sector, which maintains a higher rate of productivity than either the public or defense sectors (see also Mintz and Huang 1990, 1991).

These channels suggest a trade-off between defense expenditures and economic growth. Although the first channel suggests that the net effect of military expenditures on economic growth is likely to be positive, it remains impossible to escape the latter two channels. It is, therefore, reasonable to hypothesize a negative effect on economic growth due to any increase in a state's defense expenditures. It is also not surprising that many previous studies have shown empirical results which support not only a positive association through technology (Heo and DeRouen 1998; Phillips 1983), but also a negative effect by crowding-out investment (Heo and Eger 2005; Mintz and Huang 1991) and through a budgetary trade-off (Carroll 2006; Ohanian 1997). Between the duality of theoretical groundings for the defense–growth paradigm and the mixed results displayed in the literature, some studies have suggested that the relationship may be an empirical issue rather than a theoretical one (Alexander 1990). Though the consensus seems to be that a positive spillover may be possible, yet the majority of defense programs are not technologically related, suggesting that the spillover can have only a minor influence. Regardless of the size of the spillover, however, there is still a need to fund the programs, suggesting a relationship that is ultimately negative. Given the variety of approaches undertaken to measure the relationship, what remains to be determined is how we can best estimate the effect of an increase in a nation's defense expenditures.

Models of the Defense–Growth Relationship

The Feder–Ram Model

The most common model that is used to explain the defense–growth relationship is a variation of the Feder–Ram model (see Alexander 1990; Atesoglu and Mueller 1990; Mintz and Huang 1990; Ram 1986; Ward and Davis 1992). Derived from a neoclassical economic perspective, the Feder–Ram approach employs a supply-side explanation for aggregate output with changes in labor and capital. Following its development, a series of variations have been adopted within the literature, which are dependent on the number of sectors included and the pattern of externalities (Sandler and Hartley 1995). According to Heo, the approach holds the potential for significant contribution to the literature on the defense–growth relationship because it is "developed from a consistent theoretical structure" (1998:39) or, at least, "fairly well grounded in the neoclassical production function framework" (Biswas and Ram 1986:367). As Dunne, Smith, and Willenbockel note, the "popularity of the approach lies in the appearance of a direct link from theoretical model to econometric specification" (2005:453).

The basis for the approach was first developed by Feder, who wrote that "aggregate growth is related to changes in capital and labor through an underlying production function" (1983:60). From this, Feder divided the aggregate output of the economy into two sectors: exports and non-exports. Following Feder's division of the economy, Ram (1986) proposed a two-sector model that explains growth as comprising a government and a private sector. In a series of studies, Mintz and Huang (1990, 1991) and Huang and Mintz (1991) argued for a third sector, a defense sector, on the grounds that the effects of defense expenditures could also differ from those of non-defense-related government spending due to a different set of incentives. The literature has relied on a variety of adjustments to the Feder–Ram approach (see Heo 2000), whereas the basic three-sector version of the model distinguishes between the effects of defense expenditures (D), non-defense expenditures (N), and the rest of the economy (P). These sectors are demonstrated as follows:

$$D = D(L_d, K_d)$$
$$N = N(L_n, K_n)$$
$$P = P(L_p, K_p, D, N),$$

where subscripts denote the allocation of inputs among sectors, such that the allocation of inputs among capital, K, and labor, L, is given as:

$$K_d + K_n + K_p = K$$
$$L_d + L_n + L_p = L$$

Following Feder (1983) and Ram's (1986) sector approach to the economy, total economic output (Y) is described as:

$$Y = D + N + P,$$

and the differential of the marginal factor productivity in the defense and non-defense sectors can be captured, where δ_i denotes the difference in productivity between the three sectors, within the relationships:

$$\frac{D_1}{P_1}=\frac{D_k}{P_k}=(1+\delta_d)$$

$$\frac{N_1}{P_1}=\frac{N_k}{P_k}=(1+\delta_n)$$

Taking the proportional differential of economic output with the total differentials of sectors N, D, and P leads to the following equation:

$$\dot{Y}=\frac{P_1 L}{Y}\dot{L}+P_k\frac{I}{Y}+\left(\frac{\delta_d}{1+\delta_d}+P_d\right)\frac{D}{Y}\dot{D}+\left(\frac{\delta_n}{1+\delta_n}+P_n\right)\frac{N}{Y}\dot{N}$$

where I is equal to the derivative of capital, K, and represents net investment. Using θ to denote the externality effects of the defense and non-defense sectors, and the constant elasticity of P with regard to D, the equation can be rewritten as:

$$\dot{Y}=\frac{P_1 L}{Y}\dot{L}+P_k\frac{I}{Y}+\left(\frac{\delta_d}{1+\delta_d}+P_d\right)\frac{D}{Y}\dot{D}+\theta\dot{D}+\left(\frac{\delta_n}{1+\delta_n}+P_n\right)\frac{N}{Y}\dot{N}+\theta\dot{N}$$

The popularity of the Feder–Ram approach has led to variations of this model being used to estimate the effects of the defense sector with regard to data for individual countries (see Heo 2000; Mintz and Huang 1990; Ward and Davis 1992), cross-country data (see Heo 1998), and time-series, cross-sectional data (see McDonald and Eger 2010; Murdoch et al. 1997). Despite the preferences for the Feder–Ram model, however, the approach does draw some theoretical criticism (Alexander 1990; Dunne 1996; Dunne et al. 2005). First, there are criticisms centered on the notion that it is not possible, in reality, to divide the economy into a series of discrete sectors (Alexander 1990). We can account for sectors individually, whereas a Feder–Ram approach fails to account for the relationships between sectors. For example, it is expected that private sector growth would lead to increased tax revenue, which would lead to larger defense and non-defense government sectors. Despite the defense literature's reliance on the Feder–Ram model, the theoretical failings of a sectoral approach have led the mainstream growth literature to more advanced models of economic growth.

Second, there are criticisms that a Feder–Ram approach is subject to severe misspecification (Alexander and Hansen 2004). Central to these criticisms are issues over which sectors should be distinguished from other residual sectors within the growth equation. The difficulty of what to include can be seen early in the literature by Ram (1986, 1987) and Biswas and Ram (1986), who included two sector models but chose different sectors on which to focus. For Ram (1986, 1987), the sectors included were government expenditures and exports, respectively; for Biswas and Ram (1986), the sectors included were defense expenditures and exports. Given the variations of the models and the possibility of bias, Ram (1995) concluded that a minimum of four sectors is necessary. As Alexander and Hansen (2004) note, however, about 90% of the Feder–Ram-based studies of the defense–growth relationship include only two or three sectors. Despite advances in understanding the defense–growth relationship, the misspecification of the Feder–Ram approach continues as recent work has continued to vary the model significantly across applications, calling into question the validity of recent contributions.

The Augmented Solow Model

Although the literature on the defense–growth relationship has relied heavily on the Feder–Ram model, Dunne, Smith, and Willenbockel (2005) criticized the model, arguing that the approach ignores the mainstream growth literature. As an alternative approach to estimating the relationship, they recommend an augmented Solow model (see Dunne et al. 2002; Knight et al. 1996; Yakovlev 2007). This approach, based on the work of Solow (1956) and Swan (1956), employs a supply-side description of changes to aggregate output, which, in turn, explains the growth of the resulting changes in labor and capital. Mankiw, Romer, and Weil (1992) expanded this approach by providing an augmented Solow model, through which the accumulation of economy-wide human and physical capital provides a description for growth. The augmented Solow model, despite providing a simple explanation of economic growth, is particularly interesting in its ability to provide a realistic description of economic growth. According to Mankiw, Romer, and Weil (1992), the model can explain 80% of cross-country variation in growth, compared with the Feder–Ram model, which can explain only 66% of variation (Mintz and Huang 1990).

The estimation of the augmented Solow model relies on two assumptions. First, the causality of defense expenditures affecting growth within the literature of the Feder–Ram approach holds across other economic growth models. Second, rather than relying on a sectoral approach that measures the effects of defense expenditures, the augmented Solow model follows the first channel of influence and assumes that defense expenditures' share of growth will affect a nation's total factor productivity. This influence on productivity occurs through a leveling effect on the efficiency parameter that directs labor-augmenting technological change.

Following the neoclassical tradition, the augmented Solow model begins with a neoclassical production function that features labor-augmenting technological change which is demonstrated as:

$$Y_t = K_t^\alpha \left[A_t L_t\right]^{1-\alpha}$$

where the notation Y is aggregate real income, K is real capital output, L is labor, and A is the level of technology. It is then assumed that labor and technology grow exogenously at the rates n and g, respectively. This relation is given as:

$$L_t = L_o e^{nt}$$
$$A_t = A_o e^{gt} d_t^\theta$$

Included in the assumptions of technology is d, the share of defense expenditures in GDP, which grows at rate θ. This creates a specification of technology which suggests that a permanent change in d will not affect the long-term steady state growth. However, it does have the possibility of producing a level effect on the per-capita income along the growth path. It could also affect the transitory growth rate as it moves toward a new equilibrium.

With the traditional assumptions of the Solow model, a constant rate of savings, s, is invested. A constant growth rate of the labor force, represented by n, an advancement of knowledge, represented by g, and a given rate of depreciation, represented by δ are also witnessed. Further, y is defined as output per laborer, $y=Y/AL$, and k is defined as capital stock per laborer, $k=K/AL$. Within the model, capital accumulation is described as:

$$\dot{k}_i = sy_i - (n+g+\delta)k_i$$
$$= sk_i^\alpha - (n+g+\delta)k_i$$

This implies a steady state of k as:

$$k_i^* \left[\frac{s}{n+g+\delta} \right]^{1/(1-\alpha)}$$

After linearly adjusting around the steady state and approximating the transition dynamics of output per laborer, as it approaches the steady state, the model relates ye to the observed output per laborer through:

$$\ln y_t = e^{\psi} \ln y_{t-1} + (1-e^{\psi})\left\{\ln A_0 + \frac{\alpha}{1-\alpha}[\ln s - \ln(n+g+\delta)]\right\}$$
$$+ \theta \ln d_t - e^{\psi} \theta \ln d_{t-1} + \left[e_t^{\psi} - e_{t-1}^{\psi}\right]g$$

Using θ to represent the elasticity of income with regard to the long-run defense expenditure share of GDP, the final effects of defense expenditures on economic growth within the augmented growth model can be written as follows (see Knight et al. [1996] for a full derivation of the model):

$$\Delta \ln y_t = \beta_0 + \beta_1 \ln y_{t-1} + \beta_2 \ln s_t + \beta_3 \ln(n_t + g_t + \delta_t) + \beta_4 \ln d_t + \beta_5 \ln d_{t-1} + \varepsilon$$

According to Dunne, Smith, and Willenbockel (2005), there are three advantages of using an augmented Solow model. First, the augmented Solow model is dynamic, allowing for an understanding of the effects of defense expenditures over time. Second, the exclusion of non-defense government expenditures and various externality effects reduces the likelihood of multicollinearity that is present in other approaches. Third, the measure of human capital includes both capital depreciation and total factor productivity, suggesting that it is more theoretically specified than Feder–Ram's inclusion of the growth rate of the labor force. Notwithstanding these advantages, the augmented Solow model has failed to be adopted by most defense–growth proponents.

Data and Method

In order to compare the Feder–Ram and augmented Solow models as developed in the previous section, data from the Islamic Republic of Iran were collected for the years 1960–2007. These data are outlaid in calendar years and are expressed in 1998 constant rials. Data on total government consumption, defense expenditures,[3] GDP, and gross domestic private investment are obtained from the Central Bank of the Islamic Republic of Iran.[4] Following Alexander (1990), total government consumption is used as the government sector output. Non-defense government expenditures are obtained by subtracting defense expenditures from total government consumption, whereas private sector output is obtained by subtracting total government consumption from GDP. For labor data, I follow the previous defense–growth literature and use the population growth rate as a proxy (Alexander 1990; Heo 1998; Ram 1986). As noted by Lebovic and Ishaq, "because labor participation rates show little volatility in the short run, the population growth rate may be used instead" (1987:118). For data that are specific to the augmented Solow model, I follow the previous growth literature and fix the sum of g and δ at 0.05, assuming that any reasonable change in this assumption will have a minimal effect on the estimate (Mankiw et al. 1992). A summary of key data is given in Table 1.

Before providing the findings of the empirical analysis, there are several methodological issues that should be addressed. First, to estimate the models, I employ an ordinary least-squares approach to explain variations in the economic growth of Iran over time. The second methodological issue to be addressed is the determination of the appropriate lag for variables included within the augmented Solow model. According to Gujarati (1988), the inclusion of a distributed lag allows for the capturing of dynamic effects by including changes in variables over time. Since the specification of the growth model contains distributed lags and there is no a priori information on the lag structure, an objective criterion is needed to determine the proper number of lags. To accomplish this task, I rely on a standard information criterion (SIC), as suggested by

Table 1 Statistical Summary of Variables, 1998 rials

Variable	Mean	Std. Dev.	Min.	Max
GDP*	214,463.2	111,066.9	43,910.9	499,071.1
Defense Expenditures*	10,692.5	7,248.5	1,040.4	25,948.6
Non-defense Expenditures*	22,402.8	11,182.8	2,876.8	41,339.5
Investment*	17,581.8	8,743.8	2,539.0	35,546.4
Population**	4,4768	16,069	21,204	71,532

*Expressed in billions, **expressed in thousands.

Schwarz (1978) and Geweke and Meese (1981). As noted in Table 2, the SIC results suggest a lag structure of *t-2* as being appropriate.

Next, there is a need to discuss the econometric issues that are inherent to the models and longitudinal nature of the study. As noted by Dunne, Smith, and Willenbockel (2005) and Sandler and Hartley (1995), there is a possibility of simultaneity between economic growth and defense expenditures and between investment and non-defense government expenditures within the Feder–Ram model. In order to address this potential problem, I employ a Granger causality analysis to test for exogeneity. The results of the Granger causality analysis show no statistically significant causal effect for both relationships, suggesting the absence of simultaneity within the model.[5]

The third econometric issue to be discussed is the issue of stationarity. According to Granger and Newbold (1974), the results of a time-series regression may be spurious if any variable within the analysis is not stationary. For the augmented Solow model, the issue of stationarity is not a problem, given the use of log changes in the model. Given the design of the Feder–Ram model, however, stationarity remains a potential issue. Following Granger and Newbold, each variable within the Feder–Ram model was tested for the presence of a unit root based on the Dickey–Fuller test. The results of the Dickey–Fuller test show the absence of a unit root, suggesting that stationarity is not a problem within the model.

Lastly, there is also the potential problem of autocorrelation, given that the models are longitudinal in design.[6] I used the Durbin–Watson (D–W) statistic to test for the presence of autocorrelation. The D–W statistic indicates that there is an autocorrelation problem for the Feder–Ram model but not for the augmented Solow model (D–W = 1.59 and 1.73, respectively). To correct the serial correlation of the error terms, I used generalized least-squares (GLS) estimates of the parameters in the Feder–Ram model.

Empirical Analysis

The results of the empirical analyses are reported in Tables 2 and 3. Turning first to the comparison of the overall performance of both models, the results show that, despite the preference of the Feder–Ram model, the model failed to perform within the Iranian experience, with an R^2 of 0.34 and an F-test of 2.74. Contrary to the failure of the Feder–Ram model, the augmented Solow model performed exceptionally well at explaining Iranian economic growth, with an R^2 of 0.89 and an F-test of 965.53.[7]

Although the performance of both models is consistent with the previous literature, in which the Feder–Ram model has been shown to explain about 66% of variation (see Mintz and Huang 1990) and the augmented Solow model about 80% (see Mankiw et al. 1992), this performance is tied not to the means of estimation, but rather to the theoretical foundation on which the models are based. As noted by Dunne, Smith, and Willenbockel (2005), the Feder–Ram model lacks a strong foundation. Thus, there is no theoretical reason as to why the model should work, which is clearly demonstrated here. Alternatively, much of the high explanatory ability of the augmented Solow model can be tied to the inclusion of capital investment and labor, both of which have historically shown a significant effect on economic growth.

Next, turning to the Feder–Ram model of the defense–growth relationship, the individual estimates reflect the failed performance of the overall model. Although this article had previously hypothesized a negative

Table 2 Impact of Defense Expenditures on Economic Growth, Feder–Ram Model

Dependent Variable: Economic Growth Rate, $\hat{Y}$	Coefficient (Standard Error)
Constant	0.0943****
	(0.0370)
Capital Investment, $\frac{I}{Y}$	−0.4819
	(0.5383)
Labor, $\hat{L}$	−0.6440
	(1.5681)
Defense Expenditures, $\frac{D}{Y}\hat{D}$	−0.3953
	(1.1003)
Defense Sector Externality, $\hat{D}$	0.1109
	(0.0896)
Non-defense Expenditures, $\frac{N}{Y}\hat{N}$	2.1297
	(1.8635)
Non-defense Externality, $\hat{N}$	−0.0325
	(0.2174)

$R^2 = 0.34$
F-Test = 3.74
Durbin–Watson = 1.84

* $p < 0.10$, ** $p < 0.05$, *** $p < 0.01$

Table 3 Impact of Defense Expenditures on Economic Growth, Augmented Solow Model

Dependent Variable: Economic Growth Rate, $\Delta \ln y_t$	Coefficient (Standard Error)
Constant	1.9513****
	(0.5391)
GDP_{t-1}, $\ln y_{t-1}$	0.8297***
	(0.0473)
Capital Investment, $\ln s_t$	−0.1789***
	(0.0558)
Labor, $\ln(n + g + \delta)$	−0.1861*
	(0.3953)
Defense Expenditures, $\ln d_t$	0.0507***
	(0.0323)
Defense Expenditures$_{t-1}$, $\ln d_{t-1}$	0.0282*
	(0.0471)
Defense Expenditures$_{t-2}$, $\ln d_{t-2}$	0.0137*
	(0.0399)
$R^2 = 0.89$	
F-Test = 965.53	
Durbin–Watson = 1.73	

* $p < 0.10$, ** $p < 0.05$, *** $p < 0.01$

association between defense expenditures and economic growth, based on the Feder–Ram analysis, any change in the defense expenditures' share of GDP and its externality effect have an insignificant impact. The results appear to reflect those of both Heo and Eger (2005) and Mintz and Haung (1990, 1991). Similarly, the results follow Carroll (2006), suggesting that an increase in the non-defense expenditures' share of GDP and the subsequent externality effect also showed an insignificant effect on economic growth. Turning to the control variables, both capital investment and labor showed a negative, but insignificant, effect on economic growth.

Last, turning to the results of the augmented Solow model, we find a starkly different relationship. In addition to the model's improved overall performance, the relationship between defense expenditures and economic growth is different from that of the Feder–Ram model. The results of the estimates reveal that an increase in defense expenditures has a significant and positive effect on economic growth in the short term, and continues to do so in the next two years. Further explained, a 1% increase in the defense expenditures of the Islamic Republic of Iran is expected to result in a 0.05% increase of economic growth in the current year. In total, the increase of expenditures is expected to produce an increase of growth of 0.09%. Although this contradicts the findings of both the Feder–Ram model and the proposed hypothesis, it is consistent with what has been proposed by Atesoglu (2002), Cuaresma and Reitschuler (2004), and Mueller and Atesoglu (1993). With regard to the other control variables, as expected, the previous year's national income has a significant and positive effect on economic growth. Capital investment ($ln\ s$) and labor [represented as $ln(g+n+\delta)$], however, have a significant and negative impact. Though a negative finding is contrary to traditional macroeconomic theory, recent work on the Iranian economy suggests that a negative relationship should be expected due to the governmental restrictions on the private sector (McDonald 2009).

Analysis and Conclusion

In recent years, dramatic increases in defense expenditures around the globe are likely to continue as U.S. involvement in the Middle East and the War on Terrorism continue. Although this trend, coupled with global economic instability, has renewed public interest in the defense–growth relationship, the relationship has been an issue of interest to both academics and politicians for some time. The importance of the implications behind the defense–growth relationship has even led many researchers to dedicate their careers to finding an answer. Such dedication, however, has proved futile, as neither the direction of the relationship nor the means of expressing it has been agreed on. Although some progress has been made in recent years through a comparison of defense–growth models (see Dunne et al. 2005; Heo 2010; Sandler and Hartley 1995), these comparisons have been limited in their inferential ability due to their American focus. To assist in furthering the literature, this article has also sought to investigate the defense–growth relationship through the comparison of two leading models: a Feder–Ram model and an augmented Solow model. To complete the comparison, both models are estimated using data from the Islamic Republic of Iran from 1960 to 2007.

Although some research has compared the Feder–Ram and augmented Solow models, a core argument has been that, regardless of the approach used, the findings on the defense–growth relationship will remain consistent (Heo 2010). Within the Iranian economy, however, the empirical results of both models are clearly in disagreement. For the Feder–Ram model, defense expenditures showed a statistically insignificant effect on economic growth. Following defense expenditures, the Feder–Ram model shows itself to be incapable of explaining any economic growth, whether through non-defense expenditures, capital investment, or labor. Alternatively, within the estimates of the augmented Solow model, defense expenditures appear to improve economic growth.

One key distinction between the two approaches is the ability of the models to account for the economic performance of Iran. Based on the F-tests for the models, the augmented Solow model is more statistically significant than the Feder–Ram model (965.53 and 3.74, respectively); that is, the augmented Solow approach achieves a better fit to the Iranian experience by explaining a larger ratio of variance, as compared with the unexplained variance. A possible explanation is the likelihood of misspecification in the Feder–Ram model, which suffers from criticism on what sectors should be distinguished. The consequence of misspecification can be seen in previous works on the relationship with the Feder–Ram model, leaving researchers to consider only the direction of the relationship rather than the size (Heo 1998). Given the superior performance of the augmented Solow model, it is possible that these issues are diminished, once again allowing researchers to consider the effect size.

A second distinction is the ability of the approaches to account for the influence of defense expenditures over time. Previous literature on the defense–growth relationship in the United States has argued for a delayed effect of approximately 5 years (Heo and Eger 2005). Turning to the Iranian estimates in this article, standard information criteria show an effect from defense expenditures that can be felt approximately 2 years later. Although some uses of the Feder–Ram model involve lagged measures, the model itself is theoretically incapable of accounting for a delayed effect. It is unreasonable, however, to assume only an immediate effect, for which an augmented Solow model can easily account. This ability to account for a lingering effect clearly distinguishes the augmented Solow model as a time-series approach.

Despite the reliance on the Feder–Ram model and the growing popularity of the augmented Solow model, recent advances in macroeconomic theory have suggested more sophisticated ways of accounting for economic growth (Aghion and Howitt 1998). Though this article supports the augmented Solow model, yet work on the defense–growth relationship should continue to advance in looking for new and improved ways of accounting for the effects of the defense sector. This includes the comparison and adoption of newer models of economic growth, such as Atesolgu's (2002) Keynesian-based model and Aizenman and Glick's (2003) adaption of Barro's growth model. As noted by Mintz and Huang (1991) and Heo and Eger (2005), the real effects of defense expenditures on economic growth can be observed through indirect channels, such as employment, exportation, and investment (see also McDonald 2009). Further developments in the defense–growth relationship should strive toward better addressing these indirect effects through multi-equation modeling techniques.

Notes

1. Although the Feder–Ram and augmented Solow models are the dominant frameworks, a number of other approaches have been used throughout the literature, including a Harold–Dumar growth model, Granger causal analysis, and Keynesian-based demand-side models. Although each of these approaches has made a contribution to the understanding of the defense–growth relationship, they have been excluded from the comparison here due to their failure to obtain prominent status within the defense literature.
2. The theoretical linkage between defense expenditures and economic growth has been discussed at length in the literature; thus, only a brief encounter is provided here. For a more detailed overview of the theoretical relationship between defense expenditures and economic growth, see Dunne (1996), Dunne et al. (2002), and Sandler and Hartley (1995).
3. The definition of defense expenditures utilized in this study is from the International Monetary Fund (IMF). Expenditures are characterized as all expenditure, whether by defense or other departments, for the maintenance of military forces, including the purchase of military supplies and equipment (including the stockpiling of finished items but not the industrial raw materials required for their production), military construction, recruiting, training, equipping, moving, feeding, clothing and housing members of armed forces, and providing remuneration, medical care, and other services to them (quoted in Sen 1992:3).
4. There is some concern about the validity of data taken from the Central Bank of Iran. Data provided by the bank show a trend for defense expenditure that is similar to the trends seen in data from the Stockholm International Peace Research Institute and the World Bank. Data from the Central Bank are used in this study due to the duration of time for which the data is made available. Readers should be aware of the validity concerns and the potential effect that this may have on the results of this study.
5. The results of the Granger causal analysis are:

    Defense spending growth → Economic growth, $Ch^2 = 0.4496$ (probability $> Ch^2 = 0.799$)

    Economic growth → Defense spending growth, $Ch^2 = 2.1477$ (probability $> Ch^2 = 0.542$)

    Investment → Non-military public expenditures, $Ch^2 = 4.2651$ (probability $> Ch^2 = 0.119$)

    Non-military public expenditures → Investment, $Ch^2 = 1.1095$ (probability $> Ch^2 = 0.574$)

6. Dunne et al. (2005) and Heo (2010) have also expressed concerns about the potential for multicollinearity. To address these concerns, a bivariate correlation was conducted. The results are:

	GDP	Defense	Non-defense	Governmental
GDP	1			
Defense	0.6371	1		
Non-defense	0.7536	0.5898	1	
Governmental	0.7892	0.8376	0.9352	1

7. The root-mean-squared errors for the Feder–Ram and augmented Solow models are 0.0510 and 0.0508, respectively.

References

Adams, Gordon, and David Gold. 1987. *Defense Spending and the Economy: Does the Defense Dollar Make a Difference?* Washington, DC: Defense Budget Project.
Aghion, Phillippe, and Peter W. Howitt. 1998. *Endogenous Growth Theory.* Cambridge, MA: Massachusetts Institute of Technology Press.
Aizenman, Joshua, and Reuven Glick. 2003. *Military Expenditure, Threats and Growth.* Vol. 9618. Washington, DC: NBER Working Paper.
Aizenman, Joshua, and Reuven Glick. 2006. "Military Expenditure, Threats, and Growth." *Journal of International Trade and Economic Development* 15(2):129–155.
Alexander, W. Robert J. 1990. "The Impact of Defence Spending on Economic Growth." *Defence and Peace Economics* 2(1):39–55.
Alexander, W. Robert J., and Paul Hansen. 2004. "A Critique of the Multi-Sector Model of the Effects of Military Spending on Economic Growth." *Applied Econometrics and International Development* 4(2):35–54.
Ali, Hamid. 2011. "Military Expenditures and Human Development: Guns and Butter Arguments Revised, A Case Study from Egypt." *Peace Economics, Peace Science, and Public Policy* 17(1):1–19.
Atesoglu, H. Sonmez. 2002. "Defence Spending Promotes Aggregate Output in the United States." *Defence and Peace Economics* 13(1):55–60.
Atesoglu, H. Sonmez. 2009. "Defense Spending and Aggregate Output in the United States." *Defence and Peace Economics* 20(1):21–26.
Atesoglu, H. Sonmez, and Michael J. Mueller. 1990. "Defence Spending and Economic Growth." *Defence Economics* 2(1):19–27.
Barro, Robert J. 1990. "Government Spending in a Simple Model of Endogenous Growth." *Journal of Political Economy* 98(5): S103–S126.
Biswas, Basudeb, and Rati Ram. 1986. "Military Expenditures and Economic Growth in Less Developed Countries: An Augmented Model and Further Evidence." *Economic Development and Cultural Change* 34(2):361–372.
Carroll, Deborah A. 2006. "Guns vs. Taxes? A Look at How Defense Spending Affects U.S. Federal Tax Policy." *Public Budgeting and Finance* 26(4):59–78.
Chan, Steve. 1985. "The Impact of Defense Spending on Economic Performance: A Survey of Evidence and Problems." *Orbis* 29(2):403–434.
Chan, Steve, ed. 1987. *Military Expenditures and Economic Performance.* Washington, DC: Government Printing Office.

Cuaresma, Jesus C., and Gerhard Reitschuler. 2004. "A Non-linear Defense Growth Nexus? Evidence from the U.S. Economy." *Defence and Peace Economics* 15(1):71–82.

de Groot, Olaf J. 2011. "A Methodolgy for the Calulation of Global Economic Costs of Conflict." *Contributions to Conflict Management, Peace Economics and Development* 17:171–193.

DeGrasse, Robert W. 1983. *Military Expansion Economic Decline: The Impact of Military Spending on U.S. Economic Performance.* Armonk, NY: M.E. Sharpe.

Dunne, J. Paul. 1996. "Economic Effects of Military Spending in Developing Countries: A Survey." Pp. 439–464 in N. P. Gleditsch, O. Bjerkholt, A. Cappelen, R. P. Smith, and J. P. Dunne, eds. *The Peace Dividend.* Amsterdam, NE: North-Holland.

Dunne, J. Paul, Ron P. Smith, and Dirk Willenbockel. 2002. "Theoretical and Econometric Issues in Analysing the Military Expenditure-Growth Nexus." Presentation at the *Annual Conference of the American Economic Association.* Atlanta, GA.

Dunne, J. Paul, Ron P. Smith, and Dirk Willenbockel. 2005. "Models of Military Expenditure and Growth: A Critical Review." *Defence and Peace Economics* 16(6):449–461.

Feder, Gershon. 1983. "On Exports and Economic Growth." *Journal of Development Economics* 12(1):59–73.

Geweke, John, and Richard Meese. 1981. "Estimating Regression Models of Finite But Unknown Order." *International Economic Review* 22(1):55–70.

Gold, David. 1990. *The Impact of Defense Spending on Investment, Productivity and Economic Growth.* Washington, DC: Defense Budget Project.

Granger, C.W.J., and P. Newbold. 1974. "Spurious Regressions in Econometrics." *Journal of Econometrics* 2(1):111–120.

Gujarati, Damodar. 1988. *Basic Econometrics.* 2nd ed. New York, NY: McGraw-Hill.

Heo, Uk. 1998. "Modeling the Defense-Growth Relationship Around the Globe." *Journal of Conflict Resolution* 42(5):637–657.

Heo, Uk. 2000. "The Defense-Growth Nexus in the United States Revisited." *American Politics Quarterly* 28(1):110–127.

Heo, Uk. 2010. "The Relationship between Defense Spending and Economic Growth in the United States." *Political Research Quarterly* 63(4):760–770.

Heo, Uk, and Karl DeRouen. 1998. "Military Expenditures, Technological Change, and Economic Growth in the East Asian NICs." *Journal of Politics* 60(3):830–846.

Heo, Uk, and Robert J. Eger. 2005. "Paying for Security: The Security-Prosperity Dilemma in the United States." *Journal of Conflict Resolution* 49(5):792–817.

Hitch, Charles J., and Roland N. McKean. 1960. *The Economics of Defense in the Nuclear Age.* Cambridge, MA: Harvard University Press.

Huang, Chi, and Alex Mintz. 1991. "Defense Expenditures and Economic Growth: The Externality Effect." *Defence Economics* 3(1):35–40.

International Monetary Fund. 2008. *World Economic Outlook: A Survey by the Staff of the International Monetary Fund.* Washington, DC: International Monetary Fund.

Knight, Malcolm, Norman Loayza, and Delano Villanueva. 1996. "The Peace Dividend: Military Spending Cuts and Economic Growth." *IMF Staff Papers* 43(1):1–44.

Lebovic, James H., and Ashfaq Ishaq. 1987. "Military Burden, Security Needs, and Economic Growth in the Middle East." *Journal of Conflict Resolution* 31(1):106–138.

Mankiw, N.Gregory, David Romer, and David N. Weil. 1992. "A Contribution to the Empirics of Economic Growth." *The Quarterly Journal of Economics* 107(2):407–437.

McDonald, Bruce D. 2009. "Sanction Failure: Economic Growth, Defense Expenditures, and the Islamic Republic of Iran." Presentation at the *Annual Joint Conference of the ISSS and the ISAC.* Monterey, CA.

McDonald, Bruce D. 2011. "A Human Capital Model of the Defense-Growth Relationship." Doctoral Dissertation, Askew School of Public Administration and Policy, Florida State University, Tallahassee, FL.

McDonald, Bruce D., and Robert J. Eger. 2010. "The Defense-Growth Relationship: An Economic Investigation into Post-Soviet States." *Peace Economics, Peace Science, and Public Policy* 16(1):1–26.

Mintz, Alex, and Chi Huang. 1990. "Defense Expenditures, Economic Growth and the 'Peace Dividend'." *American Political Science Review* 84(4):1283–1293.

Mintz, Alex, and Chi Huang. 1991. "Guns Versus Butter: The Indirect Link." *American Journal of Political Science* 35(3):738–757.

Mueller, Michael J., and H. Sonmez Atesoglu. 1993. "Defense Spending, Technological Change, and Economic Growth in the United States." *Defence Economics* 4(3):259–269.

Murdoch, James C., Chung-Ron Pi, and Todd Sandler. 1997. "The Impact of Defense and Non-Defense Public Spending on Growth in Asia and Latin America." *Defence and Peace Economics* 8(2):205–224.

Ohanian, Lee E. 1997. "The Macroeconomic Effects of War Finance in the United States: World War II and the Korean War." *American Economic Review* 87(1):23–40.

Phillips, Sheena. 1983. "Trends in U.S. Military R&D Funding." Pp. 1–11 in K. Tsipis and S. Phillips, eds. *Annual Review of Military Research and Development: 1982.* New York, NY: Praeger.

Ram, Rati. 1986. "Government Size and Economic Growth: A New Framework and Some Evidence from Cross-Section and Time-Series Data." *American Economic Review* 76(1):191–203.

Ram, Rati. 1987. "Exports and Economic Growth in Developing Countries: Evidence from Time-Series and Cross-Sectional Data." *Economic Development and Cultural Change* 36(1):51–72.

Ram, Rati. 1995. "Defense Expenditures and Economic Growth." Pp. 251–273 in T. Sandler and K. Hartley, eds. *Handbook of Defense Economics.* Amsterdam, NE: Elsevier.

Russett, Bruce M. 1969. "Who Pays For Defense?" *American Political Science Review* 63(2):412–426.

Sandler, Todd., and Keith. Hartley. 1995. *The Economics of Defence.* Cambridge, UK: Cambridge University Press.

Schwarz, Gideon. 1978. "Estimating the Dimension of a Model." *Annals of Statistics* 6(2):461–464.

Sen, Somnath. 1992. "Military Expenditure Data for Developing Countries: Methods and Measurement." Pp. 1–18 in G. Lamb and V. Kallah, eds. *Military Expenditure and Economic Development: A Symposium on Research Issues.* Washington, DC: The World Bank.

Solow, Robert M. 1956. "A Contribution to the Theory of Economic Growth." *Quarterly Journal of Economics* 50(1):65–94.

Stockholm International Peace Research Institute. 2008. *SIPRI Yearbook of World Armaments, Disarmament and International Security.* London, UK: Oxford University Press.

Swan, T. W. 1956. "Economic Growth and Capital Accumulation." *Economic Record* 32(4):334–361.

Trebilcock, Clive. 1969. "'Spin-Off' in British Economic History: Armaments and Industry, 1760-1914." *Economic History Review* 22(3):474–490.

Ward, Michael D., and David R. Davis. 1992. "Sizing up the Peace Dividend: Economic Growth and Military Spending in the United States, 1948-1996." *American Political Science Review* 86(3):748–755.

Yakovlev, Pavel. 2007. "Arms Trade, Military Spending, and Economic Growth." *Defence and Peace Economics* 18(4):317–338.

Rethinking the Legacies of the Iran–Iraq War: Veterans, the Basij, and Social Resistance in Iran

Neema Noori
University of West Georgia

The existing literature on Iran has focused heavily on the Khatimi-led reformist movement in Iran and the Ahmadinejad-led conservative counter-reformation. Consequently, major structural transformations have not been taken into account. The post-revolutionary organizational rearrangements of the Iranian state took place as an unintended consequence of the Iran–Iraq War from 1980 to 1988—a long war, especially in the context of Middle Eastern wars. This article seeks to restore the centrality of war to the theoretical discussion of social class formation. Class-based mobilization in Iran has foundered. This is a consequence of not only coercion and the current system's ongoing campaign to impose limits on the public sphere, but also a product of the wartime pact between the government and veterans associations. It could be argued that the government restricted post-war distributional gains to Iran's veterans and, in doing so, linked its fate to the fate of its veterans. This article, therefore, examines how the alliance between the conservative elite and war veterans' associations has stymied class-based mobilization in Iran.

Despite the rigors with which Middle East specialists have examined regional impediments to democratization and the persistence of authoritarianism, limited attention has been paid to the impact of war on social and political change in the Middle East. As Steven Heydemann observes, "despite the now thoroughly non-controversial observation that war making, state making, and 'society making' are thoroughly interdependent, there have been no more than a handful of studies that have explored how these dynamics interact in the Middle East" (2000:1). Even more surprising is the absence of scholarly research on the Iran–Iraq War, which is the most costly and protracted regional war of the twentieth century. Having lasted eight years at the cost of an estimated 213,255 Iranian lives, the war is one of the few examples of total war in the developing world.[1] The scarcity of research on the war is only matched by a dearth of analysis on what happened to veterans after the war.[2]

This article addresses this gap in the literature by examining postwar veteran social policy in Iran. Research for this article, conducted during the summer of 2008, is based on ethnographic interviews with multiple veterans, both volunteers and draftees, in Tehran.

Curiously, participation on the frontline was not in itself a precondition for equitable postwar treatment from the government. Those who volunteered for the front, the Basij,[3] received a more expansive package of material benefits than those who were drafted to fight in the war. What accounts for this discrepancy? Since the war was framed as a struggle for the survival of the revolution, those who volunteered to fight on the frontlines were viewed as a constituency that would reliably support the regime in power. The discrepancy in the treatment of draftees and volunteers was also reflected in the public treatment that was accorded to returning members of the Basij. The Basij were lionized for their service. Those who were drafted to serve in the army were received with less enthusiasm.

Mahmoud Ahmadinejad, the current President of Iran, who is accused of rescinding many of the cultural and political reforms put in place by his predecessor, is himself a war veteran and a former member of the Basij. The success of both his election campaigns—in 2005 and 2009—was in part credited to the organizational strength of the Basij. Apart from serving as a political machine, unofficial reports suggest that the Basij engaged in ballot stuffing to engineer a victory for Ahmadinejad. Whether or not the election was rigged, the Basij have by all accounts played a similar role in the run-up to the election and its aftermath. More ominously, the Basij have reprised the role they have played repeatedly in the past two decades by violently suppressing the mass protest movement that emerged to contest the election results in 2009. Though the purpose of this article is not to provide an analysis of the post-election protest movement, it sheds light on the origins of the Basij as a coercive instrument of the state.

By directing his appeal to the Basij, Ahmadinejad has relied on a strategy of veteran co-optation with numerous antecedents in other postwar contexts. An important consequence of these policies to co-opt veterans has been the striking absence of an independently organized veterans' movement. Moreover, Iran's incipient NGO sector is curiously devoid of associations that support or advocate on behalf of veterans' affairs. In fact, more than serving as a reliable electoral block, government elites made frequent use of the Basij to forcefully hinder the formation of a nascent class-based opposition movement. Returning to the original question of this article, the discrepancy in treatment between volunteers and draftees only makes sense once class politics are taken into account. By linking the politics of class to patterns of veteran mobilization during and after the war, this article provides an explanation for the absence of a coherent class-based opposition movement in Iran.

In a country without party politics, where the conventional trope used to analyze political divisions pits conservative against reformist factions, the Basij are the closest thing Iran has to an organized political party. However, though they have features that are characteristic of political parties or interest groups, the Basij are neither a party nor an interest group. This article argues that the Basij most closely resemble an administered mass organization (AMO), an institution, according to Gregory Kasza (1995), that first came into existence after World War I and was modeled after the mass conscript army. Kasza argues that the first AMOs in Russia, Germany, and Italy were a product of war. In each case, they resulted from the failure to mobilize adequate numbers of soldiers and civilian workers during World War I. The blunders of domestic mobilization during the war convinced states of the need to organize civilians in peacetime. In each of these cases, veterans played a leading role in the formation of AMOs, the primary purpose of which was to block the formation of social and political organizations independent of the state.

According to Kasza, AMOs are characterized by the following four features. First, AMOs seek the mass membership of those comprising particular social categories. For example, by 1939, the Hitler Youth Organization had registered more than 80% of boys and girls between 10 and 18 years of age (Kasza 1995:78). Second, the organization's leadership is appointed by the government and has no capacity for independent decision making. Instead, the primary task of an AMO is to advance government policy. Third, AMOs apply organizational technologies for mobilizing armies in order to administer civilian populations during peacetime. Finally, though AMOs may appear voluntary and independent of the state to both participants and outside observers, they are, in reality, instruments of state power (Kasza 1995). This is partly what makes them such effective tools of the state.

When mobilized by the central government to either block the collective action of an opposition party or stage a counter-protest in support of the regime in power, AMOs can, under limited circumstances, project the appearance of an organic, non-coerced, and independent grassroots movement. Their utility in this capacity extends to both domestic and international audiences. In short, regardless of how AMOs are wielded, their primary purpose is to act as a prophylactic agent that counters the formation of opposition movements. The next section examines the early history of the Basij and their vital function during the war.

The lack of research and writing on the political legacies of war in the Middle East is not particularly surprising. As Kasza (1996) points out, Western social scientists, in general, and political scientists, in particular, have historically paid inadequate attention to the social and political impact of war. Kasza contends that this oversight has impeded the ability of comparative social scientists to theorize on the impact of war on social and political institutions in an adequate manner.

If social scientists have failed to adequately theorize the social and political impact of war in the West, then this failure is much more acute in the developing world. Stephen Heydemann (2000) argues that the causes and consequences of war are radically different in the Middle East. In the West, one of the salutary effects of war was that it promoted democratic reform, as evinced by Charles Tilly's (1990) research on the relationship between state formation and war in Europe. Tilly argues that the exigencies of war in terms of the increased demand for manpower and resources forced states to enlarge, to expand their reach, and eventually, when resistance is met, to bargain with their populations. Repeated iterations of bargaining have historically led to a steady increase in citizens' rights.

According to Heydemann, theories demonstrating a causal relationship between state formation, war, and democratization in the European context do not readily transfer to the Middle East. Writing about the Middle East, he observes that "the structure of revenues, the export into the region of a more fully articulated model of the nation state, and the presence of a consolidated international state system weakened the link between war making and state structure" (2000:24). Due to the region's dependence on outside sources of revenue, derived from international aid or oil exports, Middle Eastern states were never compelled to develop the extractive capacity to fund wars through the taxation of domestic populations. With regard to the need to tax, governing authorities in the region rarely experienced domestic pressure for political liberalization.

Heydemann builds on Lisa Anderson's key contributions to the relationship between the political economy of the Middle East and regional security. Anderson (1995) argues that Middle Eastern states prepare for war, go to war, and make peace with relative detachment from domestic considerations. The counterintuitive consequence of this security environment is that the production of risk can be profitable. To illustrate this point, Anderson (1995) refers to Egypt's intervention in the Yemen Civil War. Quoting Martin Malin, she argues that the conflict served as "Egypt's most important magnet for drawing resources from outside of the region" (Malin 1993:1). Further examples include Iraq's invasion of Iran and Egypt's participation with Syria and Jordan in the Arab–Israeli War of 1967. Anderson writes:

> For many of the regimes in the Middle East and North Africa, both war and peace have served as important devices used to garner infusions of revenues from the international system and thereby to purchase continuing political control at home. Decisions to wage war and sue for peace are pursued not as reflections of national interests or projections of national power, but rather because they may permit faltering authoritarian regimes renewed access to resources from the international system necessary to shore up their domestic positions. Because they have so far succeeded in producing such infusions of foreign revenues, both the initiation of war and the conclusion of peace in the Middle East and North Africa have proved inimical to political liberalization and democratization. Indeed, they have allowed—and sometimes required—the incumbent authoritarian rulers to resist and repress domestic political demands. (1995:43–44)

States reap a high dividend from manufacturing risk. By promoting insecurity or by engendering the perception of threat, regimes can persuade their regional allies and international protectors to continue to provide them with material support (Heydemann 2000: 14). "The domestic side of this strategy," according to Heydemann, "is to strengthen connections between a highly transnationalized political economy of strategic-rent seeking and the use of militarism as a means of domestic social control and social mobilization" (2000:14). Logically, a political system that thrives by perpetuating insecurity outside its borders would have no choice but to resort to authoritarianism domestically, leading to the creation of a highly militarized society.

Though it serves as a welcome contribution to improving our understanding of how preparing for war and war-making have influenced the region's politics, there are four limitations to the Heydemann volume. First, it does not explain how the post–Cold War era has altered these dynamics. Though there is ample evidence which suggests that the rentier effect still works to block democratic reform in the post–Cold War era, it is not clear that militarism continues to serve as a reliable means of extracting revenue from regional and international protectors as it did during the Cold War. Second, scant attention is directed to war veterans. Based on studies of veterans' movements in Europe and North America, it is clear that veterans have considerable political clout. They generally have the moral authority, numerical strength, and organizational capacity to extract crucial concessions from the state. In addition, the conditions under which they are demobilized have serious and long-lasting implications for domestic politics. Kasza points to the pivotal role that war veterans played "in founding the revolutionary regimes of the Soviet Union, Fascist Italy, Nazi Germany, Yugoslavia, and the People's Republic of China" (1996:362). Third, none of the case studies included in the volume examined the long-term structural and institutional effects of wartime mobilization. Fourth, limited attention is directed toward analyzing the Iran–Iraq War, which was arguably the most important regional conflict of the Modern Era.

This article's objective is to contribute to our understanding of how mobilization for the Iran–Iraq War, the prosecution of the war, and demobilization in its aftermath impact the politics of the present. As an under-examined dimension of mass politics, Kasza contends that "the incorporation of the masses into politics is an oft-noted feature of political development, but hitherto parties and interest groups have dominated research on mass organization" (1995:180). As such, students of contentious politics have overlooked the impact of AMOs in inhibiting the emergence of social movements. The fact that the most long-lived military regimes of the twentieth century have relied on AMOs is also of crucial importance.[4]

Iran's Populist Wartime Strategy

> The image of teen-age Iranians blowing themselves up on Iraqi land mines as a way to heaven should remind us that the passions of 16th to 18th-century Europe have yet to play themselves out fully in the third world of the 20th century. These passions will not often embody themselves in social-revolutionary transformations, but when they do—and when geopolitical circumstances unleash international conflicts and do not proscribe the outbreak of war—we can expect aspirations for equality and dignity, both within nations and on the international stage, to flow again and again into military mass mobilization. Arguably, this is the mission that revolutionized regimes perform best. In the face of serious (but not overwhelming) foreign threats, they excel at motivating the formerly excluded to die for the glory of their national states. (Skocpol 1988:168)

In likening Iran's revolutionary zeal to that of France, Skocpol revisits the conventional narrative, which ascribed Iran's success in mobilizing large numbers of men to post-revolutionary zeal. She contends that "because of the ways revolutionary leaders mobilize popular support in the course of struggles for state power, the emergent regimes can tackle mobilization for war better than any other task" (1988:168). Many of my informants, men who volunteered to serve at the front, echo these sentiments. In the words of one veteran, "What made this war different was religious intensity." Another veteran asserted that "Iran was fighting the world. This gave us a tremendous sense of accomplishment and pride. It also gave us the will to continue. We were fighting for the survival of our nation." However, in addition to affirming patriotic fervor, my interviews with veterans also point toward a more complex decision-making calculus.

Post-revolutionary Iran succeeded in mobilizing vast numbers of the urban and rural poor. In one campaign conducted in 1987 alone, military authorities claimed the participation of 600,000 Basij (Nezami 1993:267). In this regard, it was no different from other revolutionary regimes such as the French or the Chinese. However, as Nezami points out, it would be a mistake to attribute Iran's success in mobilizing hundreds of thousands of volunteers solely to religious or revolutionary fervor; nor would it be accurate, as Skocpol's thesis presumes, to attribute success solely to the organizational framework established before, during, and after the revolution by the movement's leaders. More important, as Nezami's dissertation on the subject documents, was the Iranian regime's efforts to provide incentives for military service by creating a robust social support system for volunteers and their families.

To counter Iraq's superiority in military hardware and regional economic support,[5] Iran capitalized on its advantage in manpower. Iran's political and economic isolation, coupled with the crippling damages inflicted on its oil industry, exacted a heavy toll on its ability to fund the war effort. In 1986, toward the end of the war, Iraq was outspending Iran nearly 2:1 on purchases of military hardware (Nezami 1993:75). All able-bodied men older than 18 years were subject to compulsory military service; exemptions were granted for cases in which the draftee was the only son, for college students, and for when a family had already lost a son to the war.

Only by making the sacrifices of war palatable by subsidizing and rationing essential goods, framing the war as a religious conflict and an extension of the revolution, and constructing a robust plan to care for veterans and their families could the government mount an effective challenge to Iraq. The bulk of Iran's oil revenue, from 1981 to 1986, was dedicated to incentivizing military service.[6]

Nezami (1993) observes that military service was promoted as a reliable and long-term employment option. In 1983, the commander of the army stated that "those who have completed their service in the army can join the Qods Reserve Brigade as volunteers, and employment will be found for those who are as yet unemployed" (quoted in Nezami 1993:240). Protections were put in place to assure volunteers and draftees that their families would be cared for while they were away. Alongside loans, families were provided subsidized healthcare and legal assistance. Nezami reports that in 1986, the judicial system was ordered to grant a five-year moratorium on the eviction of war refugees and families of fighters from rented housing (1993:273).

The Martyrs and Veterans Affairs Foundation (*Bonyad-e ShahidvaO-mur-e Janbazan*), established one month after the revolution in 1979, played a pivotal role in supporting the family members of those lost in the war. Apart from providing financial assistance, the foundation donated land and allocated housing for the families of martyrs. In 1985, a law was passed, forgiving all debts and back taxes owed by martyrs. In addition, 5% of the slots open to all incoming university students were reserved for the families of martyrs (Nezami 1993:274–275). Those who were most likely swayed by these incentives were the poor, precisely those whom the regime purported to protect. Nezami insightfully characterizes the Iranian war effort as being populist in nature (1993). In 1984, the head of the Iranian armed forces observed that "the war taught the armed forces how to draw on the coordinated activities of a society's different organs and to implement popular mobilization in the broadest sense of the term" (*Jomhuri-e Islami,* as quoted in Nezami 1993:266).

The Martyrs Foundation is one component of a larger network of overlapping organizations that continues to provide financial assistance to the families of martyrs, veterans, and the poor. For example, *Bonyad-e Mostazafan* (Foundation of the Oppressed), the largest of these parastate social support organizations, disperses 50% of its earnings to the "poor" via low-interest loans and monthly allowances (Fisk 1995; Wehrey et al. 2009:57). Critics of the *Bonyad* network object to its lack of transparency and its deepening politicization. In an article questioning the accountability of para-governmental organizations such as the Martyr's Foundation, Saeidi observes that the "foundation supports people who are most affiliated with the government. This helps provide legitimization and political authority" (2004:488). Both foundations, which are administered by former officers of the Islamic Revolutionary Guard Corps (IRGC), maintain informal ties to the IRGC (Wehrey et al. 2009:28).

Between 1981 and 1990, government funding for the Martyrs Foundation rapidly expanded, from 11.4 billion rials in 1981 to 115 billion rials in 1990. Ali Saedi, who is critical of the foundation's lack of transparency, reveals that the Shahid Investment Company, a subsidiary of the Martyrs Foundation that was established in 1994, has a controlling interest in approximately 50 private firms and has opened branches overseas (2004:488).

The social support infrastructure that encompasses the Martyrs Foundation represents an enduring and politically consequential legacy of the war. In comparative terms, it bears a resemblance to the early social support programs instituted in the United States after the Civil War. For example, Theda Skocpol reveals how the structure of the American welfare state was largely determined by veteran social policy after the Civil War. In *Protecting Soldiers and Mothers* (1992), Skocpol documents how the Republican Party, motivated by the prospect of creating a large constituency of political allies, raised protective tariffs to help fund a broad-based program that provided Civil War veterans with pensions:

> In the process of expanding Civil War benefits during the late nineteenth century, Republicans fostered the rapid growth of a supportive organized social group, the Grand Army of the Republic (GAR). Governmental openness to demands for distributive benefits encouraged the reorientation of GAR goals toward support for pensions and tariffs; and the GAR in turn achieved many legislative successes when pursuing such demands. "Old soldiers," especially Union veterans, became organizationally and ideologically central to the politics of late-nineteenth-century America. (1992:528)

With the formation of the GAR, Union Army veterans' associations successfully petitioned the state to receive pensions for themselves and more extensive state funded social support for their families. Veteran activism yielded one of the world's first social welfare programs. Curiously, an important legacy of this early welfare system was that recipients had to prove that they were morally justified to receive support. The Civil War and the particular way in which its veterans were mobilized in the aftermath of the conflict have had a lasting influence on American attitudes toward welfare and the anatomy of the American welfare state. However, it should not be forgotten that this initiative was forged from the top down by the Republican Party. As such, the veterans groups constituting GAR could be counted on to serve as a reliable source of support for Republican political causes.

Analogous to the formation of the American social welfare state, veteran social policy initiatives in Iran have left a durable footprint. The veterans' support foundations that were put in place both before and during the war not only helped cultivate a loyal following but also set limits on legitimate forms of political contestation. Those who volunteered for the frontlines, the Basij, benefited from a wider array of economic and social services. They were also expected to serve as a reliable ally of the regime.

As a corollary to these efforts to provide financial backing for volunteers and their families, the state invested heavily in supporting the symbolic status of both martyrs and the Basij. Due to the "populist" nature of Iran's wartime mobilization strategy, the Basij have come to serve as a proxy for the interests of the lower classes. As such, official efforts to co-opt class as a vehicle of social expression mean that any attempt to mobilize independently of the Basij on the basis of a class identity is forcefully challenged.

This also helps us understand why independent veterans' associations are very rare. Since the public perceives veterans to be aligned with the regime, a few civic organizations are willing to work on behalf of veterans' causes. The daughter of a veteran and an Iranian journalist who has written extensively about the war confirmed this view in an interview. She stresses that, "because of how the government has co-opted veterans movements, people are tired of the war, the whole narrative of the *shahid*, names of streets, and billboards . . . . veterans issues if dealt with in a critical manner are almost a taboo subject." A second informant, a veteran who had been drafted, states, "[A]fter the war, there was no ability to oppose the status quo or challenge how things were done. Because of how the war had been politicized, to criticize the government was tantamount to criticizing the martyrs." A third veteran echoes the same sentiment: "We went to serve. We weren't aware of our rights. We didn't know how to go about getting our due. There was pressure not to resist or to be critical of one's treatment as a veteran. We were pressured not to act. To oppose the status -quo was equivalent to being opposed to one's religion—the state religion."

In a country in which the symbolic residue of war is omnipresent, the agents of war are remarkably absent. Though murals of martyrs appear on many prominent city blocks, veterans themselves do not wear clothing that signifies their status. The most visible marker of veteran status is the checkered *keffiyeh*[7] that is wrapped around the shoulders or the neck. I repeatedly brought this to the attention of my informants, most of whom suggested that it had to do with the government's careful management of the imagery and narrative which were associated with the war and its veterans. One informant concluded, "[B]ecause of the politicization of the war, people don't want to legitimate the status quo or show that they agree with the status quo. To mark yourself as a veteran is to signify your support for the regime."

The Basij: Origins and Structure

The post-revolutionary Iranian state obviously succeeded in mobilizing vast segments of Iranian society for the war effort. The bulk of these forces were associated with the Islamic Revolutionary Guards Corps (*Sepah-e Pasdaran-e Enghelab-e Islami*), also referred to as the *Pasdaran*. After the revolution, Ayatollah Khomeini, who distrusted the army, spearheaded the creation of the Islamic Revolutionary Guard Corps (IRGC) to act as a counterweight to the regular armed forces. Khomeini ordered the creation of, in his words, a "20 million man army" to defend the revolution from internal and external threats (Nezami 1993:205). The forces that constitute the IRGC consist of two main groups: the IRGC and the Basij (*Baseej-e Mostazafin-e Sepah-e Pasdaran*), which translates into the Pasdaran's mobilization of the oppressed (Nezami 1993:205). Once the war started, the IRGC and the Basij, though initially recruited for domestic security purposes, were quickly redirected toward the frontline.

One of the important distinguishing features of the IRGC was that its ranks were predominantly filled with men and women from lower socioeconomic classes. Due to the draft, the regular armed forces were recruited from a broader range of socioeconomic strata. In 1979, the Iranian armed forces consisted of 415,000 soldiers, 1,735 tanks, and 447 combat aircrafts (Karsh 1987:84). By comparison, by 1984, the Pasdaran had swelled to 450,000 people.

The fundamental difference between the regulars of the IRGC and the Basij was that the IRGC received conventional military training. The Basij, on the other hand, received little to no training during the war. Though noted for their use of human-wave attacks to clear minefields ahead of regular infantry assaults, they played a crucial role in turning the tide in the early years of the war. Quickly trained and rapidly mobilized, they served as an indispensable component of the campaign to reverse Iraq's early advance into Iranian territory. Having proved their utility early in the war and having sacrificed so much, they had the symbolic capital to become a potent political force.

As Mehran Kamrava points out, there was nothing novel about the creation of a parallel army within the context of the Middle East. In describing the bifurcated organizational structure of many armed forces in the Middle East, he contends that each state has a conventional armed force to protect itself from external threats and a "highly ideological"militia to monitor and guard itself against internal threats (2000:82). Kamrava observes, "The armed militia essentially serves as one of the primary mechanisms through which the state institutes and perpetuates an inclusionary polity, thereby channeling popular energies and sentiments into state-supported projects. The militia is thus one of the crucial links through which the emotionally-laden nexus between the state and society is maintained" (2000:84). What is more, Kamrava suggests that the primary appeal of the Basij is that they serve as an effective path of upward mobility for the urban and rural poor. High-level officials throughout the regime are frequently recruited from the ranks of the IRGC, a much more effective means of upward mobility than service in the traditional army (Kamrava 2000:85).

Due to their numerical strength, the wide scope of activities undertaken by the Basij, and their pattern of historical development, the Basij fulfilled the established criteria for administered mass organizations described earlier. Given that the Basij, as currently constituted, were the product of a war requiring the mass mobilization of hundreds of thousands of men, the regime had an incentive to preserve their organizational capacity. Iran's war effort hinged on successfully harnessing the country's advantage in manpower; therefore, dismantling the Basij, even after the war, was never a serious option. Sustaining the Basij served several objectives: First, it helped the government maintain military readiness; second, it secured the loyalty of a military force that once demobilized could have threatened the regime; and third, it served as a useful tool for blocking the formation of anti-establishment social and political movements, a security function shared by all AMOs.

The organizational technologies pioneered during the war are visible today. In 1986, Mohzen Rezai, a presidential candidate in the electoral campaign conducted in 2009, authorized the creation of a nationwide network of military associations for the purpose of "ever greater mobilization" (Nezami 1993:268). Both now and then, the Basij claim geographical ubiquity and mass membership. Periodically, Basij commanders continue to announce initiatives to further extend the mobilizational capacities of the Basij by opening nationwide centers in new venues such as universities, factories, or primary schools. Most Basij units these days fall under the supervision of a neighborhood-based mosque or community center. The

Iranian newspaper *E'temad-e Melli*, in an article that discusses plans to unify the command structure of the Basij and the IRGC, reported that with 3000 Basij resistance units containing approximately 300 active members each, "there are almost 12 million forces in the country and a country that has 12 million Basij forces will possess extraordinary ability" (Nabi-Rudaki 2008).

Basij Week, a week-long mobilization drive held by the regime, remains intact. In 1986, during Basij Week, two years before the end of the war, the regime claimed to have recruited hundreds of thousands of people, including 1.2 million from the southern provinces of Khuzestan, Arak, and Bandar Abbas, and 500,000 who joined from the northwestern provinces of West Azerbaijan, Kurdistan, and Karaj (Nezami 1993:267). More recent iterations of Basij Week have similarly focused on the numerical strength and all-encompassing nature of the force. Though ample evidence exists that documents the regime's success in mobilizing vast armies of volunteers, the figures quoted in these publications are overstated. Similar to recent Basij recruitment numbers touted by government officials, inflated estimates such as these served symbolic objectives, signaling resilience and strong domestic support for the war to multiple publics, both domestic and international.

In December 2007, Major General Ja'fari, the supreme commander of the Guards Corps, described the function of the Basij as being all encompassing: "The Basij plays a role among all the strata [of people], on all issues and topics, and all political, security, cultural, social, and economic affairs. In fact, the Guards Corps and the Basij are two forces that listen to the orders of the leader [of the revolution] and play an effective role in an official capacity for the advancement of the goals of the revolution" (*Hemayat* 2007). Along those same lines, the supreme leader Ali Khamene'i compares the tactical skill and resolve required of Basij forces in liberating *Khoramshahr*[8] to their present versatility. In a speech celebrating Basij Week, Khamene'i extols the virtues of the Basij:

> You proved yourselves in the battlefield. And if, one day, the country again needs military, combat forces, you are in the front ranks. This is true. But war is not the Basij's total content. The Basij extends to all the arenas of life. When it is time for construction, the Basij is in the front ranks. When it is time for relief work and services, the Basij is in the front ranks. When it is time for very precise, minute, and sensitive research, Basij forces are in the front ranks.... Basij is a multi-dimensional force. (*Islamic Republic of Iran News Network* 2007)

The Basij are now estimated to number 90,000 "with an active and reserve strength of up to 300,000 and a mobilization capacity of nearly 1,000,000" (Cordesman 2007:10). Hyperbolic announcements by high-ranking IRGC officials, however, cite much higher numbers. "According to a former commander of the Basij, Brigadier General Mohammad Hejazi, the strength of the force in 2004 was 10.3 million. By 2007, during Ahmadinejad's term in office, its numbers had allegedly grown to12.6 million. The current commander of the Basij, Hassan Taeb, in a televised interview broadcast on November 28, 2008, reported that the force had grown to 13.6 million, about 20% of the total population of Iran. Of this number, 5 million were women and 4.7 million were schoolchildren" (Aryan 2008). The approximately 14 million Basijis cited by the regime fall into three categories: ordinary, active, and special. Only members of the special branch are officially considered a part of the armed forces (Zamani 2009). Only a small fraction of the Basij undergo formal military training. In addition to receiving a small stipend, Basij members are exempted from military service and receive seats in universities (MacFarquhar 2009).

As is typical of most AMOs, the Basij are called on to fulfill a wide variety of disparate tasks. For example, in addition to serving as bailiffs in court, the Basij are used to enforce moral codes such as monitoring hejab, preventing inappropriate contact between men and women, and confiscating satellite dishes (Aryan 2008). Apart from security, social control, and surveillance, the Basij are also mobilized to support humanitarian projects and disaster relief. Given their visible moral role of providing humanitarian relief in rural areas, an RAND-sponsored study of the IRGC suggests that rural populations have a more positive view of the Basij. Due to their voluntary status, their involvement in such projects is often touted as economic. Apart from the perks that are derived from affiliation with the Basij, many also receive stipends or salaries. Given the centrality of the IRGC to the Iranian economy, there are numerous material rewards that follow from membership within the Basij, a subsidiary of the IRGC. Participation in formal training is a precondition that qualifies for loans and university scholarships or for receiving welfare subsidies (Wehrey et al. 2009:28).

The next section examines what happened to veterans once they returned from the front lines. To this end, specific attention is given to the status accorded to draftees versus volunteers.

Demobilization

Though it would be a mistake to conflate the Basij with veterans, many of the Iranians I interviewed referred to men who volunteered for the war as "Basiji." In the everyday language of Iran, the designation "Basij" is used even more broadly to refer to a class of politically and culturally conservative men who are supportive of the regime. In common parlance, even formal members of the Revolutionary Guard are commonly referred to as "Basiji." In short, the term "Basij" does not only refer to formal members of the Basij Militia, but is also often used more widely to describe conservative supporters of the regime.

Both volunteers and draftees expressed dissatisfaction with the government's attempts to reintegrate veterans once they returned from the front. Amir,[9] a volunteer, describes what happened after he returned from the front as follows: "When the veterans arrived, there was no one to help them or guide them. We of course did not know how to pursue our interests. We did not and do not want material benefits. Though I would have been accepted anyway, I benefited from gaining admission to the university. This was in my view the biggest source of support." Though veterans are sensitive and quick to counter the perception that they owe their current status to government benefits, they most readily admit that the decision to volunteer was a complex one and not easily reducible to either a sense of patriotic duty or self-interest. Mostafa, another volunteer, classified volunteers as follows: "[A]mong those who enlisted, there were two types, those who saw how successful returning veterans had become and those who were truly committed."

As a whole, both categories of veterans expressed outrage with the many civilians who had profited from the war. My informants commented on how savvy war profiteers exploited state programs designed to subsidize the cost of basic goods for profit in the black market. When veterans returned home after the war, they were shocked to see how life had continued normally in their absence.

In discussing how the war altered their worldviews, Amir suggests the following: "There were four types of veterans. Twenty percent remained the same way, religiously and politically. Eighty percent returned to a normal life having changed and having adopted a more open mind—we have to live. We cannot fight everyone. Of those 80%, some are sorry that they volunteered—let's say 20%. Of the remaining number, 60% are not necessarily sad, but they do not want to return to the conditions of the past. They do not believe in what happened." Hossein, a third volunteer, concludes that since the war had ended with a military stalemate, conservative elements directed their energy inward, noting, "If we had won an absolute victory, the extremists would have gone back to their own lives. Because this was not the case, they put pressure on society.

Their efforts went toward remaking society. Groups were organized that should not have been organized. Twenty years after the war, they are still going strong."

Draftees, on the other hand, voiced frustration for what they deemed to be inequitable treatment from the government. Hamid, a draftee who currently works in a government ministry, expressed resentment over job application forms that posed questions about his military status. For example, "Were you a volunteer or were you drafted?" Shortly after the war, he remembers an interview where the employer asked, "[I]f you're a veteran then why aren't you limping? . . . Where are your injuries?" At the government agency where he now works, Hamid complains that co-workers whose records indicate that they volunteered for the war are promoted at faster rates. Referring to the Basij, Mostafa, another volunteer, adds, "After the war, they used their connections to obtain apartments and become rich. . . . After the war, many sported beards and continued to maintain the appearance and persona of veteran members of the Basij." This is a common refrain among the draftees whom I interviewed. Many assume that high-ranking members of the Basij and the Sepah (the IRGC) used these perks to amass large fortunes. There is strong resistance to veterans' perks.

Veterans and Class Politics

If the legacy of war is an under-examined component of modern Middle Eastern politics, research on class and class-based mobilization suffers from similar neglect. However, in the context of Iran, both war and the politics of class are connected. Most wars are followed by national movements that demand redistributive justice. Veterans typically command a prominent position in these movements. As discussed earlier, veteran mobilization after the American Civil War led to the creation of an incipient social welfare state. In post–World War France, veterans successfully mobilized to receive better medical care and expanded economic rights (Prost 1992).

In the aftermath of the Iran–Iraq War, the regime continued to privilege volunteers over draftees. Members of the Basij continued to reap the symbolic and material benefits of being linked to the regime in power. By cultivating ties with the Basij, the Iranian government laid the foundation for the construction of a mass-administered organization. Depicted by the regime as the crucial defender of the economically weak, the movement serves as the legitimate vehicle for representing the interests of subordinate classes. As such, conservative factions frequently portray the Basij as the preeminent defender of the poor. Ahmadinejad, as already noted, was a former officer of the IRGC and a veteran of the war. He developed a highly successful populist campaign strategy underwritten by his pledge to "deliver Iran's oil wealth to the ordinary person's *sofreh* (dining cloth)" (Bozorgmehr and Smyth 2005). Iranian analysts have credited Ahmadinejad's electoral victories in both 2005 and 2009 to the widespread mobilization of veterans, the Basij, and the IRGC. During his first campaign, Ahmadinejad pledged to improve the economic standing of veterans whose sacrifices, he claimed, had not been adequately acknowledged. According to post-election reports in 2005, the Basij served as the lynchpin of his electoral success, as the militia fanned out to "get out the vote" in south Tehran and other conservative strongholds. Since the election, Ahmadinejad has worked to solidify his position by cultivating ties with "the provincial poor, military veterans, and the other beneficiaries of state largesse" (Ehsani 2006:9). However, the chief beneficiaries of the Ahmadinejad regime appear to be the security forces, particularly the IRGC.

The IRGC has parlayed the legitimacy it earned during the war into becoming a potent political and economic force in Iran. Since 2006, the various arms of the IRGC have won billions of dollars in business contracts. In June 2006, the IRGC was awarded a $2.09 billion contract to develop the South Pars gas field, an offshore gas field under the joint ownership of Iran and Qatar. Again, in 2006, a construction company that was owned by the IRGC and associated with the Mostazafan Foundation received a $2.4 billion contract to complete the construction of Tehran's subway system. Half of the members of Ahmadinejad's cabinet are former IRGC veterans. In addition, 80 of the 290 members of parliament are veterans of the IRGC and "twenty of Iran's 30 provinces have governors from the IRGC" (Taheri 2007).

Despite the regime's populist rhetoric, there is little evidence that supports broad-based and concrete efforts toward improving the lives of the poor. In fact, the regime has repeatedly mobilized the Basij to thwart labor activists. The spike in labor activism witnessed in 2003 when thousands of teachers went on strike throughout the country, leading to the closure of 400 schools in the capital city alone, crumbled quickly in 2005 with Ahmadinejad's electoral victory (Maljoo2006:31). When threatened with a massive walkout of bus drivers, authorities mobilized the IRGC to put a quick end to the strike. More than 500 drivers were arrested. Meanwhile, members of the Basij and other government forces commandeered buses from other state institutions to maintain the flow of traffic (Maljoo 2006:32). Mohammad Maljoo also documents how new labor legislation under the populist candidate's presidency has surprisingly further eroded labor rights in Iran. In 1990, a new labor law was introduced, effectively banning the formation of independent trade unions. The 1990 law outlawed the establishment of a union when an Islamic Labor Council was already in place (Maljoo 2006:32). According to Maljoo, legislation introduced in 2006 to reform the 1990 labor legislation, in fact, reduces preexisting worker protections, making it easier for employers to fire their employees, and does nothing to ease restrictions on organizing labor unions (2006). It is indeed ironic that a president elected with a populist agenda for reform has done so much to undermine labor rights. In limiting the channels through which labor can represent its interests, the regime is, in effect, attempting to co-opt labor activists. One could similarly argue that the Basij, Khomeini's army of 20 million, meet the same criteria. It is an attempt to co-opt class and regulate the channels through which the poor can assert their interests. In other words, the Basij serve as a proxy for Iran's subordinate classes; they represent the only legitimate vehicle for expressing lower-class interests.

Despite a constitutional ban from involvement in politics and in a dramatic departure from previous election cycles, low-ranking members of the Basij were called on to play an active role in both of Ahmadinejad's presidential elections. The attempt to transform the Basij into a political machine was widely criticized by the reformist camp. The reformist newspaper *Aftab-e Yazd* published an editorial calling for the depoliticization of the Basij. The editorial states that "any move to present the Basij as closer to a particular faction or comments suggesting Basij opposition to one set of ideas can only undermine the Basij's unique position" (*Aftab-e Yazd* 2007).

In the 2009 election campaign, Mehdi Karoubi, the reformist challenger to Ahmadinejad, made the politicization of the Basij a campaign issue, calling for the militia and armed forces to refrain from intervening in the June presidential election (Jaseb 2009). This came in response to the assertion by HasanTaeb, the deputy commander of the Basij, in February 2008, that Basij members should have a "maximum presence"in the elections (Aryan 2008). In the ensuing debate, the conservative newspaper *Jomhuri-e Islami* distinguished the "special Basij," who are officially a part of the armed forces, from other Basij units. The article observes that "the majority of the people who believe in the Constitution of the Islamic Republic of Iran and the objectives of the Islamic Revolution are considered to be Basijis" (*Jomhuri-ye Eslami* 2009). An article in the youth-oriented newspaper *Javan* echoes this perspective:

> How can a teacher, a government employee, a bazaar merchant, a student, a doctor, a worker, a sportsman, a housewife, etc ... who thinks like a Basiji and has the characteristics of the Basijis, or who simply wishes to register his name in the school of love, but who does not have constant organizational contact with the Basij organization, how can one regard such a person as being a member of the armed forces? The identity of a person like that is not a military identity. The society does not regard him as a member of the armed forces, and nor does the law. In the same way, he would not be bound by any of the military regulations. Like any other member of the society, he can take part in all the four above-mentioned roles in any elections ... Truly, why are some people worried about the participation of some people who belong to the active and value-oriented body of the society (which is a general definition of the Basijis) in the election. (Zamani 2009)

In asserting that the Basij are independent of the armed forces and reflective of mainstream Iranian society, the article illustrates the utility of the AMO as an instrument of consolidation of power. One of the more insidious characteristics of AMOs is that they are designed to appear autonomous and organic. AMOs differ from political parties and interest groups in that "parties are launched to take over the government; interest groups seek to influence the government; AMOs are forged to implement policy" (Kazsa 1995:23).

Conclusion

Iran's Green Movement peaked on June 15, 2009, when hundreds of thousands of protestors converged at Azadi Square, the symbolic epicenter of the revolution in 1978. The regime, relying on both the Basij and the IRGC, used brute force to suppress the Green Movement. In February 2011, after a two-year hiatus, Egypt's Jasmine Revolution breathed new life into the protest movement. As an act of solidarity with the Egyptian movement, on February 14, thousands of Iranian protestors once again marched on Azadi Square. However, due to a massive security presence, subsequent demonstrations were less successful. Consequently, Mousavi and Karroubi have not been able to mobilize the mass numbers that emerged in the aftermath of the contested election of 2009.

This article investigates how Iran's security apparatus, itself largely a product of the Iran–Iraq War, is used to suppress opposition to the regime. As such, this article argues that the Iran–Iraq War has played an underappreciated role in determining the politics of the present. In examining the legacies of the Iran–Iraq War, this article makes the following contributions to the literature on Iranian politics. First, it identifies the Basij as an AMO rather than as a political party or interest group. Second, it argues for the centrality of war in explaining contemporary Iranian political and social institutions. Third, it demonstrates how the current regime's uses of AMOs have subverted class-based mobilization in post-war Iran.

Notes

1. The overall expense of the war is thought to be near $1,079 billion (Gongora 1997:324). A total war is one in which all of a nation's resources, both human and material, are mobilized to contribute to the war effort. As a consequence, civilians often become legitimate targets for military action.
2. There is a significant amount of Iranian scholarly research and writing in Persian on the subject of the war.
3. The Basij are a branch of the Islamic Revolutionary Guards Corps that were formed shortly after the revolution. The term "Basij" is also used more broadly to refer to military volunteers. The terminology of the group and its origins are discussed later in this article.
4. "Only one military regime in ten lasts longer than four years, but almost all military regimes that use AMOs have passed that threshold, including those in Burma, Egypt, Indonesia, Japan, Pakistan, Peru, and Spain" (Kasza 1998:188).
5. Iraq coaxed significant financial contributions from regional allies, including Saudi Arabia, Kuwait, and the UAE.
6. Nezami (1993) shows that the proportion of the budget dedicated to funding the war nearly doubled from 30% to 52% between 1983 and 1987. Nezami bases these figures on calculations from data obtained in *Jomhuri-e Islami*, Wednesday, October 4, 1983, No. 1305, Year 5, p.1 and Monday, December 28, 1987, No. 2491, Year 9, p. 1.
7. Internationally, the keffiyeh is commonly associated with Palestinian resistance fighters.
8. A strategically important city located near the border that was captured by the Iraqi army early in the war.
9. The names of my informants have been changed to protect their anonymity.

References

Aftab-e Yazd.2007. "Let Us Not Sacrifice the Basij." November 24.
Anderson, Lisa.1995. "Peace and Democracy in the Middle East, the Constraints of Soft Budgets."*Journal of International Affairs* 49(1):25–45.
Aryan, Hossein. December 7, 2008."Iran's Basij Force – the Mainstay of Domestic Security."*Radio Free Europe/Radio Free Liberty News Service*. Retrieved December 17, 2009 (http://www.rferl.org/content/Irans_Basij_Force_Mainstay_Of_Domestic_ Security/1357081.html).
Bozorgmehr, Najmeh and Garreth Smyth. 2005. "Iran's President Becomes unlikely Fashion Icon."*The Financial Times*. November 24. Retrieved March 31, 2011 (http://www.ft.com/cms/s/0/2f3ac7ac-5c8f-11da-af92-0000779e2340.html#axzz1 Gm6URHsJ).
Cordesman, Anthony. 2007. "Iran's Revolutionary Guards, the Al Quds Force, and Other Intelligence and Paramilitary Forces." Rough Draft Working Paper prepared for the Center for Strategic and International Studies. Retrieved June 9, 2012 (http://csis. org/files/media/csis/pubs/070816_cordesman_report.pdf).

Ehsani, Kaveh. 2006. "Iran: The Populist Threat to Democracy." *Middle East Report* 36(4): 4–9.
Fisk, Robert. 1995. "War Wounded Find Comfort from Billion-dollar Man." *The Independent.* May 26. Retrieved June 9, 2012 (http://www.independent.co.uk/news/world/war-wounded-find-comfort-from-billiondollar-man-1621094.html).
Gongora, Thierry. 1997. "War Making and State Power in the Contemporary Middle East." *International Journal of Middle East Studies* 29(3):323–340.
Hemayat. 2007. "Fars News Agency, Maj Gen Ja'afari announced:The Guards Corps and Basij are Prepared to Help Cultural Organizations of the Country." December 11. Retrieved June 7, 2009 (http://www.lexisnexis.com).
Heydemann, Steven. 2000. "War, Institutions, and Social Change in the Middle East." Pp. 1–30 in Steven Heydemann, ed. *War, Institutions, and Social Change in the Middle East.* Berkeley, CA: University of California Press.
Islamic Republic of Iran News Network. 2007. "There is No Force Like the Basij." November 26. Retrieved June 7, 2009 (http://www.lexisnexis.com).
Jomhuri-e Islami. 2009. "Guards Corps Announced in a Statement:The IRGC has always Urged Special Basij is not to Interfere in Elections."May 13. Retrieved June 7, 2009 (http://www.lexisnexis.com).
Jaseb, Hossein. May 9, 2009."Militia Must Stay Out of Election:Reformer." *Reuters.* Retrieved June 7, 2009 (http://www.reuters.com/article/world news).
Kamrava, Mehran. 2000. "Military Professionalization and Civil-Military Relations in the Middle East."*Political Science Quarterly* 115(1):67–92.
Karsh, Efraim. 1987. "Military Power and Foreign Policy Goals: The Iran-Iraq War Revisited." *International Affairs* 64(1):83–95.
Kazsa, J. Gregory. 1995. *The Conscription Society: Administered Mass Organizations.* New Haven: Yale University Press.
Kazsa, J. Gregory. 1996. "Review: War and Comparative Politics." *Comparative Politics* 28(3):355–373.
MacFarquhar, Neil. 2009."Shadowy Iranian Vigilantes Vow Bolder Action." *The New York Times.* June 19. Retrieved March 31, 2011 (http://www.nytimes.com/2009/06/19/world/middleeast/19basij.html).
Maljoo, Mohammad. 2006."Worker Protest in the Age of Ahmadinejad." *Middle East Report* 36 (4):30–33.
Malin, Martin. 1993. "Entrepreneurial Statecraft in Egyptian Foreign Policy: The Case of Yemen, 1962-1966."Paper presented at the annual meeting of the Middle East Studies Association, Research Triangle, NC, November 11–14.
Nabi-Rudaki, Mohammad. 2008."Former Commander Speaks of Iran Paramilitary Reform." *E'temad-e Melli.* Retrieved June 9, 2012 from Lexus Nexis Database.
Nezami, Nader. 1993."War and State Making in Revolutionary Iran." Unpublished doctoral dissertation, University of Washington.
Prost, Antoine. 1992. *In the Wake of War: 'Les AnciensCombattants' and French Society 1914-1939.* Oxford: Berg Publishers.
Saeidi, Ali A. 2004. "The Accountability of Para-governmental Organizations (Bonyads): The Case of Iranian Foundations." *Iranian Studies* 37(3):479–498.
Skocpol, Theda. 1988."Social Revolutions and Mass Military Mobilization." *World Politics* 40(2):147–168.
Skocpol, Theda. 1992. *Protecting Soldiers and Mothers: The Political Origins of Social Policy in the United States.* Cambridge, MA: Harvard University Press.
Taheri, Amir. 2007."Who Are Iran's Revolutionary Guards." *The Wall Street Journal.* Retrieved January 5, 2007(http://www.lexisnexis.com).
Tilly, Charles. 1990. *Coercion, Capital, and European States, AD990-1990.* Cambridge, MA: Basil Blackwell.

Wehrey, Frederic, Jerold D. Green, Brian Nichiporuk, Alireza Nader, Lydia Hansell, RasoolNafisi, and S. R. Bohandy. 2009. *The Rise of the Pasdaran: Assessing the Domestic Roles of Iran's Islamic Revolutionary Guards Corps.* Santa Monica, CA: Rand Corporation. Retrieved December 18, 2009 (http://www.rand.org/pubs/monographs/2008/RAND_MG821.pdf).

Zamani, Yusuf. May 16, 2009. "Basij Forces, Politics and Elections." *Javan*. Retrieved June 17, 2009 (http://www.lexisnexis.com).

Justifying War in Post–Cold War Conflicts

Molly Clever
University of Maryland

Political and Military Sociology: An Annual Review, 2012, Vol. 40: 141–170.

Justifications for war-making are a useful site to examine perceptions of legitimate political authority in particular historical contexts. Post–Cold War era political scholarship has extensively focused on the growing involvement of non-state actors in warfare, leading to assertions that a just-war revival is occurring through which the humanitarian justifications which were characteristic of pre-modern warfare are replacing modern era justifications that are rooted in the political authority of the sovereign state. The implication is that the concept of state sovereignty as the basis of international political authority is waning in the face of non-state challengers. I analyze justification frameworks used by political and military leaders in the weeks surrounding the initiation of nine conflicts from 1990 to 2008. The data do not support the claim that states are eschewing conventional state-interest arguments in favor of the greater flexibility of humanitarian arguments, or that non-state actors are more likely to use humanitarian justifications because the established state sovereignty frames are not open to them. Rather, the data indicate that state-interest frames are the predominant frame employed by both state and non-state actors, and that state actors are more likely than non-state actors to intertwine sovereign- and humanitarian-based justifications. These findings suggest that the just-war revival asserted by some scholars has been overstated and that further empirical analysis is needed.

In recent decades, claims about transformations in the nature of the sovereign state system have abounded. Arguments regarding the declining authority of state sovereignty take somewhat different forms across disciplinary boundaries, but scholars from sociology, political science, and international relations have shared a growing concern over the apparent erosion of national sovereign authority (see, for example, Axtmann 1996, 2004; Brown 2010; Kaldor 1999; Krasner 1999; Sassen 1996; Snow 2007). Much of this scholarship has been preoccupied with an image of a fracturing world in which a variety of local and global trends have coalesced to undermine the foundational power of the sovereign state system that has prevailed for the last five centuries.

Within these claims about the waning legitimacy of sovereign state power, one set of scholarship focuses on the manner in which political and military leaders justify war-making, arguing that one indication of the erosion of state sovereignty is that leaders are no longer employing conventional state-interest arguments to justify their use of organized violence. Instead, the post–Cold War era has witnessed a revival of the just-war language that was prevalent before the emergence of the sovereign state system in which the basis of political authority to engage in warfare is rooted in humanitarian and religious justifications (Dexter 2008; Falk 2004, 2005; Lawler 2002). These just-war revival arguments suggest that a shift from state sovereignist to humanitarian justifications for war in the post–Cold War era is indicative of a broader global trend away from the sovereignty of the state as the basis of political authority toward more dispersed, fractured, and overlapping bases of authority.

This study offers an evaluation of these claims and suggests that the just-war revival arguments are misdirected, as they tend to neglect two central issues. First, these just-war revival arguments have, thus far, not engaged in any systematic examination of these justifications across a broad enough set of cases to make claims about a changing pattern. Instead, they have relied on a small number of prominent recent examples which support the notion that humanitarian justifications are being employed without offering any examples to which they can be compared. Second, these arguments do not clearly define and distinguish between the different types of justifications that can be employed, and what each of these justificatory frames may indicate about how political authority is conceived. This study aims at addressing these shortcomings and provides a systematic examination of the justifications for war in the post–Cold War era.

I offer a critique of the just-war revival literature that connects these arguments with the just-war tradition as well as more recent scholarship on the changing nature of the state in a globalized context. This critique identifies a systematic evaluation of the justification frames used by both state and non-state combatants as well as the development of clearly defined justification frameworks as central components that are necessary to improve our understanding of what these justifications may indicate about the perceptions of political authority in the sovereign state system. The study proceeds to offer both these contributions. First, it develops a scheme of justification frameworks that distinguishes between logic and discourses of justification, making it possible to more clearly identify possible patterns in how justification frames may be used differently by different types of combatant actors. Second, a content analysis of these justification frames among nine combatants, representing three different types of conflict, waging war between 1990 and 2008, is conducted. The results indicate that the just-war revival claims may have been overstated. The data provide no evidence that states are eschewing conventional state-interest arguments in favor of the greater flexibility of humanitarian arguments, or that non-state actors are more likely to use humanitarian justifications because the established state sovereignty frames are not open to them. Rather, the data indicate that state-interest frames are the predominant frame employed by both state and non-state actors, and that state actors are more likely than non-state actors to intertwine sovereign- and humanitarian-based justifications. I conclude by discussing what these results may indicate about how the authority of the sovereign state is perceived in the post–Cold War era.

Justification Frames and the Just-war Revival

The *just-war revival* refers to a subset of scholarship on the transforming nature of the sovereign state system that identifies justifications for war-making as an important indicator of how legitimate political authority is conceived of in particular socio-historical contexts, and by extension, can be interpreted as a signal for broader changes in the strength and power of that system. Most prominently argued by Falk (2004, 2005), Lawler (2002), and Dexter (2008), the basic premise of these arguments is that the recent surge in humanitarian and religious-morality-based justifications for waging war, with a corresponding decline in justifications rooted in the international laws of the state system and the sovereign rights of states to promote their interests, is indicative of a transformation in the perceived authoritative power of state sovereignty. The latter type has been the conventional basis of justification since the emergence of the sovereign state system five centuries ago, whereas the former is associated with justifications for war-making in the pre- and early-modern eras before the concept of state sovereignty emerged. Before delving into the specifics of the just-war revival arguments, it is appropriate to first discuss the just-war theoretical tradition in which these arguments are rooted.

The just-war theoretical tradition draws the link between the emergence of the sovereign state system and the logic of justification for war-making. Just-war discourse underwent a major historical transformation through the seventeenth and eighteenth centuries, as European states became increasingly defined in terms of territorial delimitation and external autonomy.[1] Political entities in early modern Europe tended to be territorially ill-defined, and perceptions of legitimate warfare were broadly understood in the context of redress and vengeance and dominated by commonly held cultural values of chivalry (Parker 1995). In this context, a war was considered just only if had the features of both *jus ad bellum*—referring to a just cause for entering war—and *jus in bello*—referring to just conduct in war (Best 1994). The discourse surrounding a just cause to go to war at this time was predominantly rooted in Christian doctrine, which was most notably derived from the writings of St. Augustine in the fifth century, and largely dominated by a language of humanitarian justice and the protection of innocent Christians against wrongdoing. In essence, a leader had the right to initiate war in order to protect the innocent from harm, and those deserving protection were typically identified as such because of their membership in the same religious group as the war-waging entity. A prime example of the humanitarian discourse in *just ad bellum* claims in this period of time before the advent of the modern state is found in the speech given by Pope Urban II as he called for the start of a crusade in the year 1095:

> Since, O sons of God, you have promised the Lord to maintain peace more earnestly than heretofore in your midst, and faithfully to sustain the rights of the Holy Church, there still remains for you . . . a very necessary work. . . . For you must hasten to carry aid to your brethren dwelling in the East, who need your help, which they have often asked. For the Turks, a Persian people, have attacked them, as many of you already know . . . and, by seizing more and more of the lands of the Christians, they have already often conquered them in battle, have killed and captured many, have destroyed the churches, and have devastated the kingdom of God. If you allow them to continue much longer, they will subjugate God's faithful yet more widely. . . . Oh, what reproaches will be charged against you by the Lord Himself if you have not helped those who are counted, like yourselves, of the Christian faith! (quoted in Krey 1921:24)

This statement of justification makes apparent two components that define a framework of justification more broadly. First, it identifies the authority from which the right to wage war is drawn, in this case, the supernatural authority of the Christian God. This comprises the overarching logic of justification. Second, it identifies the reason and for whose benefit the war should be fought—in this case, it is for the safety and protection of fellow Christians living in the Holy Land. This comprises the discourse of justification. I will discuss the logic and discourses of justification in greater detail below.

After the treaty of Westphalia in 1648, the sovereign state increasingly became the dominant political authority in international relations. In correspondence with the solidification of territorial boundaries and the increasing recognition and subsequent legitimation of state authority in international law, the state became the highest authority in the war-making process, corresponding with the transfer of legitimate political authority from a sovereign body in the form of a monarch to the sovereign body of a community of citizens, defined in terms of their membership to a territorially based state government (Walzer 1977). Since a growing body of international law during the 19th and 20th centuries defined and codified the laws of war and the codes of conduct that countries should abide by when engaging in war, the logic of justification increasingly drew on the sovereign rights of states as the overarching authority to wage war; whereas discourses of justification increasingly came to invoke the interests of the states, rather than for the protection of people. During the era of the modern state, justifications framed in terms of humanitarian justice fell by the wayside in favor of justifications rooted in notions of state sovereignty and embedded in international law.

Recently, however, a number of scholars have noted an apparent revival of the just-war doctrine in which the logic of justification draws on religious and moral precepts rather than international law, and the discourses of humanitarian justice and protection of the innocent have once again come to the forefront of international relations. Richard Falk (2004) has argued that the reemergence of a just-war discourse after the Cold War is explained by the inability of international law to address the changes in technology, organization of conflict, and the emergence of powerful non-territorial actors that occurred during, and particularly after, the Cold War. Since international laws of war were based on the regulation of violence between territorial states, just-war discourse provided a "more flexible notion of permissible use of force" for states that found themselves confronted by violence waged by non-state actors. For Falk (2005), that the just-war doctrine has been revived is taken as a given and is seen as the result of processes parallel to those which have given rise to the distinction between legality and legitimacy in cases of the use of international force for the purposes of humanitarian assistance.

Peter Lawler (2002) shares the opinion that the unconventional nature of many conflicts in the post–Cold War era has spurred a reformulation of justifications. Since conventional justifications were situated in the context of wars between sovereign states, the increasing prevalence of attacks waged by non-state actors has forced state leaders to develop new justifications to fit these new conflicts. As a consequence, the moral frameworks surrounding post–Cold War conflicts have come to be characterized by a discourse of the "good war," which can take the form of the "war-waging" narrative or a "criminality" narrative. Lawler suggests that the "war-waging" narrative—which has been the dominant narrative used by the United States—reinforces the established state-centric system of war, whereas the "criminality" narrative poses a challenge to these conventions and "anticipates the ultimate transcendence of the war system as a corollary of a larger logic of global transformation" (2002:164). In other words, the logic of justification for war-making provides a concrete manifestation of broader processes of stability and transformation within a global political organization, a transformation that is marked by the emergence of a new kind of war. Lawler's account suggests that in this new war environment, states cannot simply use force in the name of their own interests and by the authority of their sovereign rights, but should instead legitimize the value of the use of force in terms of its humanitarian benefits; it should be a "good war." Helen Dexter also places these changes in the new war security environment of the post–Cold War era in which the "changing normative context that has seen attitudes towards state sovereignty and humanitarian intervention on behalf of the UN shift, has also informed the general understanding that any use of force should be for the good of humanity" (2008:58).

A prominent example of the resurgence of this understanding of justifiable war is that of the Bush administration at the start of the Iraq War in 2003, which drew on Christian references of the crusades and emphasized the potential humanitarian dangers that would result from inaction. In similar terms to those used by Pope Urban II at the start of the first crusade, Bush warned "[t]he danger is clear: using chemical, biological, or one day, nuclear weapons, obtained with the help of Iraq, the terrorists could fulfill their stated ambitions and kill thousands or hundreds of thousands of innocent people in our country, or any other" (Bush 2003). The example of the Bush administration's justification of the invasion of Iraq is heavily cited in the just-war revival arguments as evidence of the resurgence of humanitarian claims trumping those to state sovereignty in a context where a strong sovereign state government is under threat from a territorially nebulous terrorist organization. The formulations of a just-war revival center on two basic claims. First, that the use of humanitarian claims as a basis for justifying the initiation of conflict have re-emerged in the post–Cold War era, and especially after the events of 9/11, after a period of dormancy throughout most of the modern era. Second, that this revival of just-war discourse has occurred in the context of and as a response to the declining significance of the sovereign state's authority in international relations.

These two claims, the latter in particular, are likewise prominent within the new war literature that identifies a fundamental change in the nature of warfare since the end of the Cold War bipolar superpower system. The new war perspective suggests that myriad forces—including increasing globalization, the rise of terrorism, the resurgence of religious fundamentalism, and the growing prevalence of non-state combatants in war—have coalesced to undermine the conventional political authority of the sovereign state. All these changes are reflected in a new reality of warfare, war that no longer means decisive battles fought on front lines by uniformed soldiers, supplied and controlled by the government of a state, and fought for clear political goals, but rather war which is pervasive in both time and space, fought by criminals and bandits for abstract ideological goals, and waged with no clear distinction between belligerents and victims, beginning and end.

The premise of these arguments is that due to patterns of globalization, state sovereignty has become de-centered, as conflicts have become transnational (Bauman 2001; Kaldor 1999). Changes in the international environment, including a shift toward overlapping and territorially diverse economic and political interconnections, have led to a "fragmented sovereignty" with the potential to undermine national state-based sovereignties in the developing world (Davis 2010). These changing patterns of warfare also highlight a shift in motivation for war from the political to the ideological, resulting in non-state actors gaining greater influence in war-making and decreasing the ability of state organized militaries to quell violence (Keegan 1993; Van Creveld 1991). There is also a strong connection with these new patterns of war and the patterns of war-making that existed before the emergence of the sovereign state, namely, the dispersion of the control of violence among a variety of groups organized across territorial boundaries, under dispersed and overlapping loci of authority (Mueller 2004; Münkler 2005). Although many argue that such patterns pose a serious danger to global political stability and human life, not all are convinced that trends of dispersing sovereign authority warrant such pessimism. Cosmopolitans, for example, emphasize the ways in which the erosion of state sovereignty offers hope for a new kind of global political system that values universal human rights over the power of states (Held 2003; Parekh 2002; Pogge 2002). What these perspectives share is a vision of the post–Cold War global climate in which the political authority of the state is undergoing serious transformation.

Critiques of the new war perspective have largely centered on issues of measurement and definition. One set of critiques argues that empirical analyses of recent wars reveal that the surge in non-state and non-territorially bound combatants may have been overstated, and that the sovereign state has been and continues to be the dominant player in contemporary conflicts (Chojnacki 2003; Fearon and Laitin 2003). A second critique suggests that new wars are largely a matter of perception, and that greater attention to the historical variety in both current and past conflicts (Newman 2004) as well as critical engagement with how conceptual categories are employed (Kalyvas 2001), reveals that the "newness" of wars is often exaggerated and does not stand up to scrutiny.

These criticisms are similarly applicable to the just-war revival claims. These arguments, although well-grounded in the history of international law, do not offer sufficient conceptual clarity about the variety of justification frameworks that can be employed and what the use of these frameworks indicate about the political authority on which they draw. For example, language related to human rights and the protection of people is uncritically equated with just-war doctrine in these accounts, whereas these accounts fail to consider possibilities for making claims regarding the protection of people in ways that, in fact, invoke the authority of the sovereign state, such as when a state invokes its obligation to protect its citizens. In addition, the just-war revival arguments rely heavily on two prominent examples: the U.N. intervention in Kosovo in 1999 and the U.S. invasion of Iraq in 2003. Although these were two very important conflicts, relying exclusively on these two cases does not allow for sufficient comparisons across cases of different types of conflicts. Since new war and just-war revival accounts have strongly emphasized the role of non-state combatant groups in spurring the shift toward the humanitarian logic of justification, it is important to compare how combatants justify the initiation of conflict in cases of inter-state and asymmetrical wars.

This study takes as its point of departure that the discursive frameworks used by leaders to justify war provide evidence of how legitimate political authority is conceived of in particular sociohistorical contexts.

As such, these justification frames provide important pieces of evidence that can be used to make claims about broader transformations in the political authority of the state system. Understanding transformations in the sovereign state system is an extremely large and complex puzzle, and examining justification frames for war can only address one small, but important, piece of that puzzle. They provide evidence of widely held conceptions about the perceived legitimacy of state sovereignty as the basis of political authority and, therefore, can be interpreted as reflections of the status of that authority in the minds of political and military leaders. Using justifications for war-making is especially appropriate for understanding transformations in the state system for several reasons. One of the key defining features of the sovereign state in its traditional Weberian definition is its ability to monopolize the legitimate use of violence within its claimed territory and to preserve its external autonomy. It is this perceived necessity of the sovereign state to monopolize warmaking that has led many scholars to question its continued dominance. Justifications for war-making also offer a unique way for understanding how legitimate authority is conceived of in a specific historical moment and social context. War serves as a historical juncture in which authority should be publicly and explicitly articulated in order to gain both the material and moral support that is necessary to wage it. In order to gain this support, the leadership should articulate to its constituent population, in a manner that resonates with their perception of legitimate authority, why the act of war-making is appropriate. These articulations provide the necessary documentation for analyzing how legitimate political authority is conceived of in a specific moment and place. By mapping these justifications, we are able to uncover, broadly speaking, the strength of the concept of state sovereignty in contemporary modes of reasoning as well as better understand how this concept has transformed over time.

Analyzing transformations in political authority through its linguistic and discursive manifestations is particularly appropriate because political culture—and political authority specifically—is discursively constituted. Political authority is a matter of linguistic authority, "first, in the sense that political functions are defined and allocated within the framework of a given political discourse; and second, in the sense that their exercise takes the form of upholding authoritative definitions of the terms within that discourse" (Sewell 2005:334). Approaching political authority from a discursive interpretation is also a means to illuminate the connections between human agency and historical context. Human agents "find their being within language; they are, to that extent, constrained by it.

Yet they are constantly working with it and on it, playing at its margins, exploiting its possibilities, and extending the play of its potential meanings, as they pursue their purposes and projects" (Baker 1990:4). Thus, the language invoked to express political authority can reveal important details about the historical and structural context in which it is employed. To be authoritative, expressions of political authority should work within the boundaries of what is already accepted as legitimate, but can simultaneously reify boundaries while pushing them in a new direction. This understanding of political authority as expressed through linguistic frameworks proves useful for the current project. A similar understanding of linguistic frameworks is provided by Goffman (1986), whose theory of frame analysis conceives of primary frameworks as discursive expressions which render meaningful aspects that would otherwise be meaningless. Frame analysis has typically been employed in the study of social movements and the identification of processes by which frames align to produce resonance among participating individuals.[2] The goal of the current project is not to determine the resonance or effectiveness of sovereign and humanitarian justifications per se, but rather to ground these justifications in their broader social contexts. That is, the degree to which the populace accepts or rejects these justifications is not the object of analysis; rather, the fact that leaders employ the logic which they perceive to hold power within their own particular contexts is evidence of their resonance. In this regard, Goffman's concept of social frameworks provides a useful set of tools to conceive of justifications for war-making as frames that are situated in specific historical contexts.

Drawing on Goffman's theory of linguistic frameworks and Sewell's theory of the discursive constitution of politics, I develop a scheme of frameworks that maps the possible range of logic and the discourses of justification. I define the *logic of justification* as a widespread and normative pattern of reasoning which is invoked to substantiate the reasons that the initiation of a conflict by one polity against another is deemed appropriate. Drawing from the histories of the just-war tradition and modern international law from Walzer (1977, 2002) and Best (1994), I identify two central logics of justification that have been historically employed: the logic of humanitarian justice and the logic of sovereign rights. These logics encompass the authority that actors claim as the basis of their justification to engage in war-making; in contrast, the discourse of justification encompasses the reasons for the need to engage in war-making. Within these logics, the discourse of justification that is invoked can be either humancentric—referring to the obligation to protect people

Table 1 Justification Frames

		Discourse of Justification	
		Obligation to protect/ defend people	*Power to protect/ defend interests*
Logic of Justification	*Sovereign rights*	State as protector	State power-interests
	Humanitarian justice	Suffering of innocents	Group preservation

from undue harm—or interest-centric—referring to the need to protect and defend material and status interests. Within these logics and discourses of justification, four primary justification frames are identified: the state as protector, state power-interests, suffering of innocents, and group preservation. Table 1 maps this scheme of justification frames.

A justification frame that employs a logic of sovereign rights and a human-centric discourse is referred to as a *state-as-protector* frame. Here, justifications for war-making center on the responsibility of the state apparatus to protect and defend the people under its rule. This justification is based on one of the traditional defining features of the state system—that of the state holding a monopoly over the legitimate use of force. Since the state (largely) denies its citizens the right to use force for their own protection, it has a responsibility to provide protection for those citizens against any perceived threat to their safety. The state-as-protector frame is often used in the context of a state protecting its own citizens, but this is not always the case. This frame may also be used by a state to justify fighting for the protection of the citizens of another state, arguing that if a state is not fulfilling its obligation to protect its citizenry, then it becomes the responsibility of another state to step in and fill that role. Similarly, an absence-of-state argument may be used by a group within a state by claiming that since the state is not fulfilling its obligation to protect its citizenry, another polity should take on this responsibility until the state proves capable of doing so. The key component that distinguishes the state-as-protector frame from humanitarian justifications which call for the protection of innocents, which will be discussed in greater detail below, is that the identity of those who are due protection is defined in terms of a geographic location; that is, they largely occupy a distinct location which can be territorially identified and is (or is supposed to be) under the rule of a territorially delineated government. Their physical location within specific geographic boundaries warrants their protection.

A justification frame that employs a sovereign rights logic and an interest-centric discourse is referred to as a *state power-interests* frame. This frame justifies war-making in terms of the power and authority possessed by the state to protect and defend its interests, namely, material and status interests. Material interests refer primarily to territory and natural resources, whereas status interests refer to the need to establish or maintain beneficial relations with other (typically similarly organized) polities and the need to defend against threats to the status quo. In other words, the state power-interests frame is primarily concerned with the prevention of a disruption to the established system of polity organization, in this case, the international system of states. Similar to the state-as-protector frame, the state power-interests frame can invoke an absence-of-state claim, but here the absence-of-state claim is used to argue that war-making is necessary to protect the material and/or status interests of a citizen body because the state that is imbued with the authority to do so is either unwilling or unable to act.

A justification frame that employs a humanitarian justice logic and a human-centric discourse is referred to as a *suffering of innocents* frame. This frame justifies war-making in the broad context of human rights and typically invokes the idea of the prevention of suffering of innocent people as a basis for action. Let us recall the distinction made earlier between the state-as-protector and the suffering-of-innocents frames in terms of how the identity characteristics of the group warrants protection; namely, their association with territorially defined political organization. Human rights claims within the suffering-of-innocents frames are likewise distinct in the manner in which the claim invokes a fundamental right to basic security that is independent of association with any political organization.

A justification frame that employs a humanitarian justice logic and an interest-centric discourse is referred to as a *group preservation* frame. This frame justifies war-making for the protection of the interests of a group (again, based on an identity that is independent of territorial political organizations). These interest claims can be in terms of the protection of a belief system that is fundamental to the group's identity (in particular, religion), a broader claim of threat to the group's basic security and survival, the prevention of the spread of violence or security threat to other group members, or as a claim of unprovoked aggression. It is important to note that a *claim of unprovoked aggression* in the context of a humanitarian justice logic refers to the concept of a fundamental right to security that is independent of a territorial political organization. Claims of unprovoked aggression may be present within a sovereign rights logic, but in terms of national security interests, these claims are within a state power-interests frame. The essence of the unprovoked aggression claim within the group preservation frame is that the group has done nothing to deserve violence against it, but due to the aggressive actions of others, the group's fundamental right to existence is threatened, thus necessitating the use of force. This scheme of justification frameworks is used as the basis of a content analysis of the justifications for war used in the initiation of nine conflicts in the post–Cold War era.

Methods

With the aim of analyzing the frameworks used by political and military leaders to justify the initiation of these conflicts, I focus on how these logics and discourses of justification are expressed by leading political and military figures in publicly available speeches, interviews, and policy statements. "Leading political and military figures" is used somewhat vaguely, as the titles and positions of these figures vary depending on the type of government or military organization with which they are associated. Broadly speaking, leading figures include those who occupy the highest-level positions of leadership within their respective organizations and who are widely considered by other members of their organizations as representing that organization and its goals to the public. For state actors, this includes presidents and prime ministers or their official press secretaries who are responsible for disseminating their views to the public, as well as secretaries of state, foreign ministers, and the highest-level military leaders such as colonels and generals. For non-state actors, these figures might include an acknowledged official spokesperson, a founder of an organization, or a military commander who issues public statements.[3] The number of leaders identified for each case is relatively small, ranging from one to four. Given the research goals of this study, using statements from a small number of high-level leaders is preferable to sampling from a larger range of high- and mid-level political leaders and other public commentators. The justifications of high-level leaders matter because they are the official representatives of the war-waging organization and are responsible for disseminating justifications to the public in a manner that will resonate with them in order to obtain the material and moral support necessary to wage the war. Lower-level public officials, pundits, journalists, and others may express public arguments for or against the initiation of conflict, but they are ultimately not the individuals who are responsible for obtaining necessary levels of support to initiate a conflict. Therefore, it is only the justifications of the highest level of leadership, and thus a small number of individuals in each case, that is of interest to the current project. In addition to individual leaders, collective statements, such as proclamations and announcements issued to the media by military or government organizations representing each combatant group, were coded. These might include parliamentary declarations, an official statement from the office of the president, or a public declaration from a group such as Hamas. Since much of the scholarship on justifications for war-making has focused on the asymmetrical context of war as a primary cause of the shift toward greater humanitarian justifications, I will distinguish the cases I examine by the status of the initiating entity as a state or non-state actor.[4] This leads to three different types of conflict: inter-state, state vs. non-state, and non-state vs. state—the difference in these conflicts being the status of the initiating party as a state- or non-state actor.[5] By distinguishing between conflicts in this manner, I am able to determine to what extent each justification frame is associated with state or non-state actors and if states are likely to employ different justification frames when they are fighting against other states and when they are initiating conflict against a non-state actor.

Table 2 provides summary information for each of the nine cases evaluated in this study. Cases were limited to those that were initiated after 1990 and were selected from the list of conflicts between 1946 and 2008 which was provided by the UCDP/PRIO Armed Conflict Dataset (2009). From these, three conflicts of each type were purposively selected with the goal of providing a set of cases that ranged in terms of scale, geography, and start date. This variation is intended to introduce some element of control over variations in the scale of the conflict, the size and power of the combatants, as well as the stated goals of the leadership that are correlated with the justification frame used by the initiator.[6] Using the same entity in multiple positions—as the United States, Russia, Israel, and Hamas are—provides a degree of control over the particularities of these entities. Again, this is intended to demonstrate how justifications are framed in a particular historical context, namely the post–Cold War era, rather than as a consequence of the particularities of conflicts of varying scales and dynamics. In addition, several of the cases are a part of a larger series of conflicts that have been relatively continuous for several decades. Although I recognize the relationship of these conflicts to each other in the context of a longer and continuous history of conflict, for the purposes of this study, I treat these cases as independent because they

Table 2 Selected Cases

Conflict Type	Conflict Name	Side A: Initiator	Side B: Opponent	Start Date
Inter-state	Eritrean–Ethiopian War	Ethiopia	Eritrea	May 12, 1998
	U.S.–Iraq War	United States	Iraq	March 20, 2003
	South Ossetian War	Russia	Georgia	August 8, 2008
Asymmetrical, state initiator	First Russo–Chechan War	Russia	Chechan insurgents	December 11, 1994
	Afghan War	United States	Al-Qaeda, Taliban[a]	October 7, 2001
	Operation Defensive Shield	Israel	Hamas	March 29, 2002
Asymmetrical non-state initiator	Georgia–Abkhazian conflict	Abkhaz separatists	Georgia	August 30, 1992
	Second Intifada	Hamas	Israel	September 29, 2000
	July War	Hezbollah	Israel	July 12, 2006

[a] Although the Taliban was the acting governmental organization of Afghanistan until 2001, I classify this conflict as being asymmetrical for two reasons. First, the primary focus of U.S. military action in Afghanistan was, at least in name, directed against al-Qaeda. Second, the discourse used by U.S. leadership to justify the removal of the Taliban from power centered on a definition of the regime as an illegitimate governing body. Thus, according to the manner in which the war was talked about by the initiating party, both al-Qaeda and the Taliban were understood to be non-state actors.

mark a re-initiation of conflict after a period of relative peace, meaning that the leadership involved had to publicly justify their reasons for re-initiation. Similarly, I recognize that each of these conflicts is far more complex in terms of the goals and motivations of the combatant parties than I account for here. Although the specific and immediate reasons for engaging in conflict is necessarily particular to each conflict, it is the logical and discursive frameworks in which these reasons are placed that is the object of study.

Published news media accounts were used to identify the justification frames employed by political and military leaders to initiate armed conflict. Despite bias being present in news media accounts, the focus of the present analysis is not on how the journalists themselves or the readers of the accounts interpreted the justifications provided by leaders, but rather on the direct quotations from the leaders in question. The news media accounts are, thus, used not as the objects of analysis, but rather as a means to observe the objects of analysis, that is, the language used by leaders to justify conflict. Although the statements made by these leaders may be selected by the journalist in biased ways, I have no reason to believe that journalists invented quotes or attributed statements to leaders

Table 3 Codes Associated with Each Justification Frame

		Discourse of Justification	
		Obligation to protect/ defend people	*Power to protect/ defend interests*
	Sovereign rights	**State as protector**	**State power-interests**
		-Obligation to own citizens	-Material interests (territory, resources)
		-Obligation to other citizens	-Status interests (foreign relations, international or national law, general national security, and aggression against state)
Logic of Justification		-Absence of state (need to protect citizens)	-Absence of state (need to protect interests)
	Humanitarian justice	**Suffering of innocents**	**Group preservation**
		-Human rights	-Threat to group existence
		-Protection of innocents	-Preservation of belief systems
		-Prevention of future human suffering	-Prevention of spreading of violence to other group members
			-Unprovoked aggression against non-territorially defined group

which they did not actually make. The quotations uncovered in these accounts, therefore, represent the best set of information on how leaders justify war that I am able to identify. News media accounts were located using the LexisNexis Academic Major World Publications search engine, which provides the advantage of access to both U.S. and international publications, although some bias may exist due to the fact that selected publications were limited to those that were written in or translated into English.[7] The names of leading political and military leaders of each entity as well as the location of the conflict were used as search terms, and search results were restricted to the dates 30 days before and 30 days after the start of the conflict. These results were then narrowed to those news articles in which the leader was quoted with reference to the conflict in question. These documents were then coded using a content analysis coding software according to the defining features of the justification frames outlined earlier. The frequencies of each of these codes for each conflict and type of conflict were then counted in order to determine the prevalence of each justification frame. Duplicate references to identical speeches or statements were excluded from coding. A summary of the codes associated with each frame is provided in Table 3.

Results

Content analysis of the justification frames employed by leaders in the initiation of nine post–Cold War conflicts reveals that across all conflicts, state power-interests was the dominant frame used by both state and non-state combatants, comprising 269 of the 523 total statements of justification, or 51.4% of all justification frames. Altogether, sovereign rights frames comprised 61.8% of all justification frames, whereas humanitarian justice frames comprised 38.2% of all justification frames. The state-as-protector frame was the least employed justification, comprising 10.3% of all frames, whereas the suffering-of-innocents frame and the group preservation frame each comprised approximately 19% of the total frames. Summary information on the code counts of each justification frame by conflict type is provided in Table 4.

The central claim of the just-war revival perspective—that changes in the organization of conflict and the emergence of powerful non-territorial actors in the post–Cold War era has led to the increased use of humanitarian discourses which emphasize the need to protect innocent civilians—was not supported by these data. Within inter-state wars, 22.9% of the justifications employed a suffering-of-innocents frame, whereas 18.9% of justifications employed in non-state-initiated asymmetrical

Table 4 Frequency and Percentage of Justification Frames by Conflict Type

Frame Frequency (Row %) (Column %)	Inter-state	State vs. non-state	Non-state vs. state	All Conflicts
State as protector	33	16	5	54
	(6.3%)	(3.1%)	(1.0%)	(100.0%)
	(17.6%)	(11.5%)	(2.6%)	(10.3%)
State power-interests	99	90	80	269
	(18.9%)	(17.2%)	(15.3%)	(100.0%)
	(52.7%)	(64.7%)	(40.8%)	(51.4%)
Total sovereign rights frames	*132*	*106*	*85*	*323*
	(25.2%)	*(20.3%)*	*(16.3%)*	*(100.0%)*
	(70.2%)	*(76.3%)*	*(43.4%)*	*(61.8%)*
Suffering of innocents	43	21	37	101
	(8.2%)	(4.0%)	(7.1%)	(100.0%)
	(22.9%)	(15.1%)	(18.9%)	(19.3%)
Group preservation	13	12	74	99
	(2.5%)	(2.3%)	(14.1%)	(100.0%)
	(6.9%)	(8.6%)	(37.8%)	(18.9%)
Total humanitarian justice frames	*56*	*33*	*111*	*200*
	(10.7%)	*(6.3%)*	*(21.2%)*	*(100.0%)*
	(29.8%)	*(23.7%)*	*(56.6%)*	*(38.2%)*
Total	188	139	196	523
	(35.9%)	(26.6%)	(37.5%)	(100.0%)
	(100.0%)	(100.0%)	(100.0%)	(100.0%)

conflicts and 15.1% of the justifications in state-initiated asymmetrical conflicts used this frame. In addition, the state power-interests frame, which draws most directly from the sovereign rights of states rooted in international law, comprised more than half of the justification frames in inter-state wars (52.7%), but nearly two-thirds of the justification frames in state-initiated asymmetrical wars (64.7%). In other words, in this sample, states were more likely to employ justifications that were rooted in the international laws governing states when they came into conflict with non-state actors than when they fought other states.

Distinguishing between lone and combination frames is an analytically useful exercise for understanding precisely what the use of sovereign rights and humanitarian justice frames mean in terms of the conceptual authority of the sovereign state system. Combination frames, in which both humanitarian justice and sovereign rights frames are contained within a single statement of justification, may provide evidence that the logic of justification is undergoing an important transformation in the post–Cold War era. By employing both types of frames simultaneously, leaders are appealing to a conceptual reasoning in which both justification frames are given relatively equal weight; this could mean one of two things. First, the more prevalent these combination frames are, the more evidence exists that sovereignist modes of reasoning do not carry enough conceptual weight on their own, and correspondingly, that humanitarian justice frames do not carry enough conceptual weight on their own. In other words, both modes of reasoning are used to mutually support each other. Second, the use of combination frames may be indicative that both modes of reasoning are conceptually strong and that the justification is strengthened even further by employing both simultaneously. In either formulation, this use of combination frames appears to be different from the way justifications were employed in both the pre-modern and modern state-based systems in which either humanitarian justice or sovereign rights frames dominated. However, although the use of combination frames seems to provide evidence for a transformation in justification frames, without a thorough comparative analysis throughout these centuries it is impossible to tell whether this does, in fact, represent any departure from the past. It is possible that this merely represents a transformation in definition and measurement of justification frames, rather than a change in the frames themselves. Combination frames constitute a noticeable portion of the justifications employed in all conflicts, whereas lone frames are dominant. Among these nine conflicts, combination frames accounted for 15.9% of the justification statements in all conflicts. These frames were most common in inter-state conflicts, accounting for 26% of all statements of justification, followed by conflicts initiated by non-state actors in which 13% of justification statements employed combination frames, and 7% in state vs. non-state conflicts (Table 5). Although code counts are useful for revealing general patterns, it is also important to understand the historical and social context within which these justifications are made. In the remaining part of the article, three brief case studies are provided, one from each of the three types of conflicts.

Table 5 Frequency and Percentage of Lone and Combination Frames by Conflict Type

Frame Frequency (Row %) (Column %)	Inter-state	State vs. non-state	Non-state vs. state	All Conflicts
Sovereign rights frame, alone	69	79	43	191
	(36.1%)	(39.8%)	(22.5%)	(100.0%)
	(55.6%)	(76.0%)	(40.6%)	(62.8%)
Humanitarian justice frame, alone	23	18	49	90
	(25.6%)	(20.0%)	(54.4%)	(100.0%)
	(18.5%)	(17.3%)	(46.2%)	(26.9%)
Combination of sovereign rights and humanitarian justice frames	32	7	14	53
	(60.4%)	(13.2%)	(26.4%)	(100.0%)
	(25.5%)	(6.7%)	(13.2%)	(15.9%)
Total	124	104	106	334
	(100.0%)	(100.0%)	(100.0%)	(100.0%)

The U.S. Invasion of Iraq

The U.S. invasion of Iraq in 2003 is perhaps the most commonly cited example by just-war revival proponents of the resurgence of humanitarian claims. The dynamics of this case make it a particularly interesting example of what many in the new war approach consider to be typical of the changing context of war in the post–Cold War era. It represents a conflict between two members of the international system of states, but its causes are rooted in the perceived threat of terrorist networks whose organization crosses territorial boundaries and that are not under the authority of any particular state. For the Bush administration, the possibility that weapons developed by the Hussein regime could ultimately be used to support terrorist operations against citizens of the United States formed the basis of its stated cause for war. In the 60 days surrounding the initiation of conflict on March 19, 2003, the highest-level Bush administration officials (President George W. Bush, Secretary of Defense Donald Rumsfeld, and Secretary of State Colin Powell) made 73 distinct statements of justification that were reported in major international publications. Of these, 60 were lone frames, and 13 were combination frames. Although humanitarian justifications were present in these statements, they represented a minority of the justification frames employed, and were as likely to be used alone as in combination with sovereign rights frames. The suffering of innocents frame, for example, was used alone in nine instances, and in combination with sovereign rights frames in nine instances. The most commonly invoked justification frame was the state power-interests frame, specifically statements invoking the authority of international law and the right of a sovereign state to defend its national security interests. The statepower-interest frame was used alone in 19 instances, and in combination with humanitarian justice frames in seven instances. Bush often cited the authority of international law as the basis for the right to wage war. For example, in a statement to Congress on March 19, he stated that "The President of the United States has the authority—indeed, given the dangers involved, the duty—to use force against Iraq to protect the security of the American people and to compel compliance with United Nations resolutions."[8]

The state's obligation to protect its citizens was the second most commonly employed frame, which was used alone in 15 instances or in combination with other sovereign rights frames, and in combination with humanitarian justice frames in four instances. Although the obligation of the state to protect its own citizens was commonly cited, more often, the state-as-protector frame was used to justify intervention in Iraq on the basis that, since the Hussein regime was not providing for the safety of Iraq's citizens, it was necessary for other states to intervene in order to establish an Iraqi state that would fulfill this obligation in an appropriate manner. Bush commonly cited the atrocities committed by the Hussein regime against the Iraqi people and the absence of protection offered by international law, such as through the United Nations, as a reason behind the United States' obligation to intervene: "The United Nations Security Council has not lived up to its responsibilities so we will rise to ours."[9] Thus, although the protection of people was a commonly invoked justification for the Iraq War, the authority to provide this protection was more likely to be framed in terms of the authority and obligations of the sovereign state, rather than in broader humanitarian terms.

Justifications in the U.S.–Iraq case were, however, more likely to employ humanitarian justice frames than in the other two cases of interstate war in this sample. This may provide some evidence in support of the just-war revival arguments. Both the 2008 South Ossetian and 1998 Eritrean–Ethiopian wars involved territorial disputes between states as their underlying cause, whereas the U.S. invasion of Iraq contained an underlying element of the perceived threat from non-territorially based terrorist organizations. Thus, perhaps the Bush administration needed to draw on the more flexible humanitarian language to justify this war due to the involvement of issues surrounding the use of force with non-state and non-territorially based combatant actors. However, as the next case study demonstrates, state actors in this sample were, in fact, less likely to use humanitarian justice frames in wars initiated against non-state actors than in inter-state wars. This finding suggests that there may have been some unique aspects to the U.S.–Iraq War or to the Bush administration's understanding of justifiable reasons for initiating war that led to a greater use of humanitarian justifications than existed in the other inter-state wars or in the other asymmetrical state-initiated wars in this sample.

First Russo–Chechen War

The three cases of asymmetrical war initiated by a state against a non-state combatant group demonstrated remarkably similar patterns in the use of justification frames. The state power-interest frame was the dominant justification used in all three cases, with the state as protector, suffering of innocents, and group preservation frame all exhibiting five or fewer instances across all three cases. There was also relatively little use of combination frames in these cases compared with the three cases of inter-state war: Both Operation Enduring Freedom and the Russo–Chechen Wars contained five instances in which humanitarian justice and sovereign rights frames were combined, whereas there was only one instance of this kind of combination in Operation Defensive Shield.

In the 60 days surrounding the initiation of conflict in Chechnya on December 11, 1994, 67 distinct statements of justification were reported in major international publications. Most of these justifications came from Russian President Boris Yeltsin and Foreign Minister Andrey Kozyrev, who strongly argued against opposition groups in the Russian Parliament to make the case for the necessity of taking action in Chechnya. The Chechen region had a long history of antagonism with the central Russian government and, after the breakup of the Soviet Union in 1991, Chechen separatist leaders became increasingly vocal about their desire to officially secede from the Russian Federation, and reports of violence and discrimination against the non-Chechen population led the local governing authority, the Russian-backed Provisional Council, to request military assistance from Moscow.

Although the human rights violations by the Chechen insurgents against civilians were cited by Yeltsin on several occasions as a reason to send troops to Chechnya, these claims were far outnumbered by sovereign rights justifications of the state's obligation to protect its citizens from harm and the state's right to use all force that was necessary to preserve its territorial integrity. Comparing the situation with the American Civil War, Foreign Minister Kozyrev stated that the Russian constitution "provides for the unity of the Russian Federation . . . and, yes, as President Lincoln, President Yeltsin will not tolerate defection, especially defection not by popular referendum or any free and fair elections in the area, but just a military camp. . . . It is just a criminal gang . . . the state has a right to use force to restore law and order."[10] Yeltsin repeatedly cited the Russian Constitution and the laws of the Russian Federation to defend his position on the use of force in Chechnya, declaring that "Russian soldiers are there to defend Russia's unity. This is a necessary condition for the existence of the Russian state. The Chechen republic is a component part of the Russian Federation . . . Not a single territory has the right to withdraw from Russia."[11] In a televised address to the nation to explain the deployment of Russian troops to Chechnya, Yeltsin stated that "this action by the government was prompted by the threat posed to Russia's integrity, to the security of her citizens, both inside and outside Chechnya, and by the fact that the political and economic situation could be destabilized."[12]

Although human rights violations were occurring in Chechnya, and these could have easily been used by the Russian government to justify their military actions, for the most part, Yeltsin and his government instead chose to ground their arguments for the use of force in the sovereign rights of states to defend their territorial integrity and the obligation of states to protect their citizens. Since similar results were found in the other two cases of state-initiated asymmetrical war examined in this study, these findings suggest that the just-war revival claims that the involvement of non-state combatants in war requires the use of more flexible humanitarian justifications may be overstated. This conclusion is also supported by the cases of non-state-initiated asymmetrical conflict.

Second Intifada

Another major claim of the just-war revival arguments is that humanitarian logics of justification have made a resurgence because sovereign rights justifications are not available to non-state actors. Since the post–Cold War environment has witnessed an increase in the number of wars involving such actors, this can help explain why just-war discourse may be exhibiting a revival in recent decades. The findings here suggest that this claim may be overstated. Non-state combatant-initiated conflicts exhibited a much higher use of the group preservation frame compared with other types of conflicts, and these conflicts showed a greater variety in the types of justifications that were used; however, even among non-state combatant-initiated conflicts, the state power-interest frame was still the most commonly invoked justification.

The Second Intifada was precipitated by the visit of then-Israeli Prime Ministerial candidate Ariel Sharon to the Al-Aqsa Mosque, which sits atop the site of the Temple Mount, an area considered to be holy by both Jews and Muslims. Most Palestinians, including the Islamist group Hamas, viewed Sharon's visit as an act of aggression against the Palestinian people, leading to the initiation of attacks against Israel on September 28, 2000. In the 60 days surrounding the start of the conflict, 142 distinct statements of justification were reported in major international publications. Many of these statements came from Sheik Ahmad Yasin, the spiritual leader and official spokesperson of Hamas, as well as Palestinian leader Yasser Arafat, and many statements also came from group declarations released from Hamas to the media. More so than in any other conflict in this sample, the group preservation frame was employed to justify the Intifada, being the second most commonly used frame after the state power-interest frame. The group preservation frame typically portrayed the broader global Islamic community as in need of protection, as when a Hamas proclamation declared that Sharon's actions at the Al-Aqsa Mosque represented "a hostile act against our Palestinian people and the Arab and Islamic nation, as an act of war on our religion and Islamic beliefs, and as showing disregard for the feelings of more than 1.3 million Muslims."[13] Yasin commented that Sharon's visit to the Al-Aqsa Mosque represented an aggressive act against the Muslim people as a whole because it embodied "the spirit of terrorism, criminality and aggression against the holy places of others."[14]

Territorial sovereignty was the primary reason invoked for the conflict, however, with the head of the Hamas Political Bureau, Khalid Mish'al, stating that "We have the right to resist because the enemy is on our land,"[15] and a Hamas declaration stating that the primary goal of the Intifada is to "establish national sovereignty over Palestinian territories."[16] Sovereignty over Palestinian territory repeatedly emerged as the underlying reason for initiating renewed violence against Israel, with Yasin often invoking international law to support the Palestinian right to control the area surrounding Al-Aqsa: "Al-Buraq Wall belongs to the Muslims in accordance with UN resolutions, and the documents we have proving this."[17] It is perhaps not surprising, given the long history of

Israeli–Palestinian conflict, that territorial sovereignty and international law would figure strongly in the justifications for the Second Intifada. However, the patterns observed in this case were consistent with those seen in the other two cases of non-state initiated asymmetrical wars and do not align with the predictions of the just-war revival arguments. Non-state combatant initiators drew on a wider variety of justifications and were more likely to employ humanitarian logics and discourses of justification than state initiators, suggesting that there are important differences in how state and non-state actors justify war. However, the claim that conventional sovereign rights frames are only open to territorial states and that non-state actors should rely on other logics of justification may be overstated.

Conclusion

The just-war revival that has been asserted by a number of scholars appears to have more nuance than has been offered. This analysis has revealed that sovereignist logics of justification for war-making are far from fading away; rather, conventional sovereignist notions of authority remain a powerful concept among both state and non-state actors, at least in terms of the prevalence with which political leaders invoke this language to justify the initiation of conflict. The prevalence of frames in which sovereign- and humanitarian-based justifications are intertwined may be indicative of the fact that the logic of justification is undergoing a transformation; however, the nature of this transformation remains unclear. In addition, what exactly the dominance of sovereignist justifications in post–Cold War conflicts means in the context of the continuing strength of the sovereign state as the central form of political authority is unclear for several reasons and points to the need for further research on several fronts.

First, the small number of cases examined in this analysis limits the extent to which the trend outlined here can be generalized to all conflicts in the post–Cold War era. In addition, an analysis that compares the logic of justification before the advent of the international state system and throughout the modern era is necessary in order to better understand how the results outlined here can be compared over time. It is one thing to claim that non-state actors pose a challenge to the conceptual authority of state sovereignty; it is quite another thing to claim that this challenge is somehow different or more serious after 1990 than during preceding centuries. It is necessary then to expand the historical scope and number of cases in order to establish more concrete and generalizable conclusions. The scheme of justification frameworks developed here offers a structure by which such an analysis can be conducted.

Second, more in-depth research on the specific contexts of some of these conflicts are necessary to understand the reasons why certain frames are employed over others. The U.S.–Iraq War, for example, exhibited a somewhat different pattern than other inter-state wars. This may be explained by the involvement of non-state terrorist organizations alleged by the Bush administration. However, other state-initiated conflicts against non-state groups do not exhibit a similar usage of justifications, suggesting that some other factors may be at work. In addition, the use of sovereign rights justifications by non-state actors, particularly with regard to territorial sovereignty, deservesfurther attention. This analysis raises an important question as to why non-state actors are employing sovereign justifications. If they employ these frames because they perceive them as being the only way to reasonably compete and be recognized by other polities, then this is indicative of the continuing strength and dominance of the sovereign state system. However, it is possible that these non-state actors are employing seemingly sovereignist language for other reasons entirely. These reasons can only be made clear through a careful and detailed analysis of individual cases.

In addition to these analytical issues, the findings here highlight a broader set of considerations regarding the theoretical assumptions about the threat posed by non-state actors to the political authority of the state. The results of this study indicate that just-war language has not necessarily been revived. Although humanitarian logics of justification and human-centric discourses that are characteristic of this just-war language were present in these nine cases of conflict, they represented the minority of justifications employed and were less likely to be employed in those cases which the proponents of a just-war revival would predict—namely, in conflicts between state and non-state actors. Why then did scholarship in the post–Cold War era begin to perceive of a just-war revival? Non-state combatants have been an ever-present threat to the authority of the state throughout its history, but scholarly attention to these combatants has increased, as the post–Cold War political climate has made their actions more salient. In this context, the tendency to perceive of the sovereign state system as being under threat becomes heightened. Scholars thus pay greater attention to the ways in which political authority was constructed and expressed in the period before the sovereign state system came to dominate political organization, increasing the attention paid to the logic of justification that does not draw on sovereign authority. Such attention, however, cannot reveal meaningful historical patterns when not connected with more rigorous and critical historical theory.

Thus, arguments in favor of a just-war revival are rooted in assumptions about the threat posed by non-state combatants to the political authority of the state, but these arguments often fail to thoroughly consider the historical conditions and processes preceding such perceived change and theoretically engage with the dynamics of power embedded within them. As a result, many of these analyses carry an implicit presentist fallacy in which the sovereign authority of past centuries appears stable and secure, whereas the current status of this authority is under threat and precarious. In addition, although much attention is paid to non-state combatants and the threat they pose to the sovereign state system, there has been very little critical examination of the broader historical processes that underlie the formation and actions of such combatant groups—namely the processes of European state formation and expansion, colonial domination and resistance to it, and post-colonial state formation. By adopting a broader historical and theoretically critical view of these questions, it becomes possible to see that the classification of non-state actors in post–Cold War analyses typically refers to people whose experiences and identities have been shaped by resistance to particular forms of state domination, such as Western colonialism. Envisioning a world of fractured chaos in which the sovereign authority that supports the stability of the state system is under siege results from a failure to fully and critically engage with the history of state formation and the emergence and spread of the sovereign state system beyond a narrow Eurocentric vision. Employing a characterization of the emergence and spread of the sovereign state system that accounts for the ways in which this system is permeated by unequal relations of power drastically transforms this image, forcing us to more clearly articulate what has changed and what has not when it comes to the political authority of state sovereignty in a post–Cold War environment.

Notes

1. This summary of the history of just-war discourse is decidedly Eurocentric, primarily due to the fact that such a vast majority of the international laws of war were of European and American origin, and the normative discourse and literature which surrounds the just-war tradition has been rooted in the histories of European conflicts and state formation. For a further discussion of these issues, see Geoffrey Best (1994).
2. A useful review of this literature is provided by Benford and Snow (2000).
3. To identify the leading political and military figures in each case, I employed a grounded approach of first examining the secondary histories of each case, identifying

those who emerge as central figures in these accounts, and also performing preliminary searches of news accounts of each case to identify those leaders who are quoted as giving speeches or statements justifying the conflict. I moved back and forth between secondary histories and news accounts until a saturation point was reached where I was satisfied that I had identified all major figures who had provided public statements of justification in each case.
4. The term "initiator" here deserves some elaboration, as combatants in any conflict tend to point to their opposition as the true aggressors. Although it is likely that some readers will object to my definition of the initiator in some of the conflicts under study, for the purposes of the present analysis I have identified the initiator of the conflict as the polity which first made a public declaration of action against another in response to a real or perceived threat. For example, although some may view al-Qaeda as the aggressor which initiated conflict against the United States on 9/11, this attack was a clandestine operation that was not publicly declared as an act of war against the United States before its enactment. The United States viewed this attack as an act of war and subsequently publicly declared its intentions to engage in conflict against al-Qaeda and the Taliban regime in Afghanistan, leading me to identify the United States as the initiator of the war against al-Qaeda in Afghanistan in 2001.
5. Non-state vs. non-state conflicts were excluded both because of the scant information available on such conflicts and because the present study is focused on the context surrounding state and non-state combatants that come into conflict with one another. Since inter-state conflict is considered a "conventional" form of warfare, this category is used in order to compare the differences and similarities in the logic of justification between so-called "conventional" and "non-conventional" conflicts.
6. This strategy inevitably led to the exclusion of some notable and interesting cases; for example, the first U.S.–Iraq War in 1991, which would likely have been included if space and time constraints had allowed for the inclusion of more cases in each category. A future iteration of this research will include an expanded set of cases that cover a broader historical range.
7. LexisNexis Academic is a search engine of global news reports covering events since 1980. Although I was restricted to analyzing news reports which were available in English, it is not to say that those reports were strictly from English sources that report on events in a particular area from an external perspective. Although these types of sources would certainly emerge in any search, the search results also include news sources that are indigenous to the area in question and which may have either been written in English or have been translated into English. Each of the quotes analyzed was found in multiple sources from several different countries, and I found no evidence of inconsistencies in the accuracy of the reported quotations based on the country of origin of the news report. Further information on LexisNexis Academic can be found at: http://www.lexisnexis.com/hottopics/lnacademic/.
8. Kennedy, Helen and Kenneth R. Bazinet. 2003. "Saddam Stayed, So War a Go." *Daily News (New York)*. March 20. Retrieved December 1, 2010 (http://*www.lexisnexis.com*).
9. Sun Wire Services. 2003. "48 Hours to Go: Saddam Must Leave Iraq or Face U.S. Wrath." *The Toronto Sun,* March 18. Retrieved December 1, 2010 (http://*www.lexisnexis.com*).
10. McGee, Jim. 1995. "U.S., Russia Officials Stress Mutual Interests Despite Recent Tensions." *The Washington Post,* January 2. Retrieved December 5, 2010 (http://*www.lexisnexis.com*).
11. Stanley, Alessandra. 1994. "Yeltsin Limits Air Raids on the Chechen Capital." *The New York Times,* December 28. Retrieved December 5, 2010 (http://*www.lexisnexis.com*).

12. British Broadcasting Corporation. 1994. "President Yeltsin Issues Address on Chechnya." *BBC Summary of World Broadcasts.* December 13. Retrieved December 5, 2010 (http://*www.lexisnexis.com*).
13. British Broadcasting Corporation. 2000. "Hamas Founder Rejects Summit, Says There Will Be Peaceful Protests." *BBC Monitoring Middle East.* October 16. Retrieved December 3, 2010 (http://*www.lexisnexis.com*).
14. British Broadcasting Corporation. 2000. "Hamas and PFLP Leaders Meet, Call for Joint Action and Coordination." *BBC Summary of World Broadcasts.* September 14. Retrieved December 3, 2010 (http://*www.lexisnexis.com*).
15. British Broadcasting Corporation. 2000. "Hamas Leader Mish'al Comments on Sharm al-Shaykh Summit, Members Arrest." October 19. Retrieved December 3, 2010 (http://*www.lexisnexis.com*).
16. British Broadcasting Corporation. 2000. "Hamas Issues Statement on Seizure of Joseph's Tomb." *BBC Monitoring Middle East.* October 10. Retrieved December 3, 2010 (http://*www.lexisnexis.com*).
17. British Broadcasting Corporation. 2000. "Hamas Leader Yasin Says Palestinians Alone Must Have Sovereignty over Jerusalem." *BBC Monitoring Middle East.* September 7. Retrieved December 3, 2010 (http://*www.lexisnexis.com*).

References

Axtmann, Roland. 1996. *Liberal Democracy into the Twenty-First Century: Globalization, Integration, and the Nation-State.* Manchester: Manchester University Press.

Axtmann, Roland. 2004. "The State of the State: The Model of the Modern State and its Contemporary Transformation." *International Political Science Review* 25(3):259–279.

Baker, Keith Michael. 1990. *Inventing the French Revolution.* Cambridge: Cambridge University Press.

Bauman, Zygmunt. 2001. "Wars of the Globalisation Era." *European Journal of Social Theory* 4(1):11–28.

Benford, Robert D. and David A. Snow. 2000. "Framing Processes and Social Movements: An Overview and Assessment." *Annual Review of Sociology* 26(August):611–639.

Best, Geoffrey. 1994. *War and Law Since 1945.* Oxford: Clarendon Press.

Brown, Wendy. 2010. *Walled States, Waning Sovereignty.* Cambridge: MIT Press.

Bush, George W. 2003. "Message to Saddam: Washington, D.C. March 19, 2003." Retrieved February 15, 2011 (http://presidentialrhetoric.com).

Chojnacki, Sven. 2003. "Anything New or More of the Same? Wars and Military Interventions in the International System, 1946-2003." *Global Society* 20(1):25–46.

Davis, Diane E. 2010. "Irregular Armed Forces, Shifting Patterns of Commitment, and Fragmented Sovereignty in the Developing World." *Theory & Society* 39(2010):397–413.

Dexter, Helen. 2008. "The 'New War' on Terror, Cosmopolitanism and the 'Just War' Revival." *Government and Opposition* 43(1):55–78.

Falk, Richard. 2004. "The Revival of the Just War Framework." *Harvard International Review* 26(1):40–44.

Falk, Richard. 2005. "Legality and Legitimacy: The Quest for Principled Flexibility and Restraint." *Review of International Studies* 31(2005):33–50.

Fearon, James D. and David D. Laitin. 2003. "Ethnicity, Insurgency, and Civil War." *American Political Science Review* 97(1):75–90.

Goffman, Erving. 1986. *Frame Analysis: An Essay on the Organization of Experience.* New York: Harper & Row.

Held, David. 2003. *Cosmopolitanism: A Defence.* Cambridge: Polity Press.

Kaldor, Mary. 1999. *New and Old Wars: Organized Violence in a Global Era.* Oxford: Blackwell Publishers.
Kalyvas, Stathis. 2001. "New" and "Old" Civil Wars: A Valid Distinction? *World Politics* 54(1):99–118.
Keegan, John. 1993. *A History of Warfare.* New York: Vintage Books.
Krasner, Stephen D. 1999. *Sovereignty: Organized Hypocrisy.* Princeton, NJ: Princeton University Press.
Krasner, Stephen D. 2001. "Abiding Sovereignty." *International Political Science Review* 22(3):229–251.
Krey, August C. 1921. *The First Crusade: The Accounts of Eye-Witnesses and Participants.* Princeton, NJ: Princeton University Press.
Lawler, Peter. 2002. "The 'Good War' after September 11." *Government & Opposition* 37(2):151–172.
Mueller, John. 2004. *The Remnants of War.* Ithaca, NY: Cornell University Press.
Münkler, Herfried. 2005. *The New Wars.* Cambridge: Polity Press.
Newman Edward. 2004. "The 'New Wars' Debate: A Historical Perspective is Needed." *Security Dialogue* 35(2):173–189.
Pogge, Thomas W. 2002. *World Poverty and Human Rights: Cosmopolitan Responsibilities and Reforms.* Cambridge: Polity Press, 2002.
Parekh, Bikhu. 2002. "Reconstituting the Modern State." Pp. 39–55 in James Anderson, ed. *Transnational Democracy: Political Spaces and Border Crossings.* London: Routledge.
Parker Geoffrey. 1995. "Early Modern Europe." Pp. 40–58 in M. Howard, G. J. Andreopolous, and M. R, Shulman, eds. *The Laws of War: Constraints on Warfare in the Western World.* New Haven, CT: Yale University Press.
Sassen, Saskia. 1996. *Losing Control? Sovereignty in an Age of Globalization.* New York: Columbia University Press.
Sewell, William Hamilton. 2005. *Logics of History: Social Theory and Social Transformation.* Chicago, IL: University of Chicago Press.
Snow, Donald M. 2007. *National Security for a New Era: Globalization and Geopolitics.* 2nded. New York: Pearson Education.
UCDP/PRIO Armed Conflict Dataset v. 4 – 2009, 1946–2008. Retrieved December 1, 2009 (http://www.pcr.uu.se/research/UCDP/data_and_publications/datasets.htm).
Van Creveld, Martin. 1991. *The Transformation of War.* New York: The Free Press.
Wallensteen, Peter and Margaret Sollenberg. 2001. "Armed Conflict, 1989-2000."*Journal of Peace Research*38(5):629–644.
Walzer, Michael. 1977. *Just and Unjust Wars.* New York: Basic Books.
Walzer, Michael. 2004. "The Triumph of Just War Theory (and the Dangers of its Success)." *Social Research* 69(4):925–944.

Relational Dialectics in the Civil–Military Relationship: Lessons from Veterans' Transition Narratives

Christina M. Knopf
SUNY Potsdam

Political and Military Sociology: An Annual Review, 2012, Vol. 40: 171–191.

This article examines U.S. veteran narratives of transition from Iraq combat to civilian life, using relational dialectics to explore the under-studied aspects of communication and interpersonal interactions in civil–military relations theory and studies. A close reading of eight veteran narratives at SupportYourVet.org extrapolates common themes regarding veteran interaction with civilian and military communities. The lens of relational dialectics, particularly the tensions of integration–separation, stability–change, and expression–non-expression, is used to offer possible explanations for divisions between civilian and military spheres, suggesting lessons to be learned about the civil–military relationship as enacted and as studied.

With the end of the war in Iraq, tens of thousands of U.S. troops have returned home; by 2013, over 30,000 more will return from Afghanistan (Shanker et al. 2011; *Telegraph* 2011). As operations in the Middle East conclude, more than one million of these returning service members will re-enter civilian life. President Barack Obama, in conjunction with First Lady Michelle Obama's Joining Forces Initiative, has taken action to help these men and women find employment, but the return to civilian life is not as simple as hanging up dog tags and getting a job; it requires "deconditioning"—a change of attitude from the habit of subordination to the team to recognition of the individual self (Higate 2001; Jolly 1996;

Slack 2011). In the streamlined, all-volunteer, postmodern military, few service personnel have the opportunity to fully consider life after discharge, and starting over as a civilian has both drawbacks and pleasures (Jolly 1996). Civil–military relations carry with them challenges that are similar to those in any other relationship or social structure, and the move from one sphere to another is wrought with conflict—much as is the move from single to married life or from independence to parenthood, and vice versa (Higate 2001).

Civil–Military Relations and Relational Dialectics

Civil–military relations are most frequently understood as the interaction of governmental authorities and institutions with the officer corps, but also increasingly include lower-level, or more ordinary, interactions between a public and its military in the widest range of civil society (Nelson 2002). Indeed, the control and direction of the military, particularly in the American republican democracy, is intricately connected to public opinion, in which the prestige and popularity of the military are components of its might, activity, and sustainability (Huntington 1957; Albano 1994; Burk 1999; Balshaw 2001; Young 2006). The challenge is to reconcile a military that is strong enough, yet subordinate enough, to do whatever civilians ask, and only what civilians ask, effectively integrating military capabilities to collectively respond to civilian needs. Civilian control of the military is maintained through a combination of political, strategic, legal, professional, and social norms (Huntington 1957; Janowitz 1960; Feaver 1996; Franke and Guttieri 2009). Huntington (1957), however, has noted that there is not a continuum stretching from a military ethos on one end to a civilian ethos on the other; rather, the military's values are static and universal, whereas the civilians' values vary individually and, as a result, tension between the professional aspirations of the military and the politics of its society can only be managed, not eliminated (Huntington 1957; Young 2006).

"There is a tendency for current understandings of the links between military service and civilian experience to be polarized" (Higate 2001:445; see also Boëne 1990; Feaver 1996). Increased concerns about these strains arose during the 1990s, diminished in the immediate aftermath of 9/11, and returned in the midst of Afghanistan and Iraq missions (see Hoffman 2007; Szayna et al. 2007). These tensions are typically identified as military alienation from civilian leadership and society, a growing gap between the military institution and civilian society at large, increasing politicization of the military, military resistance to civilian oversight, and the inappropriate political and social influence of the officers and military institutions (Owens 2011). Ricks (1997) explores the relationship between American society and the military, raising concerns about a widening and corrosive gap between the general U.S. population and its military culture, observing that the military has started considering itself as not only separate but also superior to its public. Jolly argues that, "[t]he military ethos itself discourages thoughts about civilian life. A member of the armed forces is made to feel he or she belongs to an élite, an élite which takes pride in standing slightly apart from the society which it serves" (1996:151–152). In November 1999, the Triangle Institute for Security Studies found a growing disparity between the political and social views of service persons and civilians, prompting a major PBS News Hour inquiry into the civil–military "gap" (Dunlap et al. 1999). The aftermath of Hurricane Katrina also raised concerns about the military's domestic involvement and the health of civil–military relations (Owens 2005). Richard Kohn (2008) foreshadowed a "crisis in civil-military relations," caused by the end of the Iraq War, unsustainable military budgets, an outdated military structure, and social issues—particularly gays in the military. Even the White House's Joining Forces Initiative acknowledges a breach in understanding between the 1% of Americans fighting U.S. wars and the 99% who—many in the military believe—sacrifice nothing (see http://joiningforces.gov).

There are various explanations for the civil–military gap. Huntington (1957), for example, points out the incompatibility of liberal thought, which emphasizes individualism, with military thought, which subordinates the weaker individual to the stronger group. Similarly, Hawkins (2001) identifies contradictions between key premises of American civilian culture—atomization/individualism, pursuit of comfort, freedom of choice, equality, and deliberation—and the contrasting key premises of the military institution—unity, endurance, obedience, hierarchy, and readiness for violence. According to Hawkins, the various permutations of these premises influence definitions of society, connections of individuals, and orientations to behavior that shape civil–military relations and the lifestyles of soldiers and their families. Other explanations can be found in the military's low profile in recent decades (Harper 2001); in the air of secrecy that surrounds even routine, non-war, military operations (Brelis and Kurkjian 1997); in poor media coverage of military matters (Wiegand and Paletz 2001); or in unrealistic ideals created by military fiction (Kinney 2005). Marvin and Ingle point to the ritualistic aspect of bloodshed in war, "The community regards ambivalently the soldiers they gave up for dead, who were sent to die but did not. Soldiers likewise mistrust the community that sent them to die" (1999:122). Some blame either the absence of most of America's elite from military service (Roth-Douquet and Schaeffer 2007) or the "undemocratic" nature of an all-volunteer force (Micewski 2006).

Relational dialects may offer another explanation. A relational dialectics perspective assumes a "both/and" feature to human relations in which relationships are experienced through, and defined by, the negotiation of ongoing contradictions. "Contradiction refers to the dynamic interplay of unified opposites" (Baxter and Montgomery 1998:4), which are frequently framed in terms of binary oppositions or as centripetal forces. It is a metatheoretical perspective about communication in relationships which assumes that contradictions naturally occur in social life, that these contradictions foster change, that people are simultaneously actors and reactors of their actions (praxis), and that there is an inseparability (totality) of contradictions and praxis from other temporal, spatial, and sociocultural phenomena (Baxter and Montgomery 1996).

Contradictions and praxis strategies are theoretically most important during critical moments in a relationship (Rawlins 1991) and appear either as polarized or as a part of a continuum. Several contradictions, however, have been observed in multiple relationship types. Integration–separation occurs when group or relational loyalties infringe on the need for individuality. Negotiating both interdependence with independence creates the internal dialectic of connectedness–separateness (or autonomy–connection). The external dialectic of inclusion–seclusion appears when an affiliated couple feels the pull to spend time both with others, such as outside friends and family, and alone with each other. Stability–change appears when there is a desire to maintain order conflicts with the need to avoid tedium. Taken to its absolute, this tension is one of continuing versus ending a relationship. Internally, this acts as certainty–uncertainty—the comfort of well-worn relationships against the excitement of the unknown. The external shape of this contradiction is conventionality–uniqueness—a need to "fit in" with others and yet still stand apart as special. Expression–non-expression occurs because of people's simultaneous needs for sharing and privacy. Internally, this tension is openness–closedness—the struggle of what to divulge to another. Externally, it is revelation–concealment—the balance of support and legitimacy versus public exposure (Baxter and Montgomery 1996). Praxis patterns may be healthy or dysfunctional and vary according to relationship type, but include things such as denial to subvert a contradiction, a balance in which a compromise is achieved, segmentation or cyclical alternation of need fulfillment, or purposeful communication between partners to manage contradictions (Montgomery and Baxter 1998; Sahlstein et al. 2009).

Other studies and critiques of the civil–military dichotomy have focused on the social distance and the political forms of civil–military relations, whereas a relational dialectics approach considers the relationship contradictions as being not only about separation but also integration. Though relational dialectics has been extensively used to examine varied family, romantic, friendship, and even organizational dynamics (see, for example, Baxter, Braithwaite, and Nicholson 1999; Baxter and Erbert 1999; Braithwaite et al. 2008; Golden 2010; Harrigan and Braithwaite 2010Kellett 1999; Rawlins 1991; Sabourin 2003; Sahlstein 2006; Schrodt et al. 2006; Toller and Braithwaite 2009;), its application in the military context has been very limited. It is, however, well suited to civil–military matters, as it addresses tensions in symbiotic relationships, integration, the unity of opposites, the communication of united-yet-competing values, and the co-construction of identities, while also acknowledging the use of ritual in unification and recognizing both formal and informal cultural prescriptions for the obligations and responsibilities of relational partners (Bakhtin 1981; Baxter 2004; Baxter and Montgomery 1996).

A study conducted by Sahlstein, Maguire, and Timmerman in 2009 found that three primary contradictions emerge for military wives during the deployment cycle: uncertainty–certainty during pre-deployment, autonomy–connection during deployment, and openness–closedness at homecoming. While sharing their recognition that "Military deployment is a unique relational situation that may serve as a heuristic for future theory and research" (Sahlstein et al. 2009:422), this study is interested in the perspective of service members themselves and in what relational dialectics might offer the formulation and comprehension of civil–military relations theories, outlooks, and practices. Therefore, the following research questions guided this study: What contradictions foreground veterans' return to civilian life? What praxis strategies are most commonly used or recommended? What do these patterns suggest about the "civil–military gap?"

Method

SupportYourVet.org was created by the Iraq and Afghanistan Veterans of America (IAVA), which was founded in June 2004 as the nation's premier nonprofit group dedicated to the troops and veterans of the

Middle East conflicts and their "civilian supporters." The IAVA has more than 200,000 member veterans and civilian supporters nationwide (see http://iava.org/about). The free SupportYourVet.org Web site is specifically designed to help the friends and family of returning service personnel aid young veterans in their transition from combat to civilian life. Advertised on billboards, radio, and television, particularly in base communities, it provides information about the transition process, with tips on how to make the homecoming easiest and a guide for how to engage in conversation with a returning soldier about his or her combat duty. It also outlines the mental and emotional tolls of war and offers resources about veterans' benefits. There are discussion boards where registered users can exchange stories and seek support; as of December 2011, there were more than 160 threads, ranging from zero to 237 replies each, spanning early December 2008 to mid-September 2011. There is also a section titled "In Their Words," where site visitors can read, or even submit, "personal stories of transition and readjustment" of veterans, their family, and their friends.[1]

Eleven personal stories are posted on this portion of the site. Two were written by military wives about their experiences when their husbands returned from war, and one was written by a military father about his experience with his son in battle. Eight were written by veterans of the Iraq War—four men and four women, representing no fewer than five hometowns, five bases, and four military branches, holding different ranks and jobs in the service. These veterans' personal stories serve as the basis for understanding the military conflicts in the civil–military relationship. These accounts represent a pivotal moment in the relationship—the point at which the veterans are making a major life change of retuning to civilian society, a defining moment for the dynamics of a veteran's personal life (Jolly 1996). "Investigators often find that their best access to personal relationships is found in participants' narratives about those relationships" (Conville 1998:21). Narrative methodology uses discourse itself as the means of observation and as the data (Conville 1997, 1998). Advantages of the narrative approach in studying relational dialectics include the ability of a story to capture a moment of an ever-changing relationship, allowing for a close analysis and the ability of a narrative to depict both behaviors and perceptions within a relationship (Conville 1997). Narratives are "both a means of knowing and a way of telling about the social world," and narrative inquiry focuses on how stories function in the creation and management of social identity, sense-making, and relational dynamics (Bochner et al. 1998:43. See also Bochner 2002; Tedlock 1991). These stories at SupportYourVet.org are considered both appropriate and useful for gaining insight into the civil–military relationship, because they were selected by a large, politically successful organization (the IAVA) as representative of the veteran transition experience, and have been featured for at least three years on a continuously active Web site that has been designed to help civilians cope with and support veterans returning from Iraq and Afghanistan. As artifacts for this study, the stories' public availability gives them social and political prominence, and, therefore, added significance that would not be available in other forms of ethnography or inquiry. In addition, the use of preestablished narratives reduces the chances for observer bias and social desirability, and the public availability of the stories also avoids concerns about breaching Operations Security.[2]

This research utilizes a structural analysis of relationship narratives, relying on the Dialectics of Relational Transition—an interpretive, qualitative approach that emphasizes intelligibility, offering a particular understanding of the phenomenon in question (Conville 1998). Richard Conville (1991) developed the two-stepped procedure based on the works of Barthes and Levi-Strauss, focusing on stories that highlight relational interactions. Step one is a chronological compilation of significant episodes in a narrative, focusing on the instances that drive the story to its conclusion. As part of this initial step, this study draws out the common themes and shared structural components of the eight veteran stories, providing a narrative of the veteran experience generally, rather than that of a given individual. In doing so, rich descriptions—ones preserving the original language of the veterans—have been included so as to acknowledge the particularities of the accounts, reflecting the effort of many dialectical scholars in encouraging readers to see and feel the struggles of relational participants (Bochner et al. 1998; Ellis 1995; Ellis and Bochner 1992; Rawlins 1991). Step two classifies these episodes using a grid to reconstruct the narrative according to its functions. The grid can then suggest particular dialectical oppositions that can be used to interpret the relationship.

As a second phase to this study, elements of the veteran stories, along with the advice and recommendations provided by the IAVA, were examined for evidence of praxis in the relational dialectics—that is, practices and suggested practices for managing a veteran's return to civilian life. This phase is considered beneficial to the study for three reasons:

1. Praxis is a primary assumption of the relational dialectic perspective.
2. The focus of SupportYourVet.org is, arguably, improving praxis. In fact, one billboard advertisement, as displayed in the vicinity of Fort Drum, home of the 10th Mountain Division—the most deployed unit of the Iraq and Afghanistan conflicts—emphasized this goal. The ad appeared as a giant sheet of lined notebook paper on which a letter was being drafted. The letter read, "Honey, Welcome home from Afghanistan. ~~Are you OK? Were you scared?~~" At the bottom of the billboard was the Web address of www.SupportYourVet.org.
3. Recognition of praxis can provide additional insight into the relationship and the military experience, as evidenced by the work of Sahlstein, Maguire, and Timmerman (2009), which revealed that military rules and norms have a considerable influence on how military couples manage the contradictions of deployment.

Analysis and Findings

Description

The stories generally follow a similar format. The writer introduces himself or herself to the community, typically by providing a name, current location, and vocation and then by stating the timeframe and location of deployment, station, and/or duty. What then follows is a brief mention of life overseas, referring to vague difficulties and challenges faced; then a description of the homecoming and the feelings experienced on the return to U.S. soil, to family and friends; and then to the civilian lifestyle more broadly (including things such as schools and jobs). Five of the eight narratives conclude with an acknowledgment of a greater purpose or good.

Deployment. Mentions of deployment recognized the life-changing, or life-ending, aspects of combat engagement. Joseph wrote, "You can't go to war without being changed. Even sitting on the FOB [Forward Operating Base] doing nothing, there's always the out of the blue threat of being mortared, with no warning. That wears on you." Another said, "Time slows down." Others used phrases such as "physically and emotionally grueling," "experienced daily mortar barrages," "brushes with death," and, simply, "scary."

Anticipation. These same emotions were reflected in the ways in which the veterans described the anticipation of and experience of their homecoming as well. As frightening as the experiences of battle had been, civilian life was, in many ways, more unsure—filled with more, and more varied, uncertainties than the basic black-and-white concern of life or death. Ashling wrote, "The thought of seeing my family again was overwhelming." Joseph said:

> I was scared. Iraq was a "simple" place for me. I had a job, I went and did it. I didn't have to deal with anything else, or any other people besides other soldiers. I didn't know what to expect from people back in the United States.

Meghan expressed a mixture of eagerness and reluctance. "I played my dreams of my first week home in my head over and over again making sure that when the day came I would be set and know exactly what to do and who to see." But, ". . . as I boarded the [final] flight [home] I got nervous . . . See [sic] my family was great but I felt in a daze I no longer wanted to do anything but sleep. The first night . . . was the quietest night of my life, who would have thought getting used to quiet would take time."

Homecoming. The homecoming moment—the celebrations, the welcomes, and the ceremonies—was jarring to the veterans. Ashling wrote, "The homecoming in Texas was surreal, running into the gym through smoke with loud music blasting, to see my family waiting for me." The pomp and carnival-like atmospheres were in sharp contrast both to the difficult lives they had been leading in the proverbial trenches and to the mundane world of civilian life to which they were returning. "When we arrived to our barracks, a tent was set up for a small welcome home ceremony where family members were reunited with their soldiers. The ceremony was overdramatic and just a show for those who had loved ones in attendance. For most of us who didn't have anyone to come home to, we saw it as an obstacle between us getting on with our lives," Cara wrote. "I remember standing at parade rest, trying to figure out which was worse, war? Or being forced to be a part of that ceremony?"

Re-assimilation. This discomfort continued. Michael wrote, "I did not feel like I belonged at home. . . . There were absolutely no support mechanisms in place upon returning from Iraq." Similarly, Baldwin indicated a lack of effective transitional resources, saying "I consider myself a pretty happy person, laid back, a joker, so when I came home it didn't take me long to get back into the swing of things, even though I came home unemployed and was basically unceremoniously dumped right back into the civilian world as a reservist." Joseph had similar complaints, mentioning how horrendous it was trying to navigate the Veteran Affairs bureaucracy. Bryan "pushed the limits" of civilian life, driving too fast, drinking too much, and taking nothing seriously.

Familial Interactions. A similar displacement occurred within family life as well. "I had trouble transitioning from a man in the field to a married man," Michael said, "My wife and my grandparents met me on the parade deck. I was delighted to see them, but something had changed." Cara observed, "My friends could have very easily detached themselves from me, but they stood by me and they never let me slip, which I could have very easily." Bryan, meanwhile, detailed his sense of being outside of, even above and beyond, the civilian sphere, ". . . with each day I felt myself getting more and more out of control, I would push the limits of what was legal and appropriate just for fun. I behaved as if no laws applied to me." Transitions to civilian life were described as "rocky" or "hard," with sensations of "being comatose" or just plain "awkward." One of the hardest areas for adjustment expressed by the veterans at SupportYourVet.org was not in the physical world of employment, housing, finances, family, and laws but in the mental and emotional world of switching from what Huntington (1957) described as the singular military mind to multiple civilian minds.

The difference in worldview between military personnel and society at large was noted by several of the veterans, each in different ways. Michael commented on the lifestyle structure itself, "Eventually I got out of the Marine Corps and swore that I did not miss the structured lifestyle and the things I had to endure while enlisted. A small part of me still misses it to this day." Cara complained more about the social structure:

> I was so disconnected to everyone I love, and everything that I was looking forward to getting back to. I didn't fit in; I was a fish out of water. I didn't have anyone else to share with that would get me, I didn't even know anyone else who had served and I didn't have anybody to talk about things with.

Meghan echoed this sentiment, saying, "I didn't feel different but I felt as though I was treated different." Cara got right to the heart of the issue, "I could've cared less who supported the war and who didn't, but I couldn't stand all the complaining and complacency I would see anywhere I went. The mindset of the average American made me angry." Baldwin, likewise, wrote of annoyance at America's outlook and knowledge of military and political matters:

> When I first joined the Iraq and Afghanistan Veterans for America, a non-profit veterans advocacy group, it was out of a sense of anger and duty. Anger at how my fellow troops had been treated, and a sense of duty to get the truth out there and let America know what was being done to its' [*sic*] service members.

Such expressions reflect Ricks' (1997) finding that the military views itself as distinct from and superior to the general population.

Veteran interactions. Though the veterans often could not relate to their civilian friends and families after returning from combat, they expressed new kinship with other veterans. Meghan wrote:

> They told us before we left that there was no bond like that of those that serve together. I didn't know what they were talking about until we returned. It is a year and a half later and I consider those men I served with to be family.

Baldwin experienced the same sort of empathy and camaraderie even with veterans he did not know through his own deployment. Of his work with the IAVA, he wrote:

> So even after serving, it was just great to see other vets, hear their view of things, and hang around these people who I still have a child like [*sic*] sense of respect for. [. . .]And even if they just went through the exact same thing you did, or maybe even especially if they did, then you have someone who understands your experience in a way that no civilian will ever be able to exactly understand.

Bryan even had to remove himself from the civilian life he had known before deployment—his hometown and family—and move in with a fellow veteran in another state in order to end the self-destructive behavior he engaged in during his transition. Such sentiments suggest that true comprehension between civilians and their military, irrespective of how closely linked the spheres are, is an impossible feat. Veterans feel more closely linked to those who also served than they do to the members of the society that they served.

This becomes especially apparent in the familial terms used to describe and designate fellow soldiers and veterans. Comrades in arms are "brothers and sisters." The larger veterans community is "family" comprising strangers who act as "parents, grandparents, brothers and sisters alike" who "were so happy to see us, one would have thought they were waiting for us the entire year to return. They had food for us, hugs, and well wishes." Ashling, who had experienced the "surreal" homecoming in a Texas gymnasium, was very touched by the unanticipated welcome she and her fellow soldiers received on their first touchdown in the U.S., at the Bangor, Maine Airport, by veterans from World War II, Korea, Vietnam, and the Gulf, along with their families:

> We were complete strangers to them, but it didn't matter. . . . My gratitude for the people of that community who came together to welcome all of us back onto U.S. soil was the ultimate heartfelt surprise each one of us wanted.

Cara, who was displeased with the ceremonial return her unit received at home, was similarly moved when greeted by three Vietnam veterans on the homeward journey:

> They were determined to have each individual soldier know their service was appreciated and not in vein [sic]. It's amazing how a stranger can genuinely care and make such a big impact on you at a time when you're not even aware that you needed it.

Both women labeled the veterans they met as strangers, and yet described them as family or as having familial traits.

Friends and family, conversely, were cast as near strangers. Michael stated that he was distant from his wife; they were later divorced. Cara was unsure what her friends thought of the "dark, angry" version of herself that she was on her return. Meghan talked about the unease she felt because of the attention she received in her small town: "[E]verywhere I went people thanked me, people I didn't know came up to me and thanked me. Walking around I felt as though I had this air around me that people knew what I had been through." Bryan wrote of returning to a broken family engaged in a custody dispute for his younger brother, but being mostly unconcerned with that in comparison to the allure of the American bar scene. The contrast created by the pictures of unknown veterans as family and kith and kin as unknown entities brings the civil–military divide into sharp focus.

Higher purpose. Marie's story was one of being in and out of different branches of the military, while working different jobs, attending different schools, and working on different degrees and careers. Her tours with the military were described with two purposes—a sense of duty and a desire for adventure/work experience. After the Iraq War began, she said, "I felt that I needed to come back in the military to do my part." After returning from deployment, she sought a new job and unit and took an educational/career interest in broadcast journalism that led her to work in Mobile Public Affairs, "so [she] could get experience as a journalist in the military." Marie was again sent to Iraq:

> While stationed in Baghdad, I was able to meet many different soldiers and experience more than I was ever able to before. I loved being in the streets of Baghdad, meeting the locals and telling the soldier's story.

This suggests a sense of higher purpose that was demonstrated in each and every veteran story. As Ashling said, "I don't think I realized until later, that upon my homecoming. I was no longer just a part of my unit or the United States Army, but that I would always be part of something so much larger." The veterans speak of being a part of something larger than themselves, and they speak of a need for Americans, at large, to pay heed to the military and veteran cause. Like Marie, Joseph stated that more could be done to help America's veterans. Baldwin's narrative focused on that same cause, and information posted to the comments section following Bryan's narrative identified him as an active Iraq and Afghanistan veterans' advocate. Michael prays that there is more support now for veterans than there was when he was discharged and acknowledges that the Marine Corps forever changed his life. Meghan concluded her narrative with a direct appeal to American citizens, especially civilians, "If I could say one thing it would be to support the troops no matter what your individual views on the war are. If we know and are reminded that people are behind us it makes all the difference."

Chronology, Classification and Contradictions

Developing a concise chronology of the veteran homecoming story is somewhat challenging, because it is not a linear process. Many of the veterans described both progress and setbacks in their transitions. There is, however, a loose ordering of events that can be proposed:

1. Life-altering combat deployment
2. Wanting to see family and old friends
3. Not knowing what to expect back home
4. Joy of homecoming
5. Surrealism of homecoming
6. Challenge of re-entering civilian life
7. Desire to reconnect with friends and family
8. An inability to relate to civilians
9. Yearning to return to military life
10. Networking with veterans
11. A sense of being called to a greater purpose
12. Acceptance of a new life situation

To classify the episodes, I considered each pair of events in turn with regard to whether they are similar or different. Was Episode 1 similar to Episode 2? Was Episode 2 similar to Episode 3? If similar, they were placed in the same column; if different, they were placed in different columns. Figure 1 can be read from left to right and from top to bottom,

Table 1 The Veteran Transition Analyzed

I	II	III	IV	V	VI
(Change)	(Stability)	(Integration)	(Expression)	(Separation)	(Non-expression)
Fears of uncertainty, desire for uniqueness	Wanting to return to normalcy	Need for belonging	Being able to share war stories	Sense of being different	Not knowing how or what to talk about
1	2				
3	4				
5				6	
		7		8	8
	9	9			
			10	10	
			11		
	12				

preserving the chronology of the story. Episodes 8, 9, and 10 each appear in two columns, because the episodes share similarities with more than one other type of episode.

Stability–Change. Veterans' knowledge that combat would forever change their lives, if life for them continued, cast uncertainty—the fear of the unknown—against certainty—the comfort of the familiar. There was, however, also excitement in the new experience and pride in recognizing how combat would make them unique in comparison to those they left behind. When faced with returning to the U.S., veterans again experienced this contradiction—the desire to see the people and places they know and love and doubt about what to expect from those people. By the time the combat tour was over, the known and the unknown had changed places. The military and war had come to represent stability, and civilian life was now the change. There was nothing truly unexpected in war. As horrific as the sight of fallen comrades on the battlefield could be, it was anticipated. Mundane life-and-death events, those outside combat scenarios and/or a part of civilian life, may, therefore, be even more distressing for military personnel, including veterans, because they appear more sudden and random, and coping with them should be done at more of an individual, rather than unit, level (Holmes 1985; Tyler and Gifford 1991). This transition is acutely seen in the fantastic qualities of the homecoming moments, as described by the veterans; the ceremonies and parties assuming "surreal" qualities, alienating the veterans from the civilian life to which they were returning and making the front lines more welcoming than the home front.

Integration–Separation. Closely connected to feelings of the known and unknown were contradictions of inclusion and seclusion. Veterans feel competing responsibilities with regard to group belonging. Just as combat became routine, the military became family. Although they missed their civilian family and friends while deployed and were eager and excited to see them again, they found that they missed their military comrades and often felt that by no longer being deployed, they were shirking a responsibility. This longing to return to combat then created feelings of guilt about not being there mentally with and emotionally present for their civilian families and friends. Conflicts of integration and separation also appeared in veterans' efforts at securing civilian employment or education. Several pointed to a lack of preparation and support in the return to civilian life, but there were also admissions that they were resistant to efforts which people made to help. There are, in fact, connections between the pride, toughness, and leadership fostered in the military culture and the reluctance of veterans to seek assistance in civilian life (Higate 2001).

Expression–Non-expression. Veterans' ability and inability to foster these connections with kith, kin, and other veterans speak to contradictions of openness–closedness, as they struggled with what, how, and when to talk about combat with friends and family—typically feeling that anyone who had not experienced it would simply not understand, or fearing that it would be too upsetting for their loved ones to hear. However, the mental and emotional well-being of veterans depends on their ability to express their feelings about deployment and return—which is why many of them network with other veterans. In addition, the irritation that the veterans felt about civilians' lack of war awareness and knowledge indicated a need for them to reveal their experiences so that others will learn and understand. However, discomfort with excessive civilian attention and their recognition of military restrictions on speech simultaneously encouraged them to conceal what they knew.

Suggested and Actual Praxis

In her study of veterans transitioning from military to civilian life in Great Britain, Jolly (1996) considered why some men and women were successful at constructing new identities as civilians, whereas others were not. She discovered that there is no standard prescription for avoiding contradictions and that there will be problems upon discharge, but that efforts to mitigate the difficulties can be beneficial. SupportYourVet.org strongly recommends open communication to help expose and navigate the dialectic contradictions. The Web site's section on "Starting the Conversation" states, "Keeping the lines of communication open can help you to reconnect and overcome homecoming jitters. It can also make it easy for you to talk about problems and get help, should the need arise." It recommends that civilian friends and family take the lead and start conversations with light, open-ended questions. However, it cautions that conversations may be one sided. Operations Security, stigmas attached to mental health, and the tough, masculinized culture of the military all act as inhibitors to veteran communication (Britt et al. 2007; Higate 2001; Parker 1989), resulting in praxis of avoidance. As Joseph wrote, "I try not to talk too much about specific [combat] incidents to my family. They're not for good conversation." In addition, the communication patterns and habits of veterans may have been shaped/altered by their service; the military frequently relies on the chain of command for transmitting messages and indistinct lines between public and private, work and home often encourage taciturnity (see, for example, Hawkins 2001).

The IAVA further suggests segmentation as praxis, particularly when veterans are reluctant to discuss their experiences and feelings. They are encouraged to talk to other veterans or to log on to online veteran groups. This form of praxis was extensively seen in the veterans' stories. Baldwin, for example, claimed, "All in all, I think every veteran can benefit from hanging out and talking with other veterans. It's an experience I recommend and enjoy every time." Segmentation may be preferable, because it is a praxis pattern that is consistent with military culture and maintains the familiar set of military versus civilian distinctions. Baxter and Montgomery explain that although people make communicative choices, they simultaneously "become reactive objects, because their actions become reified in a variety of normative and institutionalized practices that establish the boundaries of subsequent communicative moves" (1996:13). As Sahlstein, Maguire, and Timmerman discovered in their analysis of deployment contradictions and praxis in military couples, "praxis patterns are situated within the network of relationships and military culture that encompass these couples and influence their communication," and are often based on the sense of restrictions and limitations imposed on them by the military's influence (2009:437; see also Drummet et al. 2003).

Discussion and Conclusion

As the U.S. welcomes home the last troops from Iraq and gears up for the return of tens of thousands more from Afghanistan, there will be increased political attention on the veteran situation. Relational dialectics can offer new and improved insights regarding this aspect of the civil–military relationship. "The transition from the military to the civilian environment tends to be understood at the level of employability, with the deeper emotional and psychological levels largely outside the routine work of resettlement agencies, unless specific problems are noted such as Post-Traumatic Stress Disorder" (Higate 2001:447). The three dialectic contradictions identified here help to shed light on a key psychological element of the "civil–military gap"—the service ethic, which is emphasized in the veterans' stories through their references to the greater good and a larger purpose.

As Janowitz articulated more than fifty years ago, "'Honor' is the basis of [the military's] belief system" (1960:215), and both military identity and ideology are rooted in the public service tradition. The frustration veterans feel at the obliviousness and griping of the average American, their anger at the treatment of veterans, the bonds they forged with strangers who had also served their country, the restlessness of returning to menial, mundane lives and tasks, and their repeated calls for action on behalf of others all speak to a distinct service ethic felt by veterans—an ethic that, for them, was missing from civilian life. For Micewski (2006), the core question of how the military integrates with society is answered by the process of personnel recruitment. The use of an all-volunteer force contributes to the professionalism and specialization of an army, providing an appearance of respect to liberal notions of individual freedom while also contributing to the decomposition of society through co-existing, though not interacting, individuals.

Civil–military relations theories suggest elements of communication in their outlines of control, such as the maintenance of a professional culture and a free press, shared social norms, military education, and celebration of the esprit de corps (Huntington 1957). However, these theories have not fully integrated or examined the communicative or interpersonal processes involved in these practices. This study has attempted to correct that oversight by suggesting that relational dialectics can inform our understanding of civil–military relations. In doing so, it points to the possibilities of mediation between the civilian and military spheres—segregation and open communication as praxis and recognition of the service ethic at the core of contradictions in the civil–military gap.

This project was a foray into the cultural and interpersonal areas of civil–military relations. Similarly, future research should place more emphasis on the experience of the enlisted person and his or her interactions with civilians. Continued attention to relational dialectics in the military experience is encouraged; not only should future studies make use of interviews, with veterans of war and peace across multiple generations and their families, but they should also give increased attention to the ways in which military culture shapes praxis, with consideration both to formal speech codes and regulations and to media influence. This research reinforces the findings of Sahlstein, Maguire, and Timmerman (2009) that there is variation in the types and availability of communication and support resources available to military personnel, and praxis patterns may be significantly influenced by relational types and outside forces, indicating a need for a greater consideration of the broader relational network and cultural history—particularly in military situations.

With few exceptions, the research that addresses the cultural and communicative elements of the civil–military relationship focuses on civilian exposure to the military via popular films and literature, news media, recruitment efforts and attitudes, and enlistment statistics. Other civil–military relations scholarship emphasizes the military and civilian elite. Addressing the multiple concerns and possibilities regarding contradictions in civil–military relations that emerged from this study, and the normative and theoretical possibilities raised by using the relational dialectics perspective as a lens on civil–military relations, can enable military social science to move in exciting new directions.

Notes

1. In 2012, the IAVA merged the SupportYourVet site with its organization's home page, and the resources analyzed here are now found at http://IAVA.org.
2. Operations Security, also referred to as OPSEC, is the identification and protection of critical information of military plans (Department of the Army 2007).

References

Albano, Sondra. 1994. "Military Recognition for Family Concerns: Revolutionary War to 1993." *Armed Forces & Society* 20(2):283–302.

Bakhtin, Mikhail M. 1981. *The Dialogic Imagination: Four Essays by M.M. Bakhtin* (Michael Holquist, Ed.; Caryl Emerson and Michael Holquist, Trans.) Austin: University of Texas Press.

Balshaw, K.S. 2001. "Spending Treasure Today but Spilling Blood Tomorrow: What are the Implications for Britain of America's Apparent Aversion to Casualties?" *Defence Studies* 1(1):99–120.

Baxter, Leslie A. 2004. "Distinguished Scholar Article: Relationships as Dialogues." *Personal Relationships* 11(1):1–22.

Baxter, Leslie A., Dawn O. Braithwaite, and John H. Nicholson. 1999. "Turning Points in the Development of Blended Families." *Journal of Social and Personal Relationships* 16(3):291–313.

Baxter, Leslie A. and Larry A. Erbert. 1999. "Perceptions of Dialectical Contradictions in Turning Points of Development in Heterosexual Romantic Relationships." *Journal of Social and Personal Relationships* 16(5):547–569.

Baxter, Leslie A. and Barbara M. Montgomery. 1998. "A Guide to Dialectical Approaches to Studying Personal Relationships." Pp. 1–15 in Barbara A. Montgomery and Leslie A. Baxter, eds. *Dialectical Approaches to Studying Personal Relationships*. New York: Psychology Press.

Baxter, Leslie A. and Barbara M. Montgomery. 1996. *Relating: Dialogues and Dialectics*. New York: Guilford Press.

Bochner, Arthur P. 2002. "Perspectives on Inquiry III: The Moral of Stories." Pp. 73–101 in Mark L. Knapp and John A. Daly, eds. *Handbook of Interpersonal Communication*, 3rd ed. Thousand Oaks, CA: Sage.

Bochner, Arthur P., Carolyn Ellis, and Lisa Tillmann-Healy. 1998 "Mucking Around Looking for Truth." Pp. 41–62 in Barbara A. Montgomery and Leslie A. Baxter, eds. *Dialectical Approaches to Studying Personal Relationships*. New York: Psychology Press.

Boëne, Bernard. 1990. "How 'Unique' Should the Military Be? A Review of Representative Literature and Outline of a Synthetic Formulation." *European Journal of Sociology*, 31(1):3–59.

Braithwaite, Dawn O., Paige W. Toller, Karen L. Daas, Wesley T. Durham, and Adam C. Jones. 2008. "Centered but not Caught in the Middle: Stepchildren's Perceptions of Dialectical Contradictions in Communication of Co-Parents." *Journal of Applied Communication Research* 36(1): 33–55.

Brelis, Mark and Stephen Kurkjian. 1997. "Confronting the Enemy Within: Safety in the US Armed Forces." *Boston Globe*:A1.

Britt, Thomas W., Tiffany M. Greene-Shortridge, and Carl Andrew Castro. 2007. "The Stigma of Mental Health Problems in the Military." *Military Medicine* 172(2):157–161

Burk, James. 1999. "Public Support for Peacekeeping in Lebanon and Somalia: Assessing the Casualty Hypothesis." *Political Science Quarterly* 144(1):53-78.

Conville, Richard L. 1997. "Between Spearheads: *Bricolage* and the Relationship." *Journal of Social and Personal Relationships* 14(3):373–386.

Conville, Richard L. 1998. "Telling Stories: Dialectics of Relational Transition." Pp. 17–40 in Barbara A. Montgomery and Leslie A. Baxter, eds. *Dialectical Approaches to Studying Personal Relationships*. New York: Psychology Press.

Conville, Richard L. 1991. *Relational Transitions: The Evolution of Personal Relationships*. Westport, CT: Praeger.

Department of the Army. 2007. *Army Regulation 530-1: Operations and Signal Security*. Washington, DC: Army Pentagon.

Drummet, Amy Reinkober, Marilyn Coleman and Susan Cable. 2003. "Military Families under Stress: Implications for Family Life Education." *Family Relations* 52(3): 279–287.

Dunlap, Charles, Mackubin Owens and Richard Kohn. 1999. "The Gap." *PBS News Hour*. Retrieved November 27, 2011 (http://www.pbs.org/newshour/forum/november99/civil_military.html).

Ellis, Carolyn. 1995. *Final Negotiations: A Story of Love, Loss, and Chronic Illness*. Philadelphia: Temple University Press.

Ellis, Carolyn and Arthur P. Bochner. 1992. "Telling and Performing Personal Stories: The Constraints of Choice in Abortion." Pp. 79–101 in Carolyn Ellis and Michael G. Flaherty, eds. *Investigating Subjectivity: Research on the Lived Experience.* Thousand Oaks, CA: Sage.

Feaver, Peter D. 1996. "The Civil-Military Problematique: Huntington, Janowitz, and the Question of Civilian Control. *Armed Forces & Society* 23(2):149–178.

Franke, Volker and Karen Guttieri. 2009. "Picking Up the Pieces: Are United States Officers Ready for Nation Building?" *Journal of Political and Military Sociology* 37(1):1–15.

Golden, Mindi Ann. 2010. "Dialectical Contradictions Experienced when Placing a Spouse with Dementia in a Residential Care Facility." *Qualitative Research Reports in Communication* 11(1):14–20.

Harper, Howard. 2001. "The Military and Society: Reaching and Reflecting Audiences in Fiction and Film." *Armed Forces & Society* 27(2):231–248.

Harrigan, Meredith Marko and Dawn O. Braithwaite. 2010. "Discursive Struggles in Families Formed through Visible Adoption: An Exploration of Dialectical Unity." *Journal of Applied Communication Research* 38(2):127–144.

Hawkins, John P. 2001. *Army of Hope, Army of Alienation.* Tuscaloosa, AL: University of Alabama Press.

Higate, Paul Richard. 2001. "Theorizing Continuity: From Military to Civilian Life." *Armed Forces &Society* 27(3):443–460.

Hoffman, Frank. 2007. "Bridging the Civil-Military Gap." *Armed Forces Journal.* Retrieved November 27, 2011 (http://www.armedforcesjournal.com/2007/12/3144666).

Holmes, Richard. 1985. *Acts of War.* New York: The Free Press.

Huntington, Samuel P. 1957. *The Soldier and the State: The Theory and Politics of Civil-Military Relations.* Cambridge: Belknap/Harvard.

Janowitz, Morris. 1960. *The Professional Soldier: A Social and Political Portrait.* Toronto: Free Press.

Jolly, Ruth. 1996. *Changing Step from Military to Civilian Life: People in Transition.* London: Brassey's.

Kellet, Peter M. 1999. "Dialogue and Dialectics in Managing Organizational Change: The Case of a Mission-Based Transformation." *Southern Communication Journal* 64(3): 211–231.

Kinney, Katherine. 2005. "The Good War and its Other: Beyond Private Ryan." Pp. 121–38 in Giles Gunn and Carl Gutiérrez-Jones, eds. *War Narratives and American Culture.* Santa Barbara, CA: American Cultures and Global Contexts Center, University of California.

Kohn, Richard H. 2008. "Coming Soon: A Crisis in Civil-Military Relations." *World Affairs Journal.* Retrieved November 27, 2011 (http://www.worldaffairsjournal.org/print/1375).

Marvin, Carolyn and David W. Ingle.1999. *Blood Sacrifice and the Nation: Totem Rituals and the American Flag.* Cambridge: Cambridge University Press.

Micewski, Edwin R. 2006. "Conscription or the All-Volunteer Force: Recruitment in a Democratic Society." Pp. 208–234 in Thomas C. Bruneau and Scott D. Tollefson, eds. *Who Guards the Guardians and How: Democratic Civil-Military Relations.* Austin: University of Texas Press.

Nelson, Daniel N. 2002. "Definition, Diagnosis, Therapy: A Civil-Military Critique." *Defense & Security Analysis* 18(2):157–170.

Owens, Mackubin T. 2005. "Hurricane Katrina and the Future of American Civil-Military Relations." *New York Post.* Retrieved December 31, 2011 (http://www.ashbrook.org/publicat/oped/owens/05/katrina.html).

Owens, Mackubin T. 2011. "U.S. Civil-Military Relations After 9/11: Renegotiating the Civil-Military Bargain." *Foreign Policy Research Institute E-Notes.* Retrieved November 27, 2011 (http://www.fpri.org/enotes/201101.owens.civilmilitaryrelations.html).

Parker, Cathy. 1989. *Freedom of Expression in the American Military: A Communication Modeling Analysis.* New York: Praeger.

Rawlins, William K. 1991. *Friendship Matters: Communication, Dialectics, and the Life Course.* New York: Aldine de Gruyter.

Ricks, Thomas. 1997. *Making the Corps.* New York: Scribner.

Roth-Douquet, Kathy and Frank Schaeffer. 2007. *AWOL: The Unexcused Absence of America's Upper Classes from Military Service – and How it Hurts our Country.* New York: Collins.

Sabourin, Teresa Chandler. 2003. *The Contemporary American Family: A Dialectical Perspective on Communication and Relationships.* Thousand Oaks, CA: Sage.

Sahlstein, Erin M. 2006. "Making Plans: Praxis Strategies for Negotiating Uncertainty-Certainty in Long-Distance Relationships." *Western Journal of Communication* 70(2):147–165.

Sahlstein, Erin, Katheryn C. Maguire and Lindsay Timmerman. 2009. "Contradictions and Praxis Contextualized by Wartime Deployment: Wives' Perspectives Revealed through Relational Dialectics." *Communication Monographs* 76(4):421–442.

Schrodt, Pauk, Leslie A. Baxter, M. Chad McBride, Dawn O. Braithwaite and Mark A. Fine. 2006. "The Divorce Decree, Communication, and the Structuration of Coparenting Relationships in Stepfamilies." *Journal of Social and Personal Relationships* 23(5):741–759.

Shanker, Thom, Michael S. Schmidt and Robert F. Worth. 2011. "In Baghdad, Panetta Leads Uneasy Moment of Closure to Long Conflict." *The New York Times*:A19.

Slack, Megan. 2011. "Fighting to Help our Heroes Find Jobs." *The White House Blog.* Retrieved November 22, 2011 (http://www.whitehouse.gov/blog/2011/11/21/fighting-help-our-heroes-find-jobs).

Szayna, Thomas S., Kevin F. McCarthy, Jerry M. Sollinger, Linda J. Demaine, Jefferson P. Marquis and Brett Steele. 2007. *The Civil-Military Gap in the United States: Does it Exist, Why, and Does it Matter?* Santa Monica, CA: RAND Corporation.

Tedlock, Barbara. 1991. "From Participant Observation to the Observation of Participation: The Emergence of Narrative Ethnography." *Journal of Anthropological Research* 47(1): 69–94.

Telegraph. 2011. "Barack Obama to Announce Withdrawal of 33,000 Troops: Troop Numbers Since 2001." *The Telegraph.* Retrieved December 8, 2011 (http://www.telegraph.co.uk/news/worldnews/asia/afghanistan/8591148/Barack-Obama-to-announce-withdrawal-of-33000-troops-troop-numbers-since-2001.html).

Toller, Paige W. and Dawn O. Braithwaite. 2009. "Grieving Together and Apart: Bereaved Parents' Contradictions of Marital Interaction." *Journal of Applied Communication Research* 37(3):237–277.

Tyler, Mary P. and Robert K. Gifford. 1991. "Fatal Training Accidents: The Military Unit as a Recovery Context." *Journal of Traumatic Stress* 4(2):233–249.

Wiegand, Krista E. and David L. Paletz. 2001. "The Elite Media and the Military-Civilian Culture Gap." *Armed Forces & Society* 27(2):183–204.

Young, Thomas-Durell. 2006. "Military Professionalism in a Democracy." Pp. 17–33 in Thomas C. Bruneau and Scott D. Tollefson, eds. *Who Guards the Guardians and How: Democratic Civil-Military Relations.* Austin: University of Texas Press.

American White Nationalism: The Ongoing Significance of Group Position and Race[1]

David Bugg
SUNY Potsdam

Dianne Dentice
Stephen F. Austin State University

Political and Military Sociology: An Annual Review 2012, Vol. 40: 193–215.

Racist individuals often express an underlying need for recognition that may result in association with groups which operate outside mainstream society and are exclusively white. We present data gathered from a survey administered to members of White Revolution, an Internet Web site for people who self-identify as white nationalists. The survey was active during the time of the survey but was closed in August 2011 by its founder and administrator, Billy Roper. In this article, we explore questions regarding racialist attitudes about group position in the broader society, prejudiced attitudes about minority groups, and nationalistic tendencies in this population of survey participants. We ground the study in Allport's classical prejudice theory and Blumer's group position model to try to make sense of what entices a segment of the population to inflate their sense of worth based on race and to align with racist organizations. We also include findings from a 2004 sample of mainstream white Americans that utilized similar questions from the General Social Survey. Both surveys reveal that respondents agree that America is better than most countries; that to be a true American, one must speak English; and that the world would be a better place if people from other countries were more like Americans.

The ideology of self-identified white nationalists is fixated on race and its importance as an in-group signifier. This segment of the population is set apart from many mainstream whites because the issue of group position based on race permeates their discourse and drives their political motivations. The racial experience also influences their interactions and motivates them to socialize with likeminded others online and at organized group activities (Brown 2009; Daniels 2009; De Koster and Houtman 2008; Futrell and Simi 2004; Simi and Futrell 2006, 2009). Since the founding of Stormfront.org in 1995, the Internet has provided a mechanism for the establishment of online forums and discussion groups that cater to white racial activists and reinforce the emergence of a symbolic form of white cultural nationalism.

In 2002, a young Arkansas white supremacist named Billy Roper formed a group called White Revolution, which was anchored by a Web site of the same name. Similar to Stormfront.org, White Revolution contained a blog, promoted events, and posted writings by Roper, his mentor William Pierce,[2] and others such as Canadian eugenicist J. Philippe Rushton. In August 2011, Roper suddenly closed the site. We believe that he will continue to be involved in the movement in some capacity and he appears to be aligning with Thom Robb's Knights Party, which is located in Zinc, Arkansas. Data for this article were gathered while White Revolution was still online with slightly more than 1,000 registered users.

We had several reasons for placing a survey in an online site for white racial activists. First, we wanted to get answers to the questions about extremist opinions regarding minority groups in the United States; white group position in American society; and nationalistic tendencies from 100 or more participants. Trying to gather this much data in a qualitative manner would take quite a long time. Even though we were fairly certain about how members of White Revolution would answer many of our questions, we were especially interested in collecting demographic information such as region of residence at the time of the survey and at age 16, age, education, and gender, among others. Demographic information is important because it provides insights into who these people are, where they come from, and what they do. We did not realize that the data we gathered would be a snapshot in time of White Revolution and its members.

Initially, we were hopeful that we would be able to do a follow-up survey which would contain specific questions about current immigration policy, how individual respondents formed opinions about minority groups, and what they perceive as the major threats to white autonomy in American society. The first survey was meant to be an "ice breaker." Unfortunately, it appears that we will not have the opportunity to explore these additional questions with participants who took the survey in May 2010. We begin our discussion with a brief review of existing literature followed by theoretical perspectives on which the article is grounded. Next, we discuss data and methodology and the results of our investigation. Finally, we discuss our findings and make some comments about indications for future research.

White Nationalism: Fueled by the Internet

The Internet is an important tool in creating networks which connect individuals with similar ideologies, regardless of their geographic location (Bowman-Grieve 2009; Bugg and Williams 2008; Daniels 2009; De Koster and Houtman 2008). The appearance of Web sites sponsored by hate groups serves a calculated purpose that is directly linked to what Castells (2004) refers to as "the network society." The mobilization of youth-oriented hate groups such as Volksfront, the popularity of the white power music industry, and the proliferation of Internet Web sites for extremists has resulted in a resurgence of activism among people who are connected with white supremacy in the United States (Adams and Roscigno 2005; Back 2002; Berlet and Vysotsky 2006; Burris, Smith, and Strahm 2000; Dobratz and Shanks-Meile 1997, 2006; Ezekiel 1995; Futrell and Simi 2004; Gerstenfeld, Grant, and Chiang 2003; McVeigh 2004; Perry 2000; Ray and Marsh 2001; Schafer 2001; Schroer 2001; Thompson 2001; Weatherby and Scoggins 2005/2006; Whine 1999). The 2008 election of Barack Obama, the first African American president, has also prompted renewed mobilization efforts among extremist groups across the country (Potok 2010).

According to Swain (2002), white nationalist leaders articulate concerns about government policies that, they say, discriminate against whites. They also support white cultural preservation in a rapidly changing multicultural society. Since they are attempting to strike a chord with mainstream whites, Swain suggests that white nationalist leaders are beginning the process of legitimating white racial politics. Some of today's most ardent "racialists" such as David Duke and Jared Taylor concentrate on social change to benefit what they view as the white minority (Swain 2002; Swain and Nieli 2003). In addition, southern cultural groups such as League of the South advocate a brand of regional nationalism that focuses on preserving white, Anglo–Celtic southern pride and heritage (Hague, Beirich, and Sebesta 2008).

Due to hate speech laws in Europe, European extremist groups take advantage of free speech in America, especially in the online environment (Whine 1999). The information revolution not only enhances the importance of extremist networks, but also facilitates network growth by enabling widely dispersed actors to communicate, consult, and coordinate efforts across greater distances. According to Dobratz and Shanks-Meile (1997), Swain (2002), and Whine (1999), the Internet allows extremist groups to reach specific target audiences as well as a broader audience of potential adherents. Brown (2009) and Meddaugh and Kay (2009) found that white supremacist discourse online also reinforces racist ideology through the construction of in-group/out-group stereotypes.

Back (2002), however, questions the ability of extremist groups to mobilize new members, as computer users often opt for virtual rather than personal interaction. In his opinion, the contemporary racist "will to power" is more virtual than real because of the isolation of online interaction. Gerstenfeld, et al. (2003), on the other hand, found that the virtual experience enables extremists to create a collective rather than a fragmented identity. Based on data drawn from six white supremacist Web sites, Adams and Roscigno (2005) found that nationalism, religion, and definitions of responsible citizenship create a sense of collective identity for these groups with the common link being race.

In an analysis of Stormfront.org, Bowman-Grieve (2009) found that social networks play an important role in political socialization and collective action for white racial activists who populate the site. Both Stormfront.org and sites such as White Revolution provide forums for white racial activists—such as the people who took our survey—to meet and exchange views. Racialist Internet sites also provide announcements and calendars of events such as Klan rallies, white power music events, and other meetings associated with the white supremacist movement. Even though White Revolution is no longer online in its original configuration, many of the people represented in the study will most likely continue similar affiliations somewhere else online and/or in groups such as Volksfront, Aryan Nations, and the Klan.

Theoretical Background

We utilize Allport's (1954) updated classical prejudice model and Blumer's group position model (1958) to help explain prejudiced attitudes of the self-identified white nationalists who participated in this survey. Our analysis refers to out-groups as racial and ethnic groups in the U.S. population. Social interaction (both positive and negative) between groups is often linked to these broad social categories especially with regard to openly racist individuals who identify as white nationalists and/or white racial activists. In addition, due to our interest in nationalistic tendencies of people who join groups that are a part of the broader white supremacist/separatist/nationalist movement, we employ a nationalist theoretical approach to help explain this particular phenomenon.

The Classical Prejudice Model

The classical prejudice theory, as originally formulated, placed heavy emphasis on individual psychological factors that relate to prejudicial attitudes and behaviors. Over the years, as Allport predicted, the theory has been transformed and updated, as American society has adapted to vast socioeconomic changes such as globalization. In our opinion, Allport's work still has much to offer in the study of prejudice. Individuals who join groups such as White Revolution, the Ku Klux Klan, and Blood and Honour are aware of social status and the importance of forming in-group allegiances (Dobratz and Shanks-Meile 1997, 2006; Ezekiel 1995, 2002). Although Allport (1954:39) maintained that prejudice is ultimately a problem of personality formation, he also acknowledged that the influence of in-group membership cannot be denied.

An updated version of Allport's model posits that interracial hostility is an individual psychological predisposition with no roots in objective reality (Duckitt 1992; Katz 1991; Kinder and Sears 1981; Pettigrew 1982). This theory suggests that since negative feelings about minority individuals and groups are socially learned, personal environment and socialization are important to consider when assessing racial conflict and prejudicial attitudes. This idea can apply to mainstream whites as well as to people who join groups such as White Revolution. Group threat due to competition may or may not be directly attributable to negative attitudes about specific groups because of their race or ethnic origins. This sociocultural approach emphasizes the influence of cultural ideas on negative or hostile responses to particular groups. In the white nationalist population, the development of personal worldviews has not necessarily followed a logical path guided by rational thought, although they are aware of the importance of gaining a mainstream audience to bolster membership in racialist groups, secure votes for political campaigns, and establish some legitimacy for their ideas (Swain and Nieli 2003:7, 66–67, 74).

A relatively large body of early work in the social sciences suggested that formal education not only decreases prejudice but also increases racial tolerance (Greeley and Sheatsley 1974; Hyman and Sheatsley 1964; Lipset 1960; Quinley and Glock 1979; Stouffer 1955). However, Swain (2002) and Swain and Nieli (2003) suggest that this finding is not necessarily true. Intellectuals in the white nationalist movement such as Jared Taylor, Michael Levin, and J. Philippe Rushton, although highly educated, believe that genetic differences between blacks and whites are largely responsible for the poorer performance of blacks in academic settings along with high crime rates in black communities (Swain and Nieli 2003:viii). Levin and Rushton are also college professors; so, it is conceivable that they have at least some ongoing contact with students of various races and ethnic backgrounds. As the white nationalist movement continues to evolve and attract a more educated following, the formal education argument for racial tolerance grows more difficult to defend. Thus, a goal of this study was to gather information about the level of education in the survey sample.

Blumer's Group Position Model

One of the assumptions of Blumer's group position model is the subjective image of where the in-group stands or, more importantly, should stand, in relation to the out-group (1958). His focus was on both the subjective and normative thrust of the sense of group position for individual members:

> Sociologically it is not a mere reflection of the objective relations between racial groups. Rather it stands for "what ought to be" rather than for "what is." It is a sense of where the two racial groups belong. . . . In its own way, the sense of group position is a norm and imperative—indeed a very powerful one. It guides, incites, cows, and coerces. It should be borne in mind that this sense of group position stands for and involves a fundamental kind of group affiliation." (1958:5)

The group position model incorporates negative feelings and beliefs as well as concerns for the material conditions of group life. Blumer identifies four elements as important in establishing a positional arrangement for the dominant racial group: (1) feelings of superiority (ethnocentrism); (2) the belief that a subordinate group is inherently different from the dominant group; (3) a proprietary claim to privilege and advantage by the dominant group; and (4) fear and suspicion that the subordinate group desires to usurp the rightful claim to scarce resources and power sources of the dominant group. The interweaving of these factors—group identity, out-group stereotyping, preferred group status, and perceived threat—constitute the fully developed "sense of group position" (1958:4).

Arguing that ideas about group position emerge as leaders or significant segments of social groups contend with one another through public discourse and political struggle, Blumer stresses that long-term social and historical processes are shaped by this exchange of ideas. Lal (1995) suggested that this exchange creates shared ideas about where the in-group ought to stand in the social order relative to other groups. Operating from a symbolic interactionist perspective, Blumer placed high value on the importance of human action in group mobilization processes. An architect of analysis of interpretive interactions between individuals, Blumer never embraced attempts to quantify racial prejudice. Instead, he argued that group conflict is as fluid as all social interactions and, therefore, not easily reducible to a few variables (Esposito and Murphy 1999). We agree with Blumer's approach; however, we also understand how difficult it is to gather data on certain hard-to-reach groups such as the one represented in this study. By administering a survey to admittedly prejudiced individuals, we use the group position model to help analyze how an openly racist group regards specific out-groups and what this means for interracial relations. In addition, a survey of this type collects the strength of attitudes held by this group of individuals at this particular moment in time. We are not the first researchers to apply Blumer's group position theory in this manner. Bobo and Hutchings (1996) used data from the 1992 Los Angeles County Social Survey and found support for Blumer's group-position framework.

Research indicates that people who identify as white nationalists are racist and harbor prejudicial attitudes toward people of color and other minority groups (Swain 2002:17, 18). Despite their historically higher ranking in the social structure, the white nationalists who participated in this study feel a sense of alienation because of their perceived loss of social status to inferior groups. In fact, the perception that whites are becoming a minority group in their own country is entrenched in extremist culture. These feelings have been shaped by a process of collective social definition that is driven by a carefully crafted racialist ideology. Following Blumer's line of thinking, this suggests that because of the history of negative relations between white racists and others, their sense of group position within the social hierarchy is more fully developed.

Nationalism Theory

Besides placing higher value on group position based on race and sharing prejudicial views about non-white minority groups, people who identify as "white separatist" or "white nationalist" also exhibit nationalistic ideas about geographical spaces and their place within the state, region, and nation. In discussion forums on Stormfront.org, an Internet site similar to White Revolution, participants hatch plans to "pioneer little Europes" in order to establish an all-white homeland somewhere within the contiguous United States. Many Stormfront discussants present their form of nationalist branding as "patriotism," which echoes Billig's (1995) description of banal nationalism or nationalism that is reproduced among the citizenry on a daily basis. Although definitions of nationalism vary greatly, we appropriate a variation of Weber's "prestige community" (Gerth and Mills 1946:171) when examining emerging nationalist tendencies and rhetoric among the white nationalists who participated in this study. The white nationalist version of "prestige communities" is based on race, and leaders such as Billy Roper are committed to creating an ideal white cultural nationalism that is reminiscent of early 1950s America.[3] The following hypotheses framed this study.

Hypotheses

H1: Racial Prejudice. Members of White Revolution who participated in this survey are more likely to harbor prejudicial attitudes about racial/ethnic minority groups than mainstream whites.

H2: Group Position. Members of White Revolution who participated in this survey believe that whites are superior to racial/ethnic minority groups.

H3: Nationalist Ideology. Members of White Revolution who participated in this survey exhibit nationalistic attitudes toward white American culture.

Data and Methods

The data for this study come from a survey administered to members of the white nationalist group called White Revolution. According to the group's leader, Billy Roper, during the time of the survey, membership consisted of approximately 1,100 individuals from various nations around the world, with the majority residing in the United States. The survey was administered online with SurveyMonkey.com through the group's Web site. A total of 148 responses were received, an estimated 13% of the group membership. The survey was available on the site for six weeks, with reminders sent to the group after two and four weeks had passed. The survey was developed to document the attitudes of people who self-identify as white nationalists with regard to minority issues in the United States along with nationalistic tendencies based on presumed ethnocentric beliefs about American culture. Questions were adapted from the National Opinion Research Center (2003). A complete list of items and the concepts that were operationalized can be found in Table 1.

Table 1 List of Items and Concepts

Concept/Theory Being Measured	Survey Item Used To Operationalize Theory	Item Code Number
Classical prejudice model	I believe that minority people are not as intelligent as Whites.	Q1
Classical prejudice model	Ethnic groups such as the Irish and Italians adapted to American culture without massive government aid programs and this is what minorities should do today.	Q2
Classical prejudice model	I am comfortable with my personal attitude toward minority groups.	Q3
Classical prejudice model	About all that is necessary to achieve racial equality in the United States has been done.	Q4
Blumer #1	In my opinion, white immigrants can easily become American.	Q5
Blumer #2	To be a real American, you have to speak English.	Q6
Blumer #2	In my opinion, minority immigrants can easily become American.	Q7
Blumer #3	The government pays more attention to minority concerns than they deserve.	Q8
Blumer #3	Minorities get more media attention than they deserve.	Q9
Blumer #3	Minority groups in America deserve to be treated fairly.	Q10
Blumer #4	Minority groups in America demand too much.	Q11
American nationalism	I would rather be a citizen of America than any other country in the world.	Q12
American nationalism	The world would be a better place if people from other countries were more like Americans.	Q13
American nationalism	Generally speaking, America is better than most other countries.	Q14

The first section of the survey comprised 15 items that addressed various topics associated with stereotypes about minority groups, an inflated sense of group worth based on race, ethnocentric attitudes about American culture, and possible nationalistic tendencies among the group being surveyed. For each of these questions, there were four possible response categories, which included: strongly disagree, somewhat disagree, somewhat agree, and strongly agree. Due to the nature of the convenience sample of white nationalist respondents, we collapsed the categories into "disagree" and "agree." This makes it easier to see the big picture without obscuring large differences.

The second section included three open-ended questions regarding the meaning of being white and white culture as well as one item on religion. The final section included eight demographic questions. We will focus on questions 1 through 14 from the first section of the survey, demographic variables, and some open-ended questions from section two. In part, due to the type of group being surveyed and its well-documented general distrust of academics, of the 148 responses, approximately one-third of the respondents did not complete all the demographic questions. Table 2 gives the White Revolution responses to the 14 survey questions.

Table 2 White Revolution Survey Responses (2010)

White Attitude Questions	Disagree	Agree	Missing Cases
I believe that minority people are not as intelligent as whites.	23 (16.3%)	118 (83.7%)	7 (4.7%)
Ethnic groups such as the Irish and Italians adapted to American culture without massive government aid programs and this is what minorities should do.	30 (21%)	113 (79%)	5 (3.4%)
I am comfortable with my personal attitude toward minority groups.	7 (4.8%)	138 (95.2%)	3 (2.0%)
About all that is necessary to achieve racial equality in the United States has been done.	47 (32.9%)	96 (67.1%)	5 (3.4%)
In my opinion, white immigrants can easily become American.	25 (17.4%)	119 (82.6%)	4 (2.7%)
To be a real American, you have to speak English.	9 (6.2%)	137 (93.8%)	2 (1.4%)
In my opinion, minority immigrants can easily become American.	99 (68.8%)	45 (31.3%)	4 (2.7%)

(continued on the next page)

Table 2 (*Continued*)

White Attitude Questions	Disagree	Agree	Missing Cases
The government pays more attention to minority concerns than they deserve.	8 (5.6%)	136 (94.4%)	4 (2.7%)
Minorities get more media attention than they deserve.	10 (7%)	132 (93%)	6 (4.1%)
Minority groups deserve to be treated fairly.	59 (41.3%)	84 (58.7%)	5 (3.4%)
Minority groups in America demand too much.	8 (5.6%)	135 (94.4%)	5 (3.4%)
I would rather be a citizen of America than any other country in the world.	43 (30.1%)	100 (69.9%)	5 (3.4%)
The world would be a better place if people from other countries were more like Americans.	83 (58.9%)	58 (41.1%)	7 (4.7%)
Generally speaking, America is better than most other countries.	45 (31.7%)	97 (68.3%)	6 (4.1%)

Four items were used to measure the updated classical prejudice model which included negative stereotypes about minority populations that group members learned at some point in their lives. An example of one of these items is: "I believe that minority people are not as intelligent as whites." To operationalize Blumer's theory, we used questions that reflect general concepts associated with the theory. For example, Blumer's first element deals with feelings of superiority. To represent this concept we used the item: "In my opinion, white immigrants can easily become American." This statement reflects the belief held by many white nationalists that whites are superior to other racial/ethnic groups. The second element of Blumer's model is that subordinate groups are inherently different from the dominant group. To represent this concept we used the following items: (1) "To be a real American, you have to speak English" and (2) "In my opinion, minority immigrants can easily become American." These statements reflect the idea that English is a symbol of the inherent superiority of white Americans and the perception that minority immigrants cannot easily become American.

Blumer's theory also deals with the proprietary claim to privilege and advantage by the dominant group. The first of three items used to measure this is: "The government pays more attention to minority concerns than they deserve." This item reflects the idea that any additional gains made by minorities come at the expense of privileges held by the dominant white group. The final element in Blumer's model is concerned with fear and suspicion held by the dominant group that the minority group will usurp scarce resources such as jobs and drive down salaries in the process. The sole item used to measure this concept is: "Minority groups in America demand too much." This item represents the belief held by many white nationalists that minority groups continue to demand more and that these demands will somehow weaken the group position of whites.

To examine the respondents' nationalistic tendencies, three survey items were used. These items addressed the perceived superiority of American culture among this particular group. An example of one of these items is: "I would rather be a citizen of America than any other country in the world." We also include some open-ended responses about white culture in this portion of the analysis.

Bivariate associations were analyzed to measure the effect of education on each of the survey items. Gamma measures were applied to test the relationships between variables. Education was used as the independent variable, whereas each survey item represented the dependent variable. We recoded education into a three-category ordinal variable as follows: (1) high school diploma or lower; (2) bachelors degree or some college; and (3) some graduate school or higher. Unfortunately, due to the convenience sample used in this research, we were unable to calculate whether any of these associations were statistically significant. It should be noted that these data are limited in their focus, as they represent only one white nationalist group and due to the nature of convenience sampling, they are not a complete representation of this group's full membership.

Mainstream White Responses (2004)

A total of seven White Revolution survey questions were adapted from the General Social Survey (GSS). Therefore, some general comparisons between our collected data and the GSS will illustrate how mainstream whites view some of the same issues. Since we adapted our questions from the GSS, the wording was slightly changed. Not all our survey questions are represented in the GSS; so, not all items can be compared. In addition, the sentiments of mainstream whites that compare to our data were collected in 2004, indicating that the data are slightly outdated and may not reflect the most current attitudes in the population. The comparison sample contains a random sample of 964 white adults living in the U.S. in 2004. Again, the strongly agree and agree categories were collapsed into one category coded agree; the strongly disagree and disagree categories were collapsed into one category coded disagree; and the neutral category was left uncoded to match the coding scheme used in the White Revolution survey.

Results

To examine the theory of the classical prejudice model, four statements were used. The first item asked for the respondent's level of agreement with item Q1. The respondents overwhelmingly agreed with this statement; however 23 (16.3%) of the sample disagreed that minority people are not as intelligent as whites. The second statement asked for agreement with Q2. Most respondents agreed that minorities should be able to adapt to American culture without massive government assistance, whereas 30 (21%) disagreed with the statement. Item 3, Q3, was overwhelmingly supported by people in the sample, indicating that there was a high level of comfort with personal attitudes about minorities. Item Q4 dealt with the issue of racial equality in the United States. Overall, 96 (67.1%) of the sample agreed that enough had been done to achieve racial equality, whereas 47 (32.9%) of the respondents disagreed.

Seven statements were included to explore Blumer's group position model. Statement Q5 was used to measure ethnocentric beliefs among respondents in the sample. A majority of respondents, 119 (82.6%), agreed that white immigrants can easily become American; whereas 25 (17.4%) disagreed. Items Q6 and Q7 were used to measure inherent differences between minorities and the dominant white group that is represented in the sample. With regard to the importance of speaking English and true Americanism, the sample of respondents overwhelmingly agreed. In response to Q7, which stated that minority immigrants can easily become American, 99 (68.8%) of the sample disagreed, while 45 (31.3%) agreed.

With regard to the measurement of Blumer's third element that deals with a proprietary claim to privilege and advantage by the dominant group, three items were used to measure the concept: Q8, Q9, and Q10. The response to Q8 which stated that the government pays more attention to minority concerns than they deserve elicited overwhelming agreement among the sample. Item Q9 also received overwhelming agreement that the media pays too much attention to minority issues. The response to item Q10 which stated that minorities deserve to be treated fairly had a mixed response with 84 (58.7%) agreeing and 59 (41.3%) disagreeing with the statement. Blumer's fourth element regarding fear and suspicion of minority groups was measured by Q10, which stated that minority groups in America demand too much. This statement resulted in overwhelming agreement from individuals who participated in the survey.

Items Q12, Q13, and Q14 were included to examine nationalistic attitudes in the survey sample. Responses to Q12 regarding attitudes about the value of American citizenship compared with citizenship in other countries were mixed with 100 (69.9%) agreeing and 43 (30.1%) disagreeing that American citizenship was better than citizenship in another country. Item Q13 stated that the world would be a better place if people from other countries were more like Americans. Only 58 (41.1%) of the sample agreed with this statement, whereas 83 (58.9%) disagreed. The final item, Q14, stated that generally speaking, America is better than most countries. Overall, 97 (68.3%) agreed with the statement, while 45 (31.7%) disagreed.

A total of 96 (64.9%) respondents answered the following open-ended question that deals with ideas about white cultural nationalism: "How do you define white culture? Do you think that most whites feel they have a distinct culture? Why or why not?" Some of the responses follow.

> Any European/early American culture most whites today identify w/alien cultures (african, indian-american) instead of their own. It is not acceptable to be proud of being European, so a lot of people have let cultural pride fall by the way side. (Response #3)
> Culture is simply the value/power expression of a homogenous group. White culture is that which is shared in common amongst all European ethnicities. Most whites know what this means: intellect, progress and strength. (Response #9)
> I define White culture as the cultures of Europe or America, or as Aryan values. I think White people are taught that they have no culture, and because of this, most would say they do not and that they are jealous of non-whites for having a culture. (Response #12)
> White culture is derived from European ancestry and nationalities. Culture is an expression of race, i.e., Jung. Whites who choose to celebrate and honor their own, European American, ancestry, rather than that of other races, have a distinct culture. Others who celebrate nonwhite culture have abdicated their own culture. (Response #22)

Bivariate Analysis

A series of gamma coefficients were performed to determine the association between level of education and the respondents' attitudes toward the survey items. According to Bobo and Hutchings (1996), whites with only a high school diploma express the strongest competitive threat with minority groups. As can be seen in Table 3, for the first four items that

Table 3 Bivariate Associations with Education and Other Items

Survey Item	Item Code Number	Concept/Theory Being Measured	Association with Education (Gamma Coefficient)	N
I believe that minority people are not as intelligent as Whites.	Q1	Classical prejudice model	.107	116
Ethnic groups such as the Irish and Italians adapted to American culture without massive government aid programs and that is what minorities should do today.	Q2	Classical prejudice model	−.017	116
I am comfortable with my personal attitude toward minority groups.	Q3	Classical prejudice model	−.053	116
About all that is necessary to achieve racial equality in the United States has been done.	Q4	Classical prejudice model	−.199	116
In my opinion, white immigrants can easily become American.	Q5	Blumer element 1	.087	116
To be a real American, you have to speak English.	Q6	Blumer element 2	.273	116
In my opinion, minority immigrants can easily become American.	Q7	Blumer element 2	.030	116
The government pays more attention to minority concerns than they deserve.	Q8	Blumer element 3	.370	116
Minorities get more media attention than they deserve.	Q9	Blumer element 3	.392	116
Minority groups in America deserve to be treated fairly.	Q10	Blumer element 3	−.187	116
Minority groups in America demand too much.	Q11	Blumer element 4	.135	116
I would rather be a citizen of America than any other country in the world.	Q12	American nationalism	.260	116
The world would be a better place if people from other countries were more like Americans.	Q13	American nationalism	.075	116
Generally speaking, America is better than most other countries.	Q14	American nationalism	.209	116

test the updated classical prejudice model, two items showed a weak association with education. Item Q1 showed a weak positive association, with more highly educated respondents being more likely to disagree. Item Q4 also showed a weak negative association with education. More highly educated respondents were more likely to agree. Items Q2 and Q3 showed no association with education.

When testing Blumer's group position model, there was no association between item Q5 and education. For the two items measuring the second element, item Q6 showed a weak-positive association with education. In this case, more educated respondents were more likely to disagree with the idea that to be a real American, you have to speak English. Item Q7 showed no association with education. All three of the items measuring the third element of Blumer's model showed some association with education. Both items Q8 and Q9 had a positive moderate association with education. For these items, more educated individuals were more likely to disagree with these statements. Item Q10 showed a weak-negative association with education. For this item, more educated respondents were more likely to agree with this item. The final item measuring Blumer's fourth element showed a weak-positive association with education. More educated respondents were more likely to disagree with item Q11 which stated that minority groups in America demand too much.

For the three items measuring nationalistic beliefs, two items show a weak-positive agreement with education, and two items showed no association. Both items Q12 and Q14 show a weak-positive association with education. For these items, more highly educated respondents were likely to disagree with these statements. Item Q13 showed no association with education.

The bivariate analysis shows some support for the influence of education on attitudes held by the respondents, which is consistent with the updated classical prejudice model (Bobo and Hutchings 1996). Approximately 60% of the items measured illustrate that education has some influence on the respondent's answer. Although most of these influences are weak, the role of education in the beliefs and attitudes of the self-identified white nationalists who took this survey cannot be completely ignored. An example is the response to the following statement (Q10): "Minority groups deserve to be treated fairly." A total of 84 (58.7%) respondents agreed with this statement. Level of education may have an impact on this response, as was discussed earlier.

Comparison with Mainstream Whites

As can be seen in Table 4, 14% of mainstream whites agreed that blacks are not as intelligent as whites as compared with 83% of White Revolution respondents who see members of minorities as being less intelligent. With regard to the issue of blacks overcoming prejudice without special favors, 73% of mainstream whites agreed with this statement as compared with 79% of the White Revolution sample. Approximately 96% of mainstream whites agreed that to be truly American, you have to speak English as compared with 93% of white nationalists. One third of mainstream white respondents did not think that people who do not share American culture and values can become fully American. By comparison, white nationalists agreed more that white immigrants could become American (82%) but were less accepting of minority immigrants becoming American (31%). Approximately 90% of mainstream whites would rather be citizens of America than any other country in the world as compared with 69% of white nationalists. For the related question that asked "Would the world be a better place if people from other countries acted more like Americans?," results indicate that 42.4% of mainstream whites and 41.1% of white nationalists agreed with this question. Finally, approximately 80% of mainstream whites thought that America is better than most countries as compared with 68% of white nationalists.

Table 4   GSS Responses (2004)

White Attitude Questions	Disagree	Agree	Neutral
I believe that Blacks are not as intelligent as Whites.	195 (27.5%)	99 (14.0%)	414 (58.5%)
Blacks should overcome prejudice without special favors.	85 (11.8%)	525 (73.0%)	109 (15.2%)
To be a real American, you have to speak English.	32 (3.3%)	939 (96.7%)	0 (0.0%)
It is impossible for people who do not share American customs and traditions to become fully American.	451 (47.4%)	316 (33.2%)	185 (19.4%)
I would rather be a citizen of America than any other country in the world.	22 (2.3%)	883 (91.6%)	59 (6.1%)
The world would be a better place if people from other countries were more like Americans.	223 (23.3%)	406 (42.4%)	329 (34.3%)
Generally speaking, America is better than most other countries.	46 (4.8%)	770 (80.2%)	145 (15.1%)

Discussion

Although the numbers of White Revolution participants is small compared with the numbers of mainstream whites represented in the GSS sample, we can still make some inferences about general attitudes represented in the two samples. It should be noted that data gathered from the White Revolution survey are not representative of the broader white nationalist movement; they merely reflect responses from this particular group and cannot be generalized. Further, the sample may have a higher representation of educated respondents than the movement in general. Due to this, respondents may have been more open to participating in a survey. We were also able to get support from the group's leader during the time the survey was conducted online.

If the demographic responses were accurate for the White Revolution survey, the results substantiated our initial expectations that men outnumber women in this particular population with the ratio of men to women being at roughly 9:1. The average age of the respondents was 39, and 80% of the people who participated in this survey were between the ages of 18 and 49. Approximately 25% of this sample stated that they had some level of higher/college education. Table 5 reveals that the majority of participants in this survey reside in the Southern region of the country, as they did at age 16.

According to the Anti-Defamation League, White Revolution was active in 17 American states from 2002 until the site shut down in August 2011 (Anti-Defamation League n.d.). The states included Alabama, Arizona, Arkansas, California, Connecticut, Florida, Georgia, Illinois, Indiana, Kentucky, Massachusetts, New Hampshire, New Jersey, North Carolina, Ohio, Texas, and West Virginia. The Southern Poverty Law Center, another watchdog group, reported that Billy Roper wanted his group to become an umbrella for various extremist organizations such as Volksfront and Blood and Honour; however, he had little success in achieving this goal.

One of the last projects undertaken by White Revolution before its demise was the White Caucus, which endorsed white nationalist candidates running for public office. In 2010, Roper tested the political waters himself as a write-in candidate for governor of Arkansas. His campaign resulted in a total of 40 votes, most of which came from remote Zinc, Arkansas, where Thom Robb's Knights Party is located. The long-term goal of the White Caucus was to establish a coalition with the Nationalist Party of America, a political party organized by Roper and heavily

Table 5 Region of Residence Table*

Region	Number	Percent
Residence at Time of Survey		
Northeast	18	17.8%
Midwest	8	7.9%
South	40	39.6%
West	24	23.8%
International	8	7.9%
Missing	3	2.9%
Total	101	99.9%**
Residence at Age Sixteen		
Northeast	23	22.3%
Midwest	12	11.7%
South	33	32%
West	24	23.3%
International	6	5.8%
Missing	5	4.9%
Total	103	100%

*Regions are defined according to the U.S. Census.
**Rounding error

promoted on the White Revolution Web site (Dentice 2011). Currently, Roper appears to be forging alliances with Thom Robb's Knights Party, which is absorbing some members who were once affiliated with White Revolution.

The data from our survey support our hypothesis that the majority of respondents from the White Revolution survey regard out-group members (minority groups) as being inferior to whites. In comparison, 14% of the GSS sample agreed that blacks are not as intelligent as whites. It is impossible to know how many of the remaining number of mainstream white respondents who disagreed were reflecting what they knew to be politically correct in their responses. We do know whether the White Revolution responses align with white racialist ideology. With regard to our group position hypothesis, respondents generally agreed that white immigrants can easily become American. Respondents from both samples support the position that in order to be a real American, one must speak English. Both samples were in agreement that no more special favors are needed to achieve racial equality in the United States. We hypothesized that the white nationalists represented in this study hold ethnocentric beliefs regarding America and American culture. A majority of respondents from both samples agree that they would rather be citizens of America than any other country. In addition, most respondents (from both samples) agreed that the world would be a better place if people from other countries were more like Americans, and the majority agreed that America is better than most other countries. The answers from both survey samples are similar with regard to ethnocentric attitudes about America and American culture.

Literature about extremist movements in the United States has shown that white racial activists are often highly critical of "unenlightened whites" (Dobratz and Shanks-Meile 1997; Swain 2002). White racial activists are also known to support separate social spaces and cultural autonomy within their communities and the nation. The idea of acculturation and assimilation of diverse groups is generally antithetical to white racialist ideology. According to Billy Roper, much of the paranoia surrounding the federal government has to do with the fact that non-white immigrants have been favored over more desirable white immigrant groups since the 1960s.[4] The resultant demographic shift is threatening the future of white children, and this force fuels the nationalist movement in the United States (Dobratz and Shanks-Meile 1997). In the past, extremist rhetoric was more blatantly hateful than mainstream dialogue with regard to immigration and other minority group issues. Since the 2008 election of President Obama, there seems to be a much more strident tone from mainstream whites and especially Tea Party activists with regard to immigrant and other minority populations in the United States.

Researchers Simi and Futrell (2009) found that forced silence in educational and work environments serves to make inner racist beliefs stronger. Because of the diversity of American society, most people (even white racial activists) have some contact with people from diverse ethnic/racial groups. The idea of multiculturalism is threatening to some segments of the population for various reasons. By joining extremist groups and participating in online forums such as White Revolution and Stormfront.org, some people find a measure of relief from forced interaction brought on by integration and affirmative action social policies.

In our opinion, the white nationalists represented in this study do not associate privilege with whiteness, although they believe that whiteness is equated with racial superiority. Rather than ignoring race, they concentrate on racial identity and all its implications. They are greatly concerned with diversity and its impact on their communities and, more importantly, the future of their children and grandchildren. Gaining research access to sites that provide sanctuary for racists is not easy. The authors tried unsuccessfully to place a survey in Stormfront.org, but our inquiries were met with silence. Although smaller and less sophisticated, White Revolution still provided an opportunity to gather data that can be added to existing studies of white supremacy. Perhaps a further investigation that focuses on the opinions and attitudes of mainstream whites who do not embrace multiculturalism and who feel threatened by the demographic shift that is occurring in the United States could help us better understand more subtle racist attitudes in contemporary American society. It would also be interesting to explore the possibility of converging extremist ideology with more mainstream ideas about immigration and securing our nation's borders.

Notes

1. Equal authorship: correspondence should be addressed to Dianne Dentice email: denticede@sfasu.edu and David Bugg email: buggd@potsdam.edu. The authors would like to thank George Gonos, Michael Kimmel, and Bob Szafran for comments on an earlier version of this article. They would also like to extend their special thanks to Jonathan Swarts and two anonymous reviewers for their critique and helpful comments. A portion of this research was supported by a grant from the Office of Research and Sponsored Programs at Stephen F. Austin State University.
2. William Pierce is the late founder of the neo-Nazi organization, National Alliance, and the author of *Hunter* and *The Turner Diaries*.
3. Personal communication with Billy Roper, May 10, 2010.
4. Personal communication with Billy Roper, October 10, 2010.

References

Adams, Josh and Vincent J. Rosigno. 2005. "White Supremacists, Oppositional Culture, and the World Wide Web." *Social Forces* 84(2):759–778.
Allport, Gordon W. 1954. *The Nature of Prejudice*. Garden City, NJ: Doubleday.
Anti-Defamation League. "Extremism in America." Retrieved May 15, 2012 (http://www.adl.org/learn/ext_us/).
Back, Les. 2002. "Aryans Reading Adorno: Cyberculture and Twenty-first Century Racism." *Ethnic and Racial Studies* 25(4): 628–651.
Berlet, Chip and Stanislav Vysotsky. 2006. "Overview of U. S. White Supremacist Groups." *Journal of Political and Military Sociology* 34(1): 11–48.
Billig, Michael. 1995. *Banal Nationalism*. London: Sage Publications.
Blumer, Herbert. 1958. "Race Prejudice as a Sense of Group Position." *Pacific Sociological Review* 1(1):3–7.
Bobo, Lawrence and Vincent L. Hutchings. 1996. "Perceptions of Racial Group Competition:Extending Blumer's Theory of Group Position to a Multiracial Social Context." *American Sociological Review* 61(6): 951–972.
Bowman-Grieve, Lorraine. 2009. "Exploring 'Stormfront' A Virtual Community of the Radical Right." *Studies in Conflict and Terrorism* 32(11):989–1007.
Brown, Christopher. 2009. WWW.HATE.COM: White Supremacist Discourse on the Internet and the Construction of Whiteness Ideology. *The Howard Journal of Communications* 20(2):189–208.

Bugg, David and James L. Williams. 2008. "Hate Groups in the Network Society: A Transnational Social Movement." Pp. 98–108 in Dianne Dentice and James L. Williams, eds. *Social Movements: Contemporary Perspectives.* Newcastle: Cambridge Scholars Publishing.

Burris, Val and Emery Smith and Ann Strahm. 2000. "White Supremacist Networks on the Internet." *Sociological Focus* 33(2): 215–234.

Castells, Manuel. 2004. *The Power of Identity.* Malden, MA: Blackwell.

Daniels, Jessie. 2009. *Cyber Racism: White Supremacy Online and the New Attack on Civil Rights.* Lanham, MD: Rowman and Littlefield.

De Koster, Willem and Dick Houtman. 2008. "Stormfront is Like a Second Home to Me: On Virtual Community Formation by Right-wing Extremists." *Information, Communication and Society* 11(8): 1155–1176.

Dentice, Dianne. 2011. "The Nationalist Party of America: Right-wing Activism and Billy Roper's White Revolution." *Social Movement Studies* 10(1): 107–121.

Dobratz, Betty A. and Stephanie Shanks-Meile. 1997. *White Power, White Pride: The White Separatist Movement in the United States.* Baltimore, MD: Johns Hopkins University Press.

Dobratz, Betty A. and Stephanie Shanks-Meile. 2006. "The Strategy of White Separatism." *Journal of Political and Military Sociology* 34(1):49–79.

Duckitt, John. 1992. *The Social Psychology of Prejudice.* New York: Praeger.

Esposito, Luigi and John W. Murphy 1999. "Desensitizing Herbert Blumer's Work on Race Relations: Recent Applications of his Group Position Theory to the Study of Contemporary Race Prejudice." *The Sociological Quarterly* 40(3): 397–410.

Ezekiel, Raphael S. 1995. *The Racist Mind: Portraits of American Neo-Nazis and Klansmen.* NY: Viking.

Ezekiel, Raphael S. 2002. "An Ethnographer Looks at Neo-Nazi and Klan Groups." *American Behavioral Scientist* 46(1): 51–71.

Futrell, Robert and Pete Simi. 2004. "Free Spaces, Collective Identity, and the Persistence of U.S. White Power Activism." *Social Problems* 51(1): 16–42.

Gerstenfeld, Phyllis B., Diana R. Grant and Chau-Pu Chiang. 2003. "Hate-online: A Content Analysis of Extremist Internet Sites." *Analyses of Social Issues and Public Policy* 3(1): 29–44.

Gerth, H. H. and C. W. Mills. 1946. *From Max Weber: Essays in Sociology.* New York: Oxford University Press.

Greeley, Andrew M. and Paul B. Sheatsley. 1974. "Attitudes toward Racial Integration." Pp. 241–50 in Lee Rainwater, ed. *Social Problems and Public Policy: Inequality and Justice.* Chicago, IL: Aldine.

Hague, Euan and Heidi Beirich and Edward H. Sebesta. 2008. *Neo-Confederacy: A Critical Introduction.* Austin, TX: The University of Texas Press.

Hyman, Herbert H. and Paul B. Sheatsley. 1964. "Attitudes toward Desegregation." *Scientific American* 211(1):16–23.

Katz, Irwin. 1991. "Gordon Allport's The Nature of Prejudice." *Political Psychology* 12(1): 25–57.

Kinder, Donald R. and David O. Sears. 1981. "Symbolic Racism Versus Racial Threats to the Good Life." *Journal of Personality and Social Psychology* 40(3): 1141–1147.

Lal, Barbara Ballis. 1995. "Symbolic Interaction Theories." *American Behavioral Scientist* 38(3):421–441.

Lipset, Seymour Martin. 1960. *Political Man.* Garden City, NJ: Anchor.

Meddaugh, Priscilla Marie and Jack Kay. 2009. "Hate Speech or Reasonable Racism? The Other in Stormfront." *Journal of Mass Media Ethics* 24(9):251–268.

McVeigh, Rory. 2004. "Structured Ignorance and Organized Racism in the United States." *Social Forces* 82(3): 895–987.

National Opinion Research Center. 2003. *General Social Surveys, 1972-2002*. Chicago: National Opinion Research Center.
Perry, Barbara. 2000. "Button-down Terror: The Metamorphosis of the Hate Movement." *Sociological Focus* 33(2):113–131.
Pettigrew, Thomas F. 1982. "Prejudice." Pp. 1–29 in Thomas F. Pettigrew, George M. Frederickson, Dale T. Knobel, Nathan Glazer, and Reed Ueda, eds. *Prejudice*. Cambridge, MA: Belknap Press.
Potok, Mark. 2010. "Rage on the Right: The Year in Hate and Extremism." Southern Poverty Law Center Intelligence Report 137:1–3.
Quinley, Harold E. and Charles Y. Glock. 1979. *Anti-Semitism in America*. NY: Free Press.
Ray, Beverly and George E. Marsh II. 2001. "Recruitment by Extremist Groups on the Internet." First Monday. Retrieved July 31, 2009 (http://www.firstmonday.org/issues6_2/ray/index.html).
Schafer, Joseph A. 2001. "Spinning the Web of Hate: Web-based Hate Propagation by Extremist Organizations." *Journal of Criminal Justice and Popular Culture* 9(2):69–88.
Schroer, Todd. 2001. "Issue and Identity Framing within the White Racialist Movement: Internet Dynamics." *Research in Political Sociology* 9:117–163.
Simi, Pete and Robert Futrell. 2006. "Cyberculture and the Endurance of White Power Culture." *Journal of Political and Military Sociology* 34(1):115–142.
Simi, Pete and Robert Futrell. 2009. "Negotiating White Power Activist Stigma." *Social Problems* 59(1): 89–110.
Stouffer, Samuel A. 1955. *Communism, Conformity, and Civil Liberties*. New York: Wiley.
Swain, Carol M. 2002. *The New White Nationalism in America: It's Challenge to Integration*. Cambridge, MA: Harvard University Press.
Swain, Carol M. and Russ Nieli, eds. 2003. *Contemporary Voices of White Nationalism in America*. New York: Cambridge University Press.
Thompson, Kevin C. 2001. "Watching the Stormfront: White Nationalists and the Building of Community in Cyberspace." *Social Analysis* 45(1): 32–52.
Weatherby, Georgie Ann and Brian Scoggins. 2005/2006. "A Content Analysis of Persuasion Techniques Used on White Supremacist Websites." *Journal of Hate Studies* 4(9): 9–31.
Whine, Michael. 1999. "Cyberspace—A New Medium for Communication, Command, and Control by Extremists." *Studies in Conflict and Terrorism* 22(3): 231–245.

The Illinois State Chapter of the Moral Majority: A Study of a Religious Right Organization at the State Level and the Perception of Power, 1980–1988

Aaron K. Davis
Kansas State University

Political and Military Sociology: An Annual Review 2012, Vol. 40: 217–241.

Over the course of the 1980s, the emergence of the voting bloc commonly referred to as the "religious right" has attracted a great deal of scholarly attention. In recent years, a handful of studies have narrowed their scope to focus on demographics, behavior, and values at the local and state level. This article discusses the activities of the Illinois state chapter of the Moral Majority and considers the actual power that it wielded. Many would consider the national parent organization to have wielded a considerable amount of political influence throughout the 1980s. This article was driven by a central question: How much power did this state chapter hold? By examining the actions and claims of the Illinois state chapter, this article also considers further questions that are crucial for gauging the legitimacy of the organization. Was the group effective? How much of the group's power can be directly credited to the media's receptiveness to the organization's desire for exposure? How strongly was the organization tied to the national group? A discussion of these questions contributes to the overall understanding of one religious right organization's activities at the state level.

The rise of the Religious Right conservative evangelical voting bloc in America is an increasingly popular area of study. Interpretations of many aspects of this collection of special interest groups are constantly shifting while, at the same time, attracting greater attention. The group that was arguably the figurehead of this movement was the Moral Majority. Although much has been written on the Moral Majority and its leader, fundamentalist pastor Jerry Falwell, many questions remain. The Illinois state chapter of the Moral Majority was active between 1980 and 1988 and, similar to most other state chapters, operated autonomously and without financial assistance from the parent organization. Despite misleading numbers of financial and membership support, the national organization retained the perception of power within the media and in the eyes of politicians. With the state chapter, a string of failures in the hopes of creating or overturning state legislation was not enough to change the same perception of power among state-level media and legislators. This study finds that the Illinois Moral Majority was not successful in its attempts to influence politics in Illinois but remained active in its efforts to affect political decisions at the local, state, and national levels.

The Moral Majority was a national organization that received its main support from Falwell's list of followers. This included members of his own Thomas Road Baptist Church, his *Old Time Gospel Hour* television program audience, and Baptist Bible Fellowship[1] members. Falwell gauged from a series of nationwide rallies between 1976 and 1979—more popularly known as "I Love America" speeches—that a large segment of Americans desired a change in the course of American politics. From his meticulously kept list of supporters, sympathizers, and financial contributors, Falwell created the Moral Majority in 1979 and set out to aid the election of conservative Republican candidates. The Moral Majority aimed at getting legislation passed that opposed pornography, homosexuality, and abortion. It also sought to establish a national Family Protection Agency. From a large network of Baptist Bible Fellowship contacts and interested church leaders across the nation, Falwell established state chapters in all 50 states by the end of 1980.

The majority of studies of the Religious Right movement, and the Moral Majority in particular, dismiss the state chapters as a whole as a set of moribund, insignificant groups (Wilcox and Larson 2006:5). Although the Illinois Moral Majority shared many similarities with other state chapters, it also registered large numbers of voters during the 1980 and 1984 presidential elections, battled against ratification of the Equal Rights Amendment, and focused on statewide church and education issues. These similarities serve as the most significant activities on the part of the chapter, yet they did not make as much of an impact as might first appear. This study of the Illinois chapter considers the public perception of power wielded by the group that was perpetuated by the media. It also raises questions as to the level of power that was held at the level of the national organization. The actions of the Illinois Moral Majority demonstrate that not every state chapter was moribund. Many were active in politics at the state level and in supporting the goals of the national organization. Illuminating the actions of the Illinois chapter also reveals that the Moral Majority was not a monolithic movement, but a national group that benefitted in the form of further media exposure from the actions of its state chapters—even if this benefit came in the form of reinforcing the media's perception of power that the national organization held.

A recent scholarly debate has taken place with regard to the Religious Right and the actual influence that these organizations have had on politics. Many works, including Patrick Allitt's *Religion in America Since 1945* (2003) and Robert Wuthnow's *The Restructuring of American Religion* (1990), discuss the support that these organizations received, such as membership numbers and funding, but neglect to consider the influence which these organizations had in politics. In a chapter of *The Christian Right in American Politics*, James W. Lamare, Jerry L. Polinard, and Robert D. Wrinkle noted that although groups such as the Moral Majority and Religious Roundtable had a strong, indirect influence on electoral politics, "there is little evidence that these organizations played a direct role in the party or electoral system" (Lamare et al. 2003:63). Although some studies examine local education, business and city policies that deal with textbooks, homosexual rights, women's rights, and free speech on the part of Religious Right organizations, they do not collectively speak to the broader, national implications of the Religious Right. For example, many publications have cited Jerry Falwell's claim of having a membership of more than four million Americans when, in reality, four hundred thousand were recorded (Liebman and Wuthnow 1983:55). Many of these studies fail to describe the voting results or other effects that these followers had at the local, state, and national levels, other than crediting this and other groups for the election of Ronald Reagan (Liebman and Wuthnow 1983:55). Work exists that does, in fact, lay out the goals and actions taken by these organizations with regard to their lobbying, direct-mail, telephone, and newsletter communications. There is little outside of case studies—which are limited in their scope, however—that considers the actual political effects which voting, donating, or political pressure has had on American society and politics in general.

For the most part, Jerry Falwell, along with his Liberty University, Thomas Road Baptist Church, and *Old Time Gospel Hour* show serves as the main focus of most discussions of the organization (Harding 2001:88–91; Martin 1996:197; Miller 2009:209; Wuthnow 1990:205). Very little is considered beyond its leader. The account of Moral Majority's creation and its subsequent activities are usually centered on Falwell, his speeches, rallies, and interactions with the media. The only other factors given attention are brief notes which acknowledge the conditions present for the creation of the group, the denominational majority that comprised Moral Majority supporters, and how the organization was constructed. In nearly all these works, the Moral Majority is one part of a larger study on the entire Religious Right (Allitt 2003; Balmer 2007; Bromley and Shupe 1984; Diamond 1989, 1995; Fishwick and Brown 1987; Green et al. 2003; Jorstad 1987; Liebman and Wuthnow 1983; Martin 1996; Noll 2007; Wilcox and Larson 2006; Wuthnow 1990). For this reason, authors usually give a brief account of its history and main figures, although more detailed studies exist (Harding 2001; Wilcox 1986, 1987).

The state chapters of the Moral Majority are an often-overlooked issue in the history of the organization. The group and its many dimensions—consisting of an education group, a lobbying arm, a legal group, and a political action committee—are examined, whereas the state chapters are given little attention (Liebman and Wuthnow 1983:54). The few times the state chapters are discussed, they are dismissed as unimportant, ineffective, and with the exception of a few chapters that were active, virtually nonexistent (Fishwick and Brown 1987:101; Wilcox and Larson 2006:41–43). This focus on the actions of the national group and its leader has neglected potentially large and meaningful areas of study. Race, class, denomination, and size are either overlooked or taken at face value from the claims of Falwell. The political involvement and impact of Moral Majority's state chapters are similarly overlooked in favor of media accounts that followed the blunders and failures of a few select state chapters. This study aims at helping fill that analytical void.

The Illinois Moral Majority

The Illinois state chapter of the Moral Majority was created in January 1980 at a meeting in Chicago, Illinois. The meeting was called by Jerry Falwell and included more than 200 pastors, not only mainly from Chicago but also from throughout the state. One of the attendees was Reverend George Zarris, a 30-year-old, married father of three who had founded his own Baptist church in suburban Aurora eight years earlier. In this meeting, Falwell revealed the platform of the Moral Majority and attempted to generate interest in the organization. Knowing that a diverse set of conservative Christian denominations were represented, Falwell declared, "Gentlemen, we have been spending a lot of our bullets shooting at one another trying to prove who is right and who is wrong. I would like to make a proposition. We can make a truce and stop shooting at each other and turn our ammunition, our focus, to the forces that are destroying the United States of America. Then when we're all done winning our country back, we can go back to shooting one another." Zarris and the rest of the room broke out in laughter, but this proposition piqued Zarris' interest.[2]

During a lunch break, Zarris approached Robert Billings, the co-founder of the Moral Majority and executive assistant to Jerry Falwell. Billings had begun the church-run elementary and high school in Hammond, Indiana, where both he and Zarris had attended the same First Baptist Church. Zarris notified Billings of his willingness to help out in any way possible. After the lunch break, Billings found Zarris and said, "George, Jerry and I just got done having a lengthy conversation and we want you to be the ad hoc chairman of the Moral Majority of Illinois." On that January day in 1980, Zarris accepted and he, along with Jerry Falwell and Robert Billings, created the Illinois Moral Majority.[3]

Zarris had grown up in the south suburbs of Chicago. He revealed his independence and perseverance early when he began attending a local Baptist Sunday School at the age of 11. He subsequently encouraged all the members of his family, including his parents, to convert from the Greek Orthodox faith to the Baptist denomination. As a teenager, George decided that the ministry was the only choice for him; so, he enrolled in the Temple Theological Seminary in Chattanooga, Tennessee. By the age of 22, George was ordained a Baptist minister. In 1972, Zarris established the Fox River Valley Baptist Church in Aurora, Illinois. Between 1972 and the beginning of his role as Moral Majority state chairman in 1980, Zarris saw his church swell to a congregation of 1,000. He fashioned his ministry after that of Dr. Jack Hyles, the pastor of the First Baptist Church in Hammond, Indiana, and Jerry Falwell. With an eye toward growth and modeling himself on Hyles, Zarris created a fleet of buses that ran six separate routes and brought in around 600 children to his Sunday School. Zarris' church created a Christian elementary school, and he eventually taped programs that were heard at six different radio stations (McClory 1981:23–24). Zarris continued to grow his church throughout his role as the presiding senior pastor at Fox River Valley Baptist Church and during his tenure as the Illinois Moral Majority state chairman.

Zarris approached his position in the newly formed Illinois state chapter of the Moral Majority with the same enthusiasm as he had while founding his church in the early 1970s. Before the 1982 congressional elections, the Illinois state chapter comprised a seven-member executive board, had set up smaller chapters in more than half of the 102 counties in Illinois, had registered a number of voters, and had raised tens of thousands of dollars (McClory 1981:25–26). The Illinois Moral Majority not only strictly followed the platform of the national organization but also focused its efforts on various state issues. Toward the end of its existence, the Illinois chapter did little in comparison to its first few years in operation and essentially faded between 1985 and its official end in 1988. In its infancy, though, the Illinois Moral Majority was very active in furthering the goals of the national Moral Majority. It raised an awareness of the issues that the group championed in Illinois. The war waged against the ratification of the Equal Rights Amendment within the state of Illinois, statewide voter registration drives, and the continued exposure to the public through various media outlets comprise the main activities of the Illinois Moral Majority.

Moral Majority's Extensive State Chapters

The Illinois state chapter shared similarities and also exhibited glaring differences in comparison to the other state chapters of the Moral Majority. After creating the Moral Majority, Falwell set out on a wave of state meetings and worked tirelessly through phone and mail exchanges, establishing state chapters in all 50 states. Falwell claimed that he had organized 50 state Moral Majority chapters and convinced 110,000 pastors, priests, and rabbis to become actively involved in the mission of the Moral Majority (Falwell 1986:1). Although the aim of the Moral Majority was to have an ecumenical, multi-denominational, and all-inclusive organization that focused solely on infusing Christian morals, the main source of support came from Baptists. The most evident example of this is found in the makeup of the state chapters. With the exception of eight states, every state chapter chairman was either a member of the Baptist Bible Fellowship or led a Baptist church (Appendix 1). The Illinois Moral Majority was no exception, as Zarris' Fox River Valley Baptist Church was an independent Baptist church.

All of Moral Majority's state chapters generally subscribed to the planks in Falwell's national platform: pro-life, pro-family, pro-traditional morality, and pro-American. Over time, a pro-Israel plank was also inserted (Martin 1996:201). Although all the state chapters championed these stances, most also pursued their own issues within their respective states. The relationship between the national and state organizations was both complimentary and distant. The national organization was able to point to its 50 state chapters as a sign of strength, and the state chapters were able to invoke the name of their parent organization during media interviews. Apart from meeting once a year, though, little communication took place as long as state chapters sought the same goals as the national organization in its activities. Since there is a lack of scholarship that analyzes individual state chapters, it is hard to attribute any sense of uniqueness to the Illinois chapter. It is surely unique in the goals it strived for during the ERA campaign, as Illinois was a final battleground for advocates both for and against its ratification across the country. However, no major successes that caught widespread media attention can be credited to any individual state chapter. If anything, the Illinois Moral Majority was typical of a well-organized state chapter: created within the first year of the national Moral Majority's appearance, headed by a Baptist pastor who was captivated by Falwell's plan, and active in its voter registration attempts.

Studies related to individual states that exist adopt either of the following approaches. The first approach examines very specific issues within a chapter and neglects to describe anything such as political impact, demographic information, or funding (Wilcox 1986:355–363, 1987:47–58). The second merely considers the Moral Majority's chapters in passing (Dochuk 2006:975–999; Lugg 2001:41–57; Moen 1996:461–464). This second approach frequently uses generalizations and dismisses all chapters as insignificant. For example, Clyde Wilcox and Carin Larson conclude, "Although the Moral Majority organization looked impressive on paper, in practice most state organizations were moribund. The few state and local groups that were active went their considerably divergent ways, often to the embarrassment of the national organization" (2006:41–42).

Indeed, state chapters were dismissed at the time as insignificant and out of touch with most Americans. In Maryland, the state chapter lobbied for a pornographic cookie control act after having objected to the sale of sexually explicit gingerbread cookies. The only result of this action was a dramatic increase in cookie sales from the targeted bakery shop. Similarly, the Indiana Moral Majority learned that the state's child welfare office had placed a child who was battered by his father under the custody of his maternal grandparents. The chapter filed a complaint, arguing that vigorous discipline was biblically sound. In California, a Moral Majority spokesperson demanded capital punishment for homosexuals. The Washington Moral Majority did not clarify how viewers would be guaranteed freedom from harassment but still demanded that the state library identify those to whom a movie titled "Achieving Sexual Maturity" was distributed (Jorstad 1981:199–200). Such highly publicized events as these illustrated the extent of the Moral Majority's forays into local and state affairs and helped create the perception that the state chapters were not terribly effective.

There were other cases of embarrassment and questionable campaigns on the part of state chapters. The case of the New York Moral Majority serves as an example of why state chapters are typically dismissed by many as being ineffective. Reverend Dan C. Fore, the New York state chairman, focused on voter registration between 1980 and 1982, but Senator Alfonse D'Amato, whose 1980 victory was seen as a New York version of the evangelical tide sweeping the country, did not credit the New York Moral Majority for any part of his victory, let alone acknowledge it as having any real leverage in the state. Both Governor Hugh Carey and Senator Daniel Patrick Moynihan were targeted by the chapter for defeat in 1982. Although Governor Carey had decided against running for reelection, Mario Cuomo, a fellow Democrat, won the office that year, while Moynihan won back his seat in 1982, 1988, and 1994 (Klein 1981:29). In December 1981, Fore was dismissed from his post as chairman of the New York Moral Majority, as his controversial remarks about Jews and Roman Catholics were an embarrassment to the group's national leadership (The Region 1981). When prodded for a response to his remarks concerning Jews' "supernatural ability to make money, control New York City, and the media," Fore responded, "I'm not an anti-Semite, I love the Jews and Christians have never been anti-Semitic." When asked about the Spanish Inquisition, Fore said, "Those weren't Christians, they were Roman Catholics" (quoted in Klein 1981:26).

Other state chapters had their share of controversies and ill-advised campaigns, but were still effective in certain areas. Although Ohio, as with most state chapters, did not have high membership numbers, the work of their activist followers was apparent in local, state, and national politics through voting or persuading others to vote in the manner the Moral Majority wanted. The Ohio membership list of around 290 names comprised people who actually attended a rally, signed a petition, contributed money, or were active in some other way. Many of these Ohio members participated in electoral activities on three or more occasions, and many more who were not directly involved with the state chapter voted in line with the sentiments of the organization (Wilcox 1986:356, 359). These examples from Maryland, Indiana, California, Washington, and New York explain why many scholars dismissed the state chapters as insignificant and conclude that the Moral Majority was a monolithic, national movement (Wilcox and Larson 2006:41–42). In contrast, similar to the Ohio chapter, the Illinois chapter proves that even without major support from the national organization, chapters existed that remained persistent and active in the attempt to insert their agendas into state politics.

"Saved, Baptized, and Registered to Vote"

An examination of the Illinois state chapter reveals that it was politically active and also focused its attention on issues beyond the election of state officials. The Illinois chapter believed in and echoed the platform of the national organization in mobilizing individuals to oppose pornography, homosexuality, immorality in schools, bills in Congress that eroded family rights, and support of legislation that supported a Family Protection Agency. However, the Illinois state chapter also largely focused on voter registration and the defeat of the Equal Rights Amendment (ERA) ratification in Illinois. It enlisted the efforts of members, pastors, and their congregations in combating other concerns, such as textbooks in schools and the curricula in public education. It did this through recruiting members from various churches across Illinois, lobbying state politicians, and utilizing the media. An analysis of the Illinois state chapter of the Moral Majority shows that the chapter was active in lobbying representatives in Springfield, registering voters for national elections, and promoting the goals of the Moral Majority in Illinois. While the state chairman identified the work against the ERA and delivered votes for Ronald Reagan in the elections of 1980 and 1984 as the biggest accomplishments of the Illinois state chapter, other actions were taken. The Illinois Moral Majority primarily not only worked toward the registration of voters for national presidential elections, but also fought for the teaching of creationism in schools and against the licensing of church day care centers as well as publicly debated anti-Moral Majority individuals.

From Falwell's national office, Zarris acquired a mailing list of 50,000 Illinois residents, of whom 5,000 were active pastors (McClory 1981:24). This list provided a starting point and signified the backbone of support for the state chapter. Zarris used the contact list to distribute pamphlets to Christian churches across the state. These 5,000 pamphlets outlined how churches could get their unregistered members on the voting rolls. At the same time, Zarris began to publish a bimonthly newsletter titled *The Moral Majority Report of Illinois,* which was mainly placed in churches and was a state-focused version of the national organization's *Moral Majority Report.* Along with a discussion of current moral issues, the newsletter contained items such as responses to questionnaires that the Illinois Moral Majority sent to every member of the Illinois General Assembly. Most of these questions centered on issues ranging from abortion and gay rights to the military draft and legalized gambling (McClory 1981:24). Although no explicit voting instructions were provided, answers supplied by legislators in the newsletters spoke volumes to the constituents within churches across Illinois and threatened to have a future electoral impact on those 95 state representatives and 22 state senators who responded.

The Illinois Moral Majority also held training seminars that taught staff and voter registration leaders how to register voters and get them to the voting booth. The training consisted of employing laymen rather than ordained ministers and church leadership in securing commitments from fellow church members that they would cast votes on election day. In bypassing any employment of church leaders and pastors in promoting political messages, the Illinois Moral Majority was able to avoid any issues related to churches publicly endorsing candidates and thereby placing their tax-exempt status at risk.

The 1980 presidential race proved to be a key event in the emergence of the Illinois Moral Majority. In March 1980, a small group of pastors met candidate Ronald Reagan at the Drake Hotel in Chicago. Having just become the chairman of the Moral Majority's Illinois state chapter two months earlier, Zarris and roughly a dozen other pastors met Reagan to discuss their major concern about the perceived moral demise of the country. In the eyes of the pastors present, it was a vetting of Reagan from prominent Illinois preachers and decisive in placing the power of conservative Christians in Illinois behind him in the voting booth. The meeting allowed the group of pastors to ask the former California governor a series of questions. Reagan answered inquiries about his spiritual background and religious upbringing to the satisfaction of those in attendance. Reagan would have seemed a rather unlikely candidate to win the approval of any group of pastors. His past included things such as a divorce, Hollywood stardom, the promotion of liberal abortion measures, and opposition as governor to legislation that would have barred homosexuals from teaching jobs (Martin 1996:208). However, Reagan held out the promise of doing what Jimmy Carter neglected to do for his evangelical constituency. Conservative evangelicals had hoped to see positions available to them in the Carter administration and were ignored. Robert Wuthnow has noted that leaders of the secular right, such as Richard Viguerie, chastised Carter "for having left them out of the political spoils while religious conservatives lambasted him for his failure to oppose abortion, promote prayer in public schools, encourage Christian schools, and allow feminists and gays to be represented at his White House Conference on Families" (Wuthnow 1990:204). Reagan represented the best choice out of all Republican candidates who could defeat Carter in the general election. There is no record of this group of pastors having any desire to back other conservative candidates, such as Illinois Representative John Anderson. At the conclusion of the cordial meeting, the group of pastors was convinced that Reagan was the most morally suitable candidate and proceeded to lay hands on him and pray for God's guidance in his life—as well as for God to allow him to become the next president of the United States.[4]

Within a few weeks of the meeting with Reagan at the Drake Hotel, a larger meeting with other nationally recognized Christian leaders took place in Chicago. Zarris, Robert Billings, and Dr. D. James Kennedy, a well-known Religious Right figure, televangelist, and mega-church pastor, along with a number of Christian leaders, met George H. W. Bush. A question and answer session ensued which mirrored that of the meeting with Reagan. When asked, Bush spoke about his Episcopalian background and denied the title "born again" Christian, yet made known his willingness to discuss his personal relationship with Jesus Christ to anyone, much to the approval of those in attendance.[5] The representation of the Illinois Moral Majority at these meetings reveals the state organization's legitimacy with regard to national politics before the voter registration drives took place. It clearly shows that presidential candidates considered meeting with them a wise decision with regard to their campaign. These meetings with Reagan and Bush also showed that larger groups within the Religious Right, such as the Moral Majority, had the ear of those within the Republican Party and were taken seriously as wielding a considerable amount of power and influence in politics.

During the years after Reagan's election, the Illinois Moral Majority waged more state-level battles. A large portion of the chapter sought to effect change through the state legislature. Others heavily invested in media exposure and placed the responsibility of enacting change on the residents of Illinois. Still others sought national change through winning the support of Illinois' senators and representatives in the U.S. Congress. None of these attempts would end in a change in the law or in seriously affecting the outcome of any targeted legislation. The Illinois Moral Majority remained active, though, following each failure with a renewed sense of action and the continued interest of the media. These battles, described next, occurred mainly within the first two years of the 1980s. The Illinois chapter maintained a strong presence in the media after these failures and still garnered a fair amount of support in the 1984 voter registration drive. It was only after the Illinois chapter scaled back its activities that the media lost attention.

The Illinois Moral Majority fought for the enactment of legislation that would mandate the teaching of creationism alongside evolution in Illinois schools. In keeping the 1925 Scopes Monkey Trial debate alive, the Illinois Moral Majority persuaded State Senator Robert Mitchler to introduce legislation that required the Illinois school system to teach the theory of creationism alongside the theory of evolution in public schools (Scopes 1980). The bill did not pass, but succeeded in creating a significant uproar in the media (Illinois General Assembly 1980). This caused the Canadian Broadcasting Corporation to go to Zarris' church and school and film students speaking out on why they believed in creationism and not evolution. It also led to a special weeklong report on the controversy that was aired on CBS News Channel 2 in Chicago. Illinois Moral Majority leaders spoke with reporters and also put media representatives in touch with the Institute of Creation Research in Naperville and its creation scientists.[6] The Illinois Moral Majority's activities did not result in the creation of a new state law, but brought the controversy between evolution and creation in the classroom back to the public spotlight and highlighted the role and views of Christian schools, colleges, and academies (Scopes 1980).

The Illinois Moral Majority also worked with other groups to influence the state government's role in the education and supervision of children. It worked alongside the Illinois Association of Christian Schools (IACS) in opposing the state licensing of church-run day-care centers. Illinois Governor James Thompson had advocated legislation that required churches in Illinois to be licensed if they provided day-care centers during Sunday services or any other time throughout the week. Representatives from the Illinois Moral Majority and the IACS would meet with the Republican governor in his office and chastise him for imposing legislation on a tax-exempt organization and for violating the separation of church and state. They also lobbied members of the Illinois legislature in the hopes of keeping state licensing away from church operations.

Senate Bill 524 (SB 524) essentially sought to separate church-run day-care centers from non-church-operated day-care centers. SB 524 was aimed at changing the existing Child Care Act in a way that conformed to the requests of the Illinois Moral Majority. An amendment to the bill, proposed by Senators W. Timothy Simms, John J. Nimrod, and James Gitz, aimed to "exclude from definitions of day care center programs which are operated as an integral part of a local church ministry or a religious nonprofit elementary school, provided that appropriate state health and fire safety standards are maintained" (Legislative Reference Bureau 1981:329). The bill drew much debate and dialogue on the floor of the General Assembly that centered on the question of church and state separation (Illinois General Assembly 1981a:30). It proved to be a victory from those within the ranks of the Illinois Moral Majority and from churches that did not wish to conform to state licensing procedures. The bill passed the legislature in the months of May and June 1981 by votes of 47 to 2 in the Senate and 95–57 in the House (Legislative Reference Bureau 1981:329–330).

This victory claimed by the Illinois Moral Majority and Illinois churches, though, was short-lived when the bill made its way to Governor Jim Thompson's desk for approval. In August 1981, Thompson vetoed SB 524, and the bill faced an uncertain future, as its survival rested on the three-fifths vote required in both the House and the Senate to override the governor's veto. The veto override made its way back into the legislature and sailed through the Senate in mid-October on a 38–15 vote. It died abruptly at the end of the month, however, in a close House vote that failed to override the veto, with 98 in favor and 75 opposed (Legislative Reference Bureau 1981:330).

However, the Illinois Moral Majority maintained a presence in Springfield despite this setback. Rather than taking an aggressive and hostile stand on issues important to their organization, the state chapter approached the state capitol with a positive attitude and managed to put on a constructive and friendly face when conversing with elected officials. George Zarris declared,

> When we were down in Springfield with the state senators and representatives, even those who would be classified as liberal and Democrats still displayed common decency and appreciation that we were there to voice our opinion. Among those that were conservative, some even born-again Christians, they were so appreciative. They would say, "You don't understand, you people are like a breath of fresh air."

Normally, the people who went to Springfield or Washington, D.C. were the people pushing some cause that they wanted to advance or simply get more money. They were so appreciative that here were honest, hard-working, employed, tax-paying people who were conservative and were saying, "We're tired of this, turn it around and make it right." We developed some lifelong friendships going to Springfield and being involved in just petitioning our elected leaders.[7]

The Illinois Moral Majority actually employed a full-time field representative to help in forming county chapters and lobbying in Springfield in 1980 and 1981. After 1981, the state chapter felt that they could offer no more than what already occurred in the state legislature as they made more progress through the media and with voter registration. In addition, the Illinois legislature consistently passed stiff anti-abortion bills without pressure from pro-life lobby organizations (McClory 1981:25). Illinois Representative Nord Swanstrom compared the efforts of the Illinois Moral Majority with the tactics of other groups such as Phyllis Schlafly's Eagle Forum:

It seemed like the Moral Majority was always in Springfield. Sometimes they would have things like coffee parties, petitions, post-card mailings, and other things like that. Other more aggressive groups like Eagle Forum and NOW [National Organization for Women] were harder to read. One minute, they were the sweetest, kindest people you would ever want to meet. They would leave a plate of cookies in your office. The next minute you would see them doing things like spelling out ERA in the capitol lawn with weed killer. One time I was in an executive meeting having a discussion about an abortion measure when they entered the capitol building and poured animal blood all through the hallways.[8]

Although Swanstrom preferred the more genteel lobbying tactics of the Moral Majority, he also noted that there were senators and representatives, such as Representative Penny Pullen, who actually enjoyed the tactics and pressure from groups such as the Eagle Forum, who were often meeting with leaders of the organization.[9] The state capitol, however, was also not the only place where the Illinois Moral Majority made its voice heard. They also lobbied the U.S. Congress.

The Illinois Moral Majority occasionally sent leaders to Washington, D.C. as well. Apart from making their presence known with state senators and representatives, they also wished to establish a relationship with the state's U.S. senators and representatives. Most of the time, they merely showed support for legislators when they supported a measure that the Illinois Moral Majority favored. They also arranged meetings to discuss concerns and remind them of the public constituency that adhered to the perspective of the Moral Majority. Between the lobbying in Springfield and

Washington, D.C., the Illinois Moral Majority established relationships with key elected officials and consistently made its stances known at both the state and national levels.

The group's willingness to publicly comment on their positions and agenda along with their consistent activity at the capitol in Springfield accounts for the power that was credited to them from the media. Another reason for the perception of power and influence came from the organization's participation in events which gave the impression that the Illinois Moral Majority contributed significantly to an outcome they desired. The affiliation with these larger and self-described victories can be seen in two specific instances. The first was the reversal of a piece of out-of-state legislation that had been passed in Washington, D.C. The second was the case of the ERA in Illinois in 1982.

In October, 1981 a sexual assault bill was introduced in the U.S. House that sought to broaden the legal definition of rape while, at the same time, repealing the criminal penalties for many sexual acts, including adultery, fornication, sex with animals, and sodomy between consenting adults. What Illinois Moral Majority members specifically disagreed with were the provisions that both lowered the age of consent to 14 for sexual acts between teenagers and also revoked any penalties for teachers having sex with students aged 16 years or older. Along with many politicians, special interest groups, and the D.C. Moral Majority chapter, the Illinois Moral Majority put pressure on the Illinois delegation. Representatives Phillip Crane, John Porter, Dan Rostenkowski, Paul Simon, and Robert Michel helped defeat the bill in a 281–119 tally (Isikoff and Kurtz 1981). Although it paled in comparison to the registration drives conducted by the Illinois Moral Majority and also affected the citizens of Illinois less than the previous examples, the reversal of this legislation claimed to reveal the extent of the state chapter's power in the eyes of Illinois representatives.

A second, more significant example of the Illinois Moral Majority's ability to claim more power and influence than it actually possessed can be seen in a description of the course of the ERA in Illinois in 1982. The ERA was first drafted by women's suffrage activist Alice Paul in 1923. Paul saw passage of the ERA as the next step in legally solidifying equal justice to all citizens after the ratification of the Nineteenth Amendment, which provided the right to vote to women. The years between 1923 and 1970 saw one form or another of the ERA introduced into every session of Congress to no avail (National Archives 1970). Its intention was clear: "Equality of rights under the law shall not be denied or abridged by the

United States or by any state on account of sex." Nearly every time the Amendment was introduced, it was held up in a committee. However, the ERA passed the House of Representative in 1971 and then the Senate, in 1972. It was then sent to the states for ratification with 38 states required within the seven-year deadline. In 1978, the ERA still lacked the required number of state ratifications, and Congress extended the time limit to June 1982. By the time the 1982 deadline was upon the ERA, several states were involved in an eleventh-hour push to ratify the amendment, and Illinois was the primary focus of those for and against the ERA.

Phyllis Schlafly's Eagle Forum, the leading anti-ERA organization at the time, joined forces with the Illinois Moral Majority in attempting to halt ratification in Illinois. These groups worked feverishly in Springfield, lobbying state representatives and senators. Both groups pled their case and tried to push state lawmakers to vote against ratification. In the end, Illinois failed to ratify the amendment. The push to gain the 38 states needed to ratify fell short with 35 states voting for it. Since becoming a state in 1818, the Illinois General Assembly had never turned down a constitutional amendment, until the ERA (Dinges 1977:23). Zarris was so relieved that the ratification of the ERA did not occur in Illinois that he later invited Mr. and Mrs. George Ryan to his church in Aurora to thank them for their opposition to the ERA.

Zarris may not have understood how effective Ryan was in stopping the ERA from ratification in Illinois. Ratification of the ERA in the state required a two-thirds vote from the Illinois state legislature. The vote was close enough to have succeeded if the ratification only required a three-fifths majority. Ryan alone had the power at the time to allow a change to the three-fifths vote rule, but refused to do so. One newspaper editorial from 1982 quoted NOW president Eleanor Smeal as identifying George Ryan as the "symbol of opposition to the ERA" (Manning 1982b:11). Another cited Phyllis Schlafly's Eagle Forum as having run an "effective grassroots campaign" that helped keep Ryan from eliminating the three-fifths vote rule in favor of a simple majority vote which would have assured ERA ratification (Manning 1982a:5).

All these events cover the years between the formation of the Illinois Moral Majority's chapter in early 1980 to just after Reagan's second inauguration in early 1985. This was roughly half of the Illinois Moral Majority's lifespan but constituted the most active years of its existence. From 1985 until the dissolution of the organization in 1988, the Illinois state chapter made little noise. Perhaps sensing the end of the national organization, gauging the lack of interest from Illinois citizens who were content with their analysis of the country's moral direction, or a decline in funding, the Illinois Moral Majority scaled back the number of battles it waged. At both the national and state levels, the Illinois state chapter began to fade away from the public spotlight and the halls of Congress. In 1988, Zarris left his Fox River Valley Baptist Church to begin an international radio ministry, with which he is still involved today, gave up his post as the state chairman, and closed the Illinois Moral Majority in 1988.

My Kingdom is Not of This World

Describing such activities of the Illinois Moral Majority as voter registration drives, ERA opposition, the promotion of creationism in public schools, the publication and distribution of voter guides and advertisements, the establishment of county chapters, and the reaction to the effort to license church day-care centers shows that the organization was persistent in its activity and seemed to wield more power than it actually had in the eyes of the media and politicians. By following the series of challenges, victories, and losses of the Illinois Moral Majority, it is plain to see that the state chapter was extremely active, covered a large area, and worked to resolve several issues simultaneously. Similar to the national organization and all the state chapters, the Illinois Moral Majority was at its height in the first half of the 1980s. Voter registration drives, a widely distributed newsletter that mirrored that of the national organization's *Moral Majority Report*, aggressive lobbying against Equal Rights Amendment legislation, and high media exposure describe the major activities of the Illinois Moral Majority. The shifting political scene in Reagan's two elections, C. Everett Koop's confirmation as the surgeon general, the inability to ratify the Equal Rights Amendment, and the overall belief in Reagan's claim that it was, in fact, "morning in America" left many believing that the Religious Right had succeeded in restoring morality to America. These reasons, along with the discovery on the part of those within the Republican Party that larger evangelical conservative groups did not have the influence which they claimed, led to the loss of funding and support that brought down the Moral Majority. As interest in the organization waned, so did its support. The Moral Majority was in substantial financial trouble by the end of the 1980s, as supporters steadily stopped contributing money. A loss of membership and support signaled the decline of the Moral Majority and all its state chapters. Before the 1980s gave way to the 1990s, the Moral Majority and its state chapters lost their effectiveness within the Religious Right movement and faded away.

Conclusion

Across the nation, many Americans desired a break from what they perceived as the immoral direction of the country. Fundamentalist churchgoers desired a break from the path the United States appeared set on in the supposedly sex and drug-ridden 1960s, the political disappointments of Watergate and the Vietnam War, and such perceived threats to Christianity as abortion, homosexuality, and secular humanism. The Moral Majority and groups similar to it commanded the attention of politicians and political pollsters alike in helping shape a new voting demographic. This ultimately led to the ushering in of Ronald Reagan and an increased public debate over social issues. The Moral Majority, its national supporters, and its state chapters were instrumental in the new wave of Christian political involvement.

However, the Moral Majority was not monolithic. It focused on change at a national level and chartered its state chapters in the hopes of building its support for the national cause. Since all of the state chapters were financially independent and operated autonomously, they attempted to make an impact at both the state and national levels. The Illinois Moral Majority claimed to have registered over 100,000 voters who would have otherwise not participated in the political process. It exerted pressure on state lawmakers at a time when the Equal Rights Amendment faced a serious ratification challenge and supported the passage of legislation that would keep the state government out of the operation of church business. The Illinois Moral Majority argued its case in the media and challenged those with different worldviews in the hopes of shedding light on the evangelical worldview with regard to many things, from what was being taught in the classroom to homosexuality and abortion. None of these accomplishments had any substantive impact apart from the false sense of power that was attributed to the state chapter. Despite its appearance of success, the Illinois state chapter was weak. It had no political influence, and the media attention that it attracted can be directly attributed to the perseverance of its leadership in securing a presence on television, radio, and in print. The frequency of the Illinois Moral Majority's appearance in newspapers, magazines, and on television elevated the amount of power that audiences and politicians considered the organization to possess. The diverse and expansive battles that the state chapter was involved in created the perception of influence and power within the media, despite falling short in its goals repeatedly.

The Illinois Moral Majority no longer maintains any records of its existence, and any impact it might have had is not apparent in Illinois today. Through the sources consulted for this study, it is apparent that those within the organization considered the Illinois Moral Majority as having accomplished major goals and shaping the politics of Illinois and even the nation in the 1980s. The manner in which the organization was treated in the media at the time made many believe that this was the case. However, in reviewing the outcomes of proposed legislation, it is apparent that the Illinois Moral Majority was not as influential as many at the time believed. This makes it all the more impressive that the state chapter was able to continue its lobbying efforts and maintain its legitimacy with state and national leaders for years. The overestimation of the state chapter also raises the question of power within the national organization. The figures given by Falwell with regard to his following, funding, and supporters do not match up with what research has shown those numbers to actually be (Falwell 1986; Fitzgerald 1989; Martin 1996:213; Tamney and Johnson 1988:235). An area for future research would be to question the power and influence of the national Moral Majority and find out why the organization became so popular in the media and so catered to by Republicans in the 1980s. In the case of the Illinois Moral Majority, the media's coverage generated the illusion of power that kept it involved in political activity, despite never having exerted any consequential influence. The group's claim to have registered 100,000 voters was impressive, but not decisive. In the 1980 election, Ronald Reagan garnered 2.3 million votes in Illinois to incumbent Jimmy Carter's 1.9 million votes. Although the number of voters the Illinois Moral Majority claimed to have registered is large—had the 100,000 Illinois residents not been intent on voting before the group's registration efforts—if it had done nothing, the state's election results would have had the same result: a victory and 26 electoral votes for Reagan. The actions of the Illinois chapter just illustrated show that the media should have discredited or lost interest in the state chapter long before it began to disseminate. This was not the case. Similar to the national organization, the Illinois Moral Majority consistently attracted the attention of the media, which gave it legitimacy and the belief that it was important to or influential in the political process.

Notes

1. The Baptist Bible Fellowship is a collection of conservative Baptist churches. This group traces its origins to 1950, when the BBF split from the General Association of Regular Baptist Churches (GARBC). The GARBC was established as a reaction against liberalism in the Northern Baptist Convention. By 1980, the BBF (or the Baptist Bible Fellowship International) directory listed nearly 3,000 churches that were affiliated to it.

2. Personal interview with George Zarris, Hammond, Indiana, October 18, 2009.
3. Personal interview with George Zarris, Hammond, Indiana, October 18, 2009.
4. Personal interview with George Zarris, Hammond, Indiana, October 18, 2009.
5. Personal interview with George Zarris, Hammond, Indiana, October 18, 2009.
6. Personal interview with George Zarris, Hammond, Indiana, October 18, 2009.
7. Personal interview with George Zarris, Hammond, Indiana, October 18, 2009.
8. Telephone interview with Nord Swanstrom, April 5, 2010.
9. Telephone interview with Nord Swanstrom, April 5, 2010.
10. "Moral Majority State Chairmen," *Moral Majority Report,* January 13, 1981. Reprinted with denominational identifications in Liebman and Wuthnow 1983: 62–65.
11. Baptist Bible Fellowship (BBF).

References

Allitt, Patrick. 2003. *Religion in America since 1945.* New York: Columbia University Press.
Balmer, Randall. 2007. *Thy Kingdom Come: How the Religious Right Distorts Faith and Threatens America.* New York: Basic Books.
Bromley, David and Anson Shupe. 1984. *New Christian Politics.* Macon: Mercer University Press.
Diamond, Sara. 1989. *Spiritual Warfare: The Politics of the Christian Right.* Boston, MA: South End Press.
Diamond, Sara. 1995. *Roads to Dominion: Right-Wing Movements and Political Power in the United States.* New York: The Guilford Press.
Dinges, Sue. 1977. "Equal Rights Amendment." *Illinois Issues* (March):22–23. Retrieved October 14, 2009 (http://www.lib.niu.edu/1977/ii770322.html).
Dochuk, Darren. 2006. "Revival on the Right: Making Sense of the Conservative Moment in Post-World War II American History." *History Compass* 4(5):975–999.
Falwell, Jerry. 1986. "Statement by Jerry Falwell." Delivered at the National Press Club. Washington, DC. January 3.
Fishwick, Marshall and Ray B. Brown, eds. 1987. *The God Pumpers: Religion in the Electronic Age.* Bowling Green: Bowling Green State University Popular Press.
Fitzgerald, Michael. 1989. "Falwell Closes Moral Majority," *USA Today,* June 12.
Green, John C., Mark J. Rozell, and Clyde Wilcox, eds. 2003. *The Christian Right in American Politics: Marching to the Millennium.* Washington, DC: Georgetown University Press.
Harding, Susan Friend. 2001. *The Book of Jerry Falwell: Fundamentalist Language and Politics.* Princeton: Princeton University Press.
Illinois General Assembly. 1980. "81st General Assembly: Transcript of June 18, 1980." Retrieved March 20, 2010 (http://www.ilga.gov/senate/transcripts/strans81/ST061880.pdf).
Illinois General Assembly. 1981a. "House of Representatives Transcription Debate." Retrieved January 21, 2010 (http://www.ilga.gov/house/transcripts/htrans82/HT102981.pdf).
Illinois General Assembly. 82nd General Assembly Transcripts. 1981b. "Transcript of October 15, 1981." Retrieved January 21, 2010 (http://www.ilga.gov/senate/transcripts/strans82/ST101581.pdf).
Isikoff, Michael and Howie Kurtz. 1981. "DC Bill Explodes Land Mine on Home Rule Battlefield." *Washington Post,* October 26.
Jorstad, Erling. 1981. "The New Christian Right." *Theology Today* 38(2):193–200.

Jorstad, Erling. 1987. *The New Christian Right, 1981-1988.* Lewiston: Edwin Mellen Press.
Klein, Joe. 1981. "The Moral Majority's Man in New York." *New York* 14(May 18):26–30.
Lamare, James, Jerry Polinard, and Robert Wrinkle. 2003. *Texas: Religion and Politics in God's Country.* Pp. 59–78 in John C. Green, Mark J. Rozell, and Clyde Wilcox, eds. *The Christian Right in American Politics: Marching to the Millennium.* Washington: Georgetown University Press.
Legislative Reference Bureau. 1981. "Legislative Synopsis and Digest of the 1981 Session of the Eighty-Second General Assembly: Action on All Bills and Resolutions Received Through December 18, 1981." Volume 20, No. 1. Springfield, IL: State of Illinois.
Liebman, Robert C. and Robert Wuthnow. 1983. *The New Christian Right.* New York: Aldine Publishing Company.
Lugg, Catharine. 2001. "The Christian Right: A Cultivated Collection of Interest Groups." *Educational Policy* 15(1): 41–57.
Manning, Al. 1982a. "Page Five." *Springfield State-Journal Register*, June 21.
Manning, Al. 1982b. "Tough to Pass Anything This Session." *Springfield State-Journal Register*, June 23.
Martin, William. 1996. *With God on Our Side: The Rise of the Religious Right in America.* New York: Broadway Books.
McClory, Robert. 1981. "Rev. George Zarris: Moral Majority Leader in Illinois." *Illinois Issues* 7(11):23–26.
Miller, Stephen P. 2009. *Billy Graham and the Rise of the Republican South.* Philadelphia: University of Pennsylvania Press.
Moen, Matthew C. 1996. "The Evolving Politics of the Christian Right," *PS: Political Science and Politics* 29(3):461–464.
"Moral Majority State Chairmen." *Moral Majority Report*, January 13, 1981.
National Archives. 1970. "Martha Griffiths and the Equal Rights Amendment." The Center for Legislative Archives. Retrieved October 14, 2009 (http://www.archives.gov/legislative/features/griffiths).
Noll, Mark. 2007. *Religion and American Politics: From the Colonial Period to the Present.* Oxford: Oxford University Press.
"Scopes Controversy Revived: Man vs. Monkey in Illinois." 1980. *Chicago Tribune.* March 3.
Tamney, Joseph and Stephen Johnson. 1988. "Explaining Support for the Moral Majority." *Sociological Forum* 3(2): 234–255.
"The Region; Fore 'Going Back to Preach Gospel'." 1981. *New York Times.* December 2.
Wilcox, Clyde and Carin Larson. 1986. "Evangelicals and Fundamentalists in the New Christian Right: Religious Difference in the Ohio Moral Majority." *Journal for the Scientific Study of Religion* 25(September No. 3):355–363.
Wilcox, Clyde and Carin Larson. 1987. "Seeing the Connection: Religion and Politics in the Ohio Moral Majority." *Review of Religious Research* 30 (September No. 1): 47–58.
Wilcox, Clyde and Carin Larson. 2006. *Onward Christian Soldiers: The Religious Right in American Politics.* Boulder: Westview Press
Wuthnow, Robert. 1990. *The Restructuring of American Religion.* Princeton: Princeton University Press.

Appendix 1

Moral Majority State Chairmen[10]

State	Chairman	Location	Denomination
Alabama	Rev. Dick Vignuelle	Shades Mt. Independent Church Birmingham (School)	Conservative Evangelical
Alaska	Dr. Jerry Prevo	Anchorage Baptist Temple (School)	BBF[11]
Arizona	Dr. J. C. Joiner	New Testament Baptist Church Tucson (School)	BBF
Arkansas	Rev. Roy McLoughlin	First Baptist Church Vilonia	Baptist
California	Dr. Tim LaHaye	Scott Memorial Baptist San Diego	BBF
Colorado	Mr. Ed McKenna	(Not Available) Parker	(Not Available)
Connecticut	Rev. Robert Crichton	Colonial Hills Baptist Danbury	Independent Baptist
Delaware	Dr. R. H. Hayden	Pine Creek Baptist Temple Newark (School)	BBF
Florida	Dr. Bob Gray	Trinity Baptist Church Jacksonville (School)	BBF
Georgia	Dr. Bill Pennell	Forest Hills Baptist Church Decatur	Baptist
Georgia	Dr. Charles Stanley	First Baptist Church Atlanta	Southern Baptist
Hawaii	Dr. Don Stone	Lanakila Baptist Church Waipahu (School)	BBF
Idaho	Rev. Buddy Hoffman	Treasure Valley Baptist Church Boise	Independent Baptist
Illinois	Rev. George Zarris	Fox River Valley Baptist Church Aurora	Independent Fundamentalist
Indiana	Dr. Greg Dixon	Indianapolis Baptist Temple Aurora	BBF

(continued on the next page)

Moral Majority State Chairmen[10] (*Continued*)

State	Chairman	Location	Denomination
Iowa	Dr. Olin Adams	Quint City Baptist Temple Davenport (School)	BBF
Kansas	Rev. Ray Melugin	Wichita Baptist Tabernacle (School)	BBF
Kentucky	Dr. W. Robert Parker	Kosmosdale Baptist Church Louisville	Baptist
Louisiana	Rev. Bob Buchanan	Central Baptist Church Baton Rouge	Baptist
Maine	Dr. Harry Boyle	Grace Baptist Church Portland	BBF
Maryland	Dr. Herbert Fitzpatrick	Riverdale Baptist Church Upper Marlboro	BBF
Massachusetts	Dr. Thomas Ward	(Not Available) Boston	(Not Available)
Michigan	Dr. David Wood	Heritage Baptist Church Grand Rapids	Independent Baptist
Minnesota	Rev. Rich Angwin	Temple Baptist Church St. Paul (School)	BBF
Mississippi	Dr. James Johnson	Capitol City Baptist Church Jackson (School)	BBF
Missouri	Dr. W. E. Dowell	Springfield Baptist Temple (School)	BBF
Montana	Don Jones	(Not Available) Billings	(Not Available)
Nebraska	Rev. Gene Hutton	Marshall Drive Baptist Church Omaha (School)	BBF
Nevada	Rev. Duane Pettipiece	Gateway Baptist Church Las Vegas (School)	BBF
New Hampshire	Dr. Arlo Elam	Tabernacle Baptist Church Hudson (School)	BBF
New Jersey	Dr. Harry Vickery	Heritage Baptist Temple Saddle Brook (School)	BBF

(*continued on the next page*)

Moral Majority State Chairmen[10] (*Continued*)

State	Chairman	Location	Denomination
New Mexico	Dr. Curtis Goldman	Temple Baptist Church Albuquerque (School)	BBF
New York	Dr. Dan Fore	Staten Island Baptist Church New York City	Independent Baptist
North Carolina	Rev. Lamar Mooneyham	Tri-City Baptist Church Durham	BBF
North Dakota	Rev. Ken Schaeffer	New Testament Baptist Church Larimore	Independent Baptist
Ohio	Rev. Thomas Trammell	Deer Park Baptist Church Cincinnati (School)	BBF
Oklahoma	Rev. Jim Vineyard	Windsor Hill Baptist Church Oklahoma City (School)	BBF
Oregon	Rev. Mike Gass	Harvest Baptist Temple Medford	Independent Baptist
Pennsylvania	Dr. Dino Pedrone	Open Door Baptist Church Chambersburg	Baptist
Rhode Island	Rev. Tom Crichton	Greater Rhode Island Baptist Temple Johnston	BBF
South Carolina	Dr. Bill Monroe	Florence Baptist Temple (School)	BBF
South Dakota	Rev. R. L. Tottingham	Bible Baptist Church Sioux Falls (School)	BBF
Tennessee	Dr. Bobby Moore	Broadway Baptist Church Memphis	Baptist
Texas	Dr. Gary Coleman	Lavon Drive Baptist Church Garland (School)	BBF
Utah	Rev. Robert Smith	(Not Available) Salt Lake City	(Not Available)
Vermont	Rev. David Buhman	(Not Available) Milton	(Not Available)

(*continued on the next page*)

Moral Majority State Chairmen[10] (*Continued*)

State	Chairman	Location	Denomination
Virginia	Rev. Danny Cantwell	Open Door Baptist Church	BBF
		Richmond (School)	
Washington	Rev. Tom Starr	Valley Forth Memorial	Community
		Spokane	
West Virginia	Dr. Fred Brewer	Fellowship Baptist Church	BBF
		Huntington	
Wisconsin	Dr. Harley Keck	First Bible Baptist Church	Independent
		Green Bay	Baptist
Wyoming	Dr. Morgan Thompson	First Baptist Church Cheyenne	Baptist

Book Reviews

War! What Is It Good For? Black Freedom Struggles and the U.S. Military From World War II to Iraq by Kimberley L. Phillips. Chapel Hill: University of North Carolina Press, 2012 (343 pages; cloth).

Reviewed by Marcus S. Cox
The Citadel: The Military College of South Carolina

    The modern civil rights movement can be described as one of the most significant crusades in world history. It not only changed the course of American history during the post–World War II era, but also arguably became the template of activism for dozens of other social movements, such as the women's liberation movement, the gay and lesbian movement, the Native American movement, the environmental movement, the antiwar movement, and many others. The modern civil rights movement is a window not only to the social events of the 1950s and 1960s, but also to a world movement for social change and independence. At the heart of the struggle for African American self-determination are African American soldiers who returned from the battlefields of Europe, the South Pacific, Korea, and Southeast Asia to lead grassroots struggles and national organizations, because they emphatically believed that their sacrifices and contributions to the welfare of the country had earned them the right to be first-class citizens.

    On the other hand, many African American veterans and conscripts questioned the sensibility of serving in the armed forces for a nation and federal government that worked to emasculate and humiliate them while promoting the contradictory Cold War image of a beacon of liberty and opportunity to people of color from around the world. Though military service historically reflected an avenue to full citizenship for native-born white men, European immigrants, and some racial minorities, African Americans continued to fight for the "right to fight" but to no avail. *War!*

What Is It Good For?: Black Freedom Struggles and the U.S. Military from World War II to Iraq by Kimberley L. Phillips attempts to document how African Americans resisted embracing the link between military service and citizenship and subsequently fashioned an antiwar black freedom movement.

According to the author, *War!* not only examines African American military history in the context of civil rights struggles, but also seeks to answer two significant questions. "How did African Americans' overlapping experiences as perpetrators and victims in America's wars and occupations while they also participated in freedom struggles shape their critiques of racial and colonial violence? And how did their experiences with militarism and wars reshape their struggles for full citizenship, freedom, and racial justice?" (p. 6)

These questions are addressed in the form of six chapters, beginning with a discussion of the *Double V Campaign* during World War II and culminating in a brief conversation on the war in Iraq and an in-depth analysis of the correlation between black freedom struggles and antiwar activism. Although the 1940s and 1950s reflect a period when African Americans passionately fought for the "right to fight," Phillips correctly suggests that "by the 1960s, the idea of combat as a 'right' and a declaration of black citizenship and military as 'equal opportunity' no longer retained its rhetorical and organizing power for civil rights struggles as it had in the previous two decades. On the contrary, many African Americans considered their high presence in the military and combat as evidence of their political and economic inequality in American society" (p. 14). Although African Americans continue to participate with pride and distinction in America's armed forces, they disproportionately suffer from high unemployment, extraordinary incarceration rates, and lack of economic opportunity, and they no longer see military service as a civil rights imperative and an avenue to enhanced political opportunity.

War! What Is It Good For? not only reflects a valuable addition to the collection of significant works on the black experience in the post–war era but also makes a important contribution to our understanding of the African American antiwar movement of the 1960s and how African American attitudes toward military service and militarism changed in succeeding decades. This book is well written, meticulously researched, and a must read for interested scholars and students of the civil rights era and African American military history enthusiasts of the twentieth century.

Accumulating Insecurity: Violence and Dispossession in the Making of Everyday Life edited by Shelley Feldman, Charles Geisler, and Gayatri A. Menon. Athens, GA: University of Georgia Press, 2011 (318 pages; cloth).

Reviewed by Edward J. Laurance
Monterey Institute of International Studies

A book with the title *Accumulating Insecurity: Violence and Dispossession in the Making of Everyday Life* has the potential to provide evidence and explanations for the rise in human insecurity in the United States and throughout the world. It arrives at a time when the international community has begun to embrace the concept of human security, that is, "a concern with the everyday security of individuals and the communities in which they live rather than the security of states and borders."[1] How does this book connect with this movement?

The book "examines the relationship between two vitally important contemporary phenomena: a fixation on security that justifies global military engagements and the militarization of civilian life, and the dramatic increase in day-to-day insecurity associated with contemporary crises in health care, housing, incarceration, personal debt, and unemployment. Contributors to the volume explore how violence is used to maintain conditions for accumulating capital" (book cover). The editors are sociologists engaged in critical theory, that is, the examination of modernity and its concomitant limitations and negative effects. Topics addressed include the fear experienced by illegal immigrants, the rehabilitation of victims of sex trafficking, protest-as-violence associated with extractive industries, the decline of the welfare state into a "pull yourselves up by your bootstraps" reality, recruiting criminals into the U.S. military, national security versus public safety in Mexico, and arbitrary non-judicial detention of citizens.

During the 1990s, the traditional realist concern with the security of the state came under challenge for several reasons. First, the end of the Cold War saw a dramatic decline in interstate wars and the rise of intrastate conflict and armed violence. Second, with declining support from their Cold War mentors and arms suppliers, the phenomenon of the failing state highlighted the inability of states to practice social responsibility and to protect their own citizens. In many cases, states became the enemy of their citizens. The result was the birth of the concept of human security. The first major illumination of this concept was the 1994 Human Development Report, which identified human insecurities in health, hunger, persistent poverty, environmental degradation, personal (violence, crime, terrorism, and domestic violence), community and political repression, and human rights violations. In a sense, *Accumulating Insecurity* adds to this conversation, as it deals with demonstrating the fear associated with unemployment, lack of healthcare, and the loss of human rights. The difference, of course, is that this book attempts to demonstrate that there is one major cause for all these insecurities—namely the pursuit of capital. As might be expected, the world of practitioners dealing with improving human security cannot wait for this "pursuit" to change in the short term. Hence, they search for more proximate causes to provide entry points for policies that are designed to improve human security, producing efforts to reform the security sector, reduce malaria, control the flow of the tools of violence, and so on. One exception might be the efforts to control the trade in "conflict diamonds." We also see this issue raised by Paul Collier in his work on greed and grievance, in which he explains that civil wars are due more to greed (both dependence on primary commodity exports and a large diaspora substantially increase the risk of conflict), than to grievance (focusing on ethnic and religious divisions, political repression, and inequality).[2]

The book also fits with the ongoing debate about freedom from fear and freedom from want. In 2005, the United Nations developed a policy that separates the two concepts for the purpose of insuring freedom from want, e.g., the Millennium Development Goals.[3] The main focus on "fear" in this U.N. context is on armed violence, terrorism, and the repressive tactics and corruption associated with state security forces. *Accumulating Insecurity* demonstrates that conditions such as unemployment and lack of health care generate their own version of fear, thereby fusing the two freedoms. This growing fear has led to the inability of people to socially reproduce themselves.

From the perspective of the global discourse on human security, this book is of limited utility. First, it is written by critical theorists for other critical theorists and their students. The book can certainly be praised, and has been, for its contribution to that field of sociology. Second, since the main thrust of critical theory is criticism, the authors do not feel obligated to propose solutions—and they don't. Third, the time period for the case studies is almost always the Bush administration. Some things have already changed since then. One is the effect of the global recession that began in 2007. Although the book covers the unemployment issue, nowhere does it mention the significant efforts, some successful, to achieve greater corporate social responsibility. There have been some very specific efforts with regard to developing voluntary codes of conduct for the extractive industries to improve the conditions discussed in this book. Overlooking these efforts is understandable for critical theorists whose main premise about corporations would automatically dismiss them. In addition, the well-documented problem of recruiting criminals for the armed forces has changed for the better, given the recession. Statistics show that today's U.S. military is filling its ranks with better educated and smarter people. Finally, the main thesis of the book, that the growing human insecurity in the world "is increasingly framed by a concern with war and the protection of corporate finance," remains debatable. The guns versus butter argument has raged since the end of World War II. We all await the peace dividend that never comes. This book sheds considerable light on that debate and in the end is its greatest strength.

Notes

1. Mary Kaldor. 2011. "Human Security in Complex Operations," *PRISM* 2(2) Retrieved June 1, 2012 (http://www.ndu.edu/press/human-security-complex-operations.html).
2. Paul Collier and Anke Hoeffler. 2004. "Greed and Grievance in Civil War." *Oxford Economics Papers* 56(4):563–595.
3. Interestingly, these goals do not include reduction of violence.

Proxy Warriors: The Rise and Fall of State-Sponsored Militias by Ariel I. Ahram. Stanford: Stanford University Press, 2011 (208 pages; cloth).

Reviewed by Daniel M. Masterson
United States Naval Academy

For centuries, militias have been integral components of both the evolution and devolution of nations. Witness the roles of militias in the anti-colonial revolutions in the Americas after 1775. The diversity of these militias can be quite stark. Northern Ireland's B-Specials, formed as a reserve militia to aid the Royal Ulster Constabulary in maintaining British rule after 1920, seem to have little in common with Peru's Rondas *Campesinas* (Peasant Self Defense Brigades), which fought the terrorist front *Sendero Luminoso* for a decade after 1985. Both operated with government support, because the ability of the state in both cases to confront

IRA or *Senderista* terrorism was decidedly inadequate. Ariel Ahram's cogent and highly thoughtful study of state-sponsored militias confronts prevailing wisdom regarding the supposedly destructive consequences of militias in what he refers to as late-developing states.

Ahram builds his analysis around three case studies: Indonesia, Iraq, and Iran. These are obvious, but certainly complex, scenarios for review. In a book whose text runs less than 150 pages, Ahram deals with the complexity of case studies remarkably well. In all instances, he is careful to build a helpful historical background in order to create a framework for his analysis of contemporary issues involving the militias of these three states. For instance, Ahram clearly notes the failures of British policy in Iraq and how they were replicated by U.S. policymakers after 2004. He argues, as have many others, that the insufficient size of the initial U.S. invasion force in 2004 and the decision to force the Iraqi army to stand down led to a virtually lawless Iraq. Similar to Britain in Iraq and Palestine in the 1920s, the United States wanted to limit the cost and size of its invasion and occupying forces in Iraq, as its military personnel were spread so thin around the world. Ahram concludes, "As the British had in the 1920s, it was soon clear that U.S. officials badly underestimated the amount of blood and treasure required to rebuild Iraq" (p. 89).

One of Ahram's key observations in this book is that militias in a failing state are not always the predatory warlord armies portrayed in films such as Sylvester Stallone's *Rambo*. He insists that militias have consistently provided stability and security to failing states. This was certainly true in Peru when 300,000 lightly armed *Ronderos* augmented a badly undermanned Peruvian army. It was also true in Iraq after 2004, when U.S. forces could not protect citizens against brutal sectarian violence, but local militias did. In the 1970s, the Provisional IRA in Northern Ireland tried to present itself as a militia protecting Catholics in the region. However, the British security state was too strong to make this a believable argument. Ahram tries hard to debunk the idea that militias try to weaken or eliminate aspects of central state control with their own territory. He insists, on the contrary, that militias routinely cooperate with state authorities when their interests are mutual. He argues further that there is little reason to believe that states confronting violence and threats to stability will be any more tolerant of the human rights of its citizens than local-based militias charged with protecting their own ethnic groups. The present situation in Syria is a tragic example of this. These are interesting and provocative assertions that Ahram argues with conviction.

This book would be appropriate for an upper-level undergraduate course. It is short, very well written, mostly free of jargon, and its arguments are clearly made. I would suggest, however, that it might have been a better book if Ahram had isolated a few of these militias for more in-depth study when he developed the case histories of Indonesia, Iraq, and Iran. What were the internal dynamics of the PKI fighters in Indonesia, for example? How old were they? In what ways were they recruited? What happened to them after militia service?

Apart from these suggestions, there is a good deal worth pondering at some length in this study on militias. They are not well understood today, and our vital interests require that they should be.

Hyper-Conflict: Globalization and Insecurity by James H. Mittelman. Stanford, CA: Stanford University Press, 2010 (256 pages; paper)

Reviewed by Stephen J. Scanlan
Ohio University

The dynamics of globalization and its implications for conflict in the twenty-first century present multiple challenges for understanding international security. In *Hyper-Conflict: Globalization and Insecurity*, James H. Mittelman takes on complex questions akin to whether globalization is an arbiter of peace or a catalyst for violence. Theoretically informed and grounded in recent historical evidence from multiple case studies, Mittelman's work establishes an important new direction in understanding insecurity in the contemporary world through the lens of what he terms *hyper-conflict*.

Mittelman begins with what he describes as tension between globalization processes that essentially weaken borders and promote deterritorialization versus state needs to maintain national security in the protection of territorial domains, national interests, and citizens. Although some argue that global commerce, the spread of democracy, and the expansion of education, transportation, and international communication systems, among other processes, may foster peace in a globalized world, the flipside is that insecurity and conflict may be promoted through such routes as well—particularly if non-state actors and transnational networks become increasingly empowered and disgruntled or contribute to problematic concerns. For example, arms proliferation, cybercrime and identity theft, terrorist threats, and trafficking in both humans and narcotics are all seemingly promoted by the interconnectedness of the globalized world and can contribute to conflict.

Alluding to economic historian James Beard, Mittelman notes that we are thus left in the quandary of being in a state of "perpetual war for perpetual peace" to protect us from insecurity in many forms—both old and new—and an increasingly intertwined global and local. Such uncertainty is exacerbated in the globalization era by what he considers the intense *hypercompetition* and *hyperpower* of the times. Mittelman's conceptualization of these ideas is the key to understanding hyper-conflict and ultimately disentangling globalization's impact on insecurity and the future world order. Hypercompetition is derived from the economic forces of globalization ("geoeconomics"), whereas hyperpower is primarily geopolitical in nature, involving the global struggle for power that is dominated by the United States. Their interaction creates greater tension and ultimately hyper-conflict—a byproduct of the concentration of wealth, the hierarchy of power, and the further marginalization of those nations and individuals deemed to be on the fringes of society, all of which contribute to the questioning of globalization and who benefits the most from the system.

In what he portrays to be a less-than-rosy scenario, Mittelman argues that the end result is a state of postnational security in which "national security and global security, often regarded as counterpoints, are becoming a single stream . . . and hyper-conflict turns into a seemingly chronic condition" (p. 165). He further notes that insecurity is widespread, connecting to both military and civilian sources of conflict and new and increasingly sophisticated forms of combat. The deterritorialization of threat from climate change, global pandemics, immigration, international terrorism, and transnational crime, among other forces, thus shape the way insecurity manifests itself in the future.

Building on to his solid command of international relations theory and incorporating significant themes from global studies, Mittelman presents the case for heightened global insecurity by examining in detail what at first may seem four disparate conflicts: the 1995 Multilateral Agreement on Investment; the Asian economic crises of 1997 and 1998; the 1999 Battle of Seattle anti-World Trade Organization protests; and the attacks of September 11, 2001. As Mittelman notes, "the connective tissue among the cases is conflict over the governance of globalization" (p. 19). He examines each separately in a detailed fashion while also drawing connections between them. He provides sound evidence for the prevalence of hypercompetiton and hyperpower's reinforcing dynamics in generating hyper-conflict within globalization's creation of a multilevel governance structure where the state is "but one actor pressured by many" (p. 172), including corporations, individuals, international organizations, and social movements. A shift to a new *nomos* (a term denoting a framework of order and orientation, attributed to philosopher Carl Schmitt) has thus ensued, moving us from an old to a new world order predicated on a state of perpetual fear derived from economic, legal, military, normative, political, social, and spatial threats to the future of security.

In sum, Mittleman provides a wealth of ideas and a thorough analysis of the complex issues pertaining to his conceptualization of hyper-conflict that also serves as an early warning for future insecurity scenarios. His insightful work will command the attention of policy-makers and academics alike, particularly those in the areas of international relations and security studies. Political and military sociologists, in particular, will find that *Hyper-Conflict* is important in its efforts to engage militarization with the political economy and power dimensions of globalization as well as the forces of social change that have both created and challenged this dynamic. Hyper-conflict and its roots in globalization are of vital interest to contemporary peace and if understood and addressed appropriately, future and ongoing threats to security can be effectively addressed.

***

Ground Wars: Personalized Communication in Political Campaigns by Rasmus Kleis Nielsen. Princeton: Princeton University Press, 2012 (220 pages; paperback).

Reviewed by Todd M. Schaefer
Central Washington University

In *Ground Wars*, Rasmus Kleis Nielsen examines a resurgent—and yet, academically neglected—aspect of political campaign communication, namely the direct canvassing and get-out-the-vote (GOTV) efforts at the core of election contests at all levels of government, which often make the difference in close races. He makes the case that face-to-face communication, or "people as a medium," is exhibiting a rebirth in recent years, in part because of the over-saturated and fragmented media environment in which people now live. This is especially true for elections "below the radar screens" of most voters.

He chooses as his subject two Democratic campaigns for the U.S. House of Representatives in competitive districts in the 2008 election. He employs an ethnographic approach by actually working as a grassroots volunteer for the campaigns and by interviewing participants in the process, from fellow canvassers to party leaders. The work thus provides an in-depth and front-line account of how contemporary "ground wars" are waged. It also places the subject in historical context by showing how this age-old technique has been adapted to the high-tech marketing of today, noting how it is different from the political machine efforts of the strong-party era. Campaigns now utilize state and national computer databases to find high-value targets, those voters most likely to be favorably disposed to the candidate, and yet less likely to turn out to vote. He concludes that this process is neither the idealistic grassroots democracy that some envision, nor the manipulative persuasion of communication professionals, but rather represents a key participatory and civic engagement piece of American democracy.

Nielsen also emphasizes the struggles of turning ground war strategies into tactics. Again and again, the campaign professionals, or at least the mid-level managers of the canvassing operation, attempt to stress uniformity in the message presentation and data collection by their armies of foot soldiers. However, whether due to variance in training, motivation, skills, or simply the unique circumstances of each encounter, such consistency is often not what really happens on the doorsteps or telephones.

Anecdotes and vignettes from "real people" talking appear throughout the book, providing both supporting evidence and a more colorful picture of the subject. This material added to the authenticity of the work, though at times the discussions of chapter-opening illustrative quotes in the text itself required flipping back a few pages to comprehend the case at hand.

As someone who has worked as a precinct captain and "walked my own turf" before elections, as well as done phone-banking, I could certainly relate to the stories Nielsen told and can attest that the nature of these encounters and their descriptions in the book ring true. That direct voter contact is a stressful enterprise and one which does not lend itself to highly scripted interactions, unlike paid advertisements, is likewise an important and valid contribution.

In fact, it is the use of these standardized political messages (the "scripts" canvassers are to deliver) that leads me to take issue with calling this (as in the sub-title) *personalized* communication. The author admits that beyond using past voting behavior measures targeting likely supporters and "persuadables," the use of truly individualized messages to sway voters such as might be developed through marketing and demographic data-mining techniques—estimated guessing that a given voter might be more concerned about particular issues, and not others, for example—is not employed. Indeed, one of the problems he documents is that canvassers, especially paid ones brought in to supplement volunteers, often do not know much about the candidates for whom they are stumping, complicating their ability to address individual voters' concerns. Personal, for sure, but personalized communication is still apparently a way off. Still, this is a minor quibble.

Second, his use of two Democratic campaigns in the New York metro area, of course, raises questions about generalizability, given the differences in party organizations and electoral laws across the U.S. (for example, in some states, such as Washington, there is no party voter registration or identification, changing the nature of the ground war). Republican operations might differ as well. However, he makes the case that these activities are more similar than different nationwide, and such would be an issue with any case study approach.

All in all, the work is a very welcome addition to the reams of quantitative election studies and those that only analyze mass-media efforts at persuasion. The book should be read by all who are interested in how campaigns are implemented in the twenty-first century. I plan to assign it my students doing internships on campaigns in the future, at least to give them a better idea of what they are in for.

In This Issue

David Bugg is Assistant Professor of Sociology at SUNY Potsdam. His research interests include gun culture, white nationalism, and policing.

Molly Clever is a Ph.D. candidate in the Department of Sociology and a research assistant at the Center for Research on Military Organization at the University of Maryland. She would like to thank Meyer Kestnbaum and David Segal for their helpful advice on this research as well as three anonymous reviewers for their constructive feedback.

Aaron K. Davis received his M.A. in history from Western Illinois University and is currently a Ph.D. candidate in American Religious History at Kansas State University where he serves as a graduate teaching assistant. His dissertation research focuses on religion and Cold War foreign policy during the Eisenhower administration.

Dianne Dentice is Associate Professor of Sociology at Stephen F. Austin State University. Her research interests include extremist social movements, white racial activism, and white nationalist identity formation.

Orlee Hauser is Assistant Professor of Sociology at the University of Wisconsin Oshkosh. She has published work on organizational belonging in the IDF and has now turned her attention to issues of belonging in a very different institution—the family! Her recent focus is on parenting, maternal gatekeeping, maternal identity, and paternal identity.

Christina M. Knopf is Associate Professor of Communication at SUNY Potsdam. Her research on communication and the military appears in several edited collections and is regularly presented at conferences, such as the National Communication Association and the American Sociological Association conventions.

Udi Lebel is Senior Lecturer and Head of the Department of Sociology and Anthropology at Ariel University Center as well as a research fellow at the Samaria and Jordan Rift R&D Center, Israel. His main research interests include the political psychology of bereavement, death, and dying; civil–military relations; and the politics of memory and commemoration.

Maria Markantonatou is Lecturer in Political Sociology at the University of the Aegean in Lesvos, Greece. Her research interests include state theory and the transformation of the modern state as related to welfare deregulation, the internationalization of the economy, and the privatization of formerly state activities in the field of security and warfare.

Bruce D. McDonald, III is Assistant Professor of Public Administration at Indiana University South Bend. His previous work has appeared in a variety of journals, including the *Journal of Policy Modeling*, *Peace Economics, Peace Science and Public Policy*, and *Administration & Society*. His areas of interest including defense administration, economic policy, and public policy methodologies.

Neema Noori is Assistant Professor of Sociology at the University of West Georgia. He specializes in the comparative politics and political economy of the Middle East and Central Asia. His research interests include authoritarian governance, social policy, higher education, and globalization.